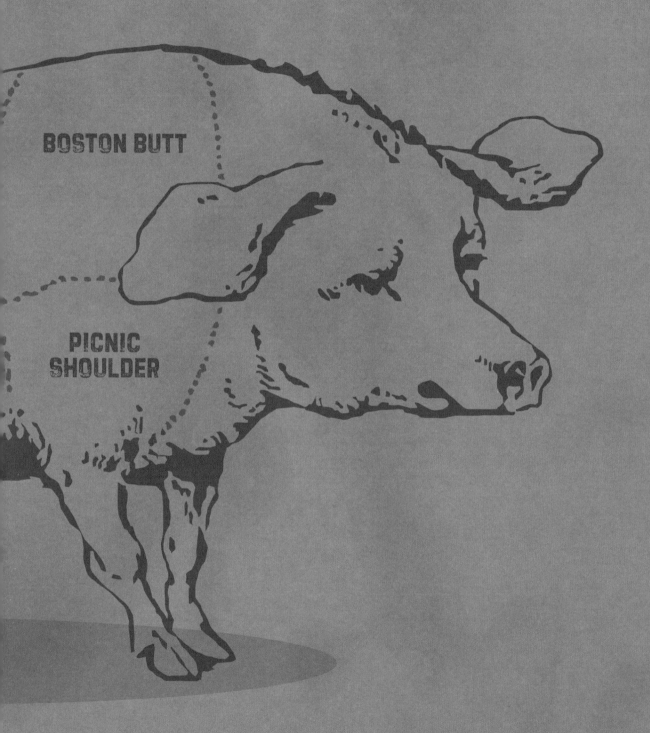

BOSTON BUTT

PICNIC
SHOULDER

PRIMAL CUTS

COOKING WITH AMERICA'S BEST
BUTCHERS

MARISSA GUGGIANA

FOREWORD BY DARIO CECCHINI
INTRODUCTION BY ANDREW ZIMMERN

WELCOME BOOKS / NEW YORK

CONTENTS

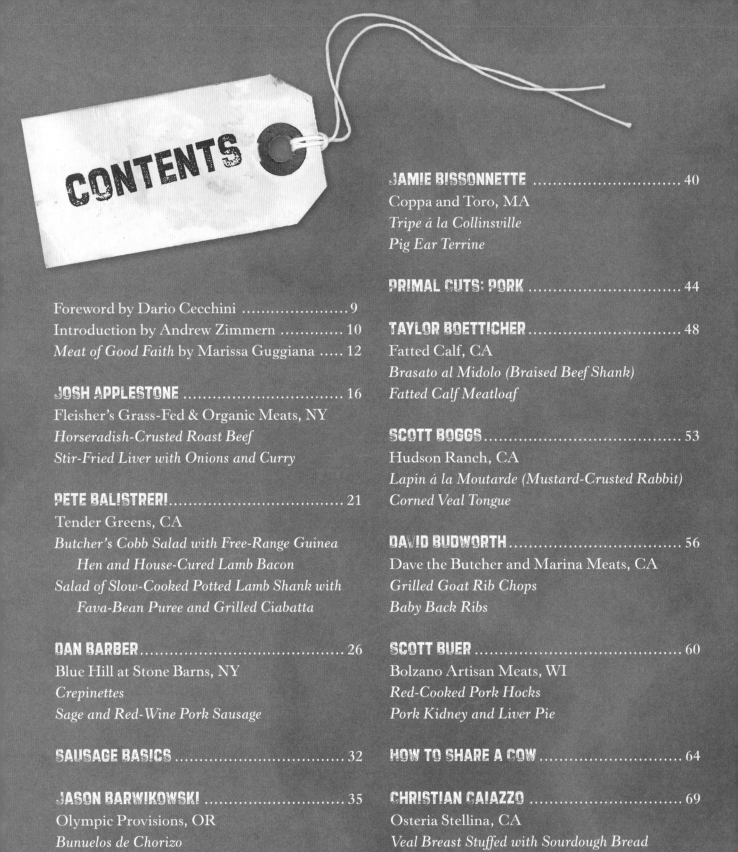

FOREWORD

Some time ago, maybe ten years, a butcher of about eighty and on the verge of retirement came to find me in my shop. He shook my hand and thanked me, telling me that my pride and passion in butchery had restored the dignity of the craft in the eyes of the people, and, therefore, in himself. Though I never saw him again and wish him the best for years to come, I will never forget what he told me: "I once was filled with the doubt that I had wasted my life, but now, thanks to you, I now know my doubts were wrong."

Here is the essence of our craft as butchers: a task crude and compassionate, strong yet delicate, always respectful toward the killed animal, with the ethical imperative of always using the meat in the best manner possible, knowing that, since the beginning of time, these animals were given to mankind as a gift from God.

The true butcher, like the artists of the Tuscan Renaissance, walks the never-ending path in search of bettering his own art and reaching his fullest potential.

A true butcher looks to use the whole animal and hopes, as one would hope for themselves, that the animal had a comfortable life full of good food, necessary space to live and a respectful death.

The true butcher knows that his work is a piece of art, the most delicate craft of all that we eat and all that nurtures us.

A true butcher knows that his objective is not the pursuit of expansion or profit, but rather to become the master of his own art.

These were the inspirations of the artists of the Renaissance and these, surely, are the same inspirations of the American butchers who, with confidence and pride, have paved the way for a rebirth in this noble and ancient craft. In the end, the question will always be simple: *To beef or not to beef . . .*

—DARIO CECCHINI

INTRODUCTION

The book you hold in your hands is one of the keys to de-coding, understanding, and preserving culture on our planet as we know it. Sounds like a big idea and a lot of responsibility. Don't let that stop you. Just because Marissa's book is important doesn't make it any less fun than taking a break at the family barbecue, tying up your cousin to the nearest ant hill, and basting him with honey. This tome is a collection of superb stories about the men and women who make the meat world go round, with recipes and buckets of undiluted butcher worship thrown in for good measure. It's a paean to the meat cutting art. Its primacy is immediate, and because the return toward a renaissance of snout-to-tail eating is upon us, this book is supremely relevant. On the more amusing side of the equation, *Primal Cuts* accurately depicts the life and lessons of the meat world and profiles some of the more amusing vagabonds and legends in the business.

Primal Cuts does what other books of this type don't, it connects its subject to you and your daily life. For thousands of years, everyone ate from necessity. Fancy food, restaurants, food movements, and the like were nonexistent. Many dishes from those times still remain, from black pudding to head cheese to *dinaguan* (a Southeast Asian stew of innards thickened with blood), from haggis to *slátur* to kalua wild pig and even *asado con cuero*. But in the main, those dishes have never been popular here in America. For the last seventy-five years, we have moved away from traditional eating and cooking in America. We have sped up our food chain, and cheapened and mechanized it to the point where we have endangered the health of our children. And along the way, we have placed the onus of feeding the most people for the least money on the shoulders of the factory farms and commodity producers, who are slowly but surely sucking away every last drop of our culinary heritage. Can you feel a "but" coming?

Good news: this book represents the rebirth of a time when we were connected to our food sources. For the last fifteen years a handful of committed purveyors, chefs, restaurateurs, butcher shops, farmers, and meat cutters have helped push us back toward a time when we ate all parts of the animal. We were healthier, and I think happier, and we had more in common with our forefathers, which is important to be aware of as we navigate through our nightmarishly disposable culture. *Primal Cuts* represents in a meaningful tangible way that eating a variety of proteins is better for our world because it eases pressure off the mainstream supply chain and onto a more sustainable way of eating. Told you it was an important book.

The men and women chronicled in these pages, the recipes and tips, and most importantly the food, are all easily recognizable by our grandparents. That's a barometer for a real-food life that Michael Pollan so famously raves about, and *Primal Cuts* gives you access to that world. And let's face it, I think it's also a lot of fun to be inspired to feed and care for a plump little piglet and know how to dispatch it and utilize every part of the animal—and I mean every part—to feed your family. That kind of connection to the food pathways in our world has been shrinking and disappearing. *Primal Cuts* is emblematic of a tradition saved.

I worry about this kind of stuff. I spend my life on the road and chronicling more than my share of dying breeds makes me skittish about our future food life. *Primal Cuts* gives me hope. When I read about Brooklyn's Tom Mylan, a knife-slinging, young, barley-pop loving butcher who can hack up a pig and put it back together like a jig saw puzzle, I get a huge whopping food-on. San Francisco's Ryan Farr shows you what is possible for

the classic American tube steak. Guys like Dan Barber, Joel Salatin, and Josh Applestone are stars in the food world, but Marissa also brings to life farmers who are unknown outside of their own terroir, like Jim Reichardt, the duck guru of Sonoma. There is a new wave of young meat-a-holic twenty-something youngsters who are opening butcher shops, offering classes, and teaching their peers all about meat. Enterprising entrepreneurs are renting smokers and meat grinders and throwing block parties. All over our country, the malaise of years past has given way to a new energy and every day I meet more and more Americans who are really into learning about where their food comes from. Most importantly they are supporting local butchers, farm markets, and regional suppliers, and diving head first into the nose-to-tail movement. Pig's heads and trotters, beef hearts, and lamb kidneys are becoming popular again. Chefs have been eagerly embracing the nearly lost arts of charcuterie and salumi, but notably, home cooks are becoming more interested in making their own bacon these days than finding a recipe that utilizes the store-bought variety.

I was in Philadelphia recently, walking down the street thinking of the butchers I have come to know and love around the world. I had just pounded down a tongue sandwich bathed in red "gravy" and spiked with fried chiles at George's on 9th Street. That may have had something to do with it. I was daydreaming about the camel butchers I befriended in the souk in Syria, the Czerw brothers in Port Richmond, my pal Mike Lorentz in Cannon Falls Minnesota or Sandy Crombie, the haggis king of Edinborough. I stumbled into DiBrunno's and the manager there stuffed me silly with La Quercia lardo and guanciale . . . I was in heaven. Ames, Iowa, is giving Parma, Italy, a run for its money, believe me. And then, as I was leaving, he gave me a slice of Southwark Restaurant's pig's head *testa*, a white-and-pink ovaline shaving of cured meat and fat that Chef Sheri Waide creates, butchering pig heads from scratch in her kitchen. She kicks back some of the product to the guys at the salumeria. I couldn't help but think how far we've come as a food culture. This book, the one in your hands right now, proves it.

—ANDREW ZIMMERN

MEAT OF GOOD FAITH

Standing before a dusty pile of pig testicles on a hot April morning, I realized that my life had come to a place from which it will never return.

After a boozy and beautiful Easter Sunday in Richmond, Virginia, with Tanya Cauthen of Belmont Butchery, I had hightailed to Polyface Farms in Swoope to meet Joel Salatin. When I arrived, I headed to a tent, where two people were quietly inventorying chest freezers filled with Cryovac bags of meat.

Something about the giant farmhouse—tilting into the earth with age—the solemnity of the employees, and the earnestness of my respect for Joel Salatin gives my memory of the afternoon a certain Dust Bowl glamour.

"Is Mr. Salatin here?"

"He expecting you? He's up there."

"Up where?"

"You'll see."

If that isn't just how every fairytale begins.

"Follow that path, young lady, the one with the destination just out of sight."

Sure enough, once I took a few steps I heard the visceral, gut-wrenching sound of a pig screaming. When I came around the corner, I watched this hero of mine, bent over, with a helper (so dirty from his physical work that he had mud on his teeth), castrating a young pig. Once Joel noticed me, he came right over, dropped a steaming set of testes at my feet, gave me the biggest shit-eating grin east of the Mississippi, and put out a hand. And I shook that hand without the slightest flinch.

There's a flea-bitten old saw that says you should never meet a hero. If you think that seeing Joel emasculate a pig proves that to be true, well then, you just don't know me at all. I was utterly charmed that after a flight from New York that morning, he had gotten right back into the grubby, squealing labor of being a farmer. Salatin is one of the great thinkers and mouthpieces of the good food movement, and the integrity of his opinions comes from the deep well of his hard work.

Joel Salatin, like every single butcher in this book is a mirror for me. Eating is a daily prayer, an act of care that passes from the earth into our every cell. Those that spend their lives in devotion to righteous food are my people. Every butcher in *Primal Cuts* is different, which is why I selected them, but we all share a mission to make food that is meaningful and that respects the earth and nourishes its inhabitants.

I run a meat plant in Sonoma County, California. The job of my company, Sonoma Direct, is to butcher whole animals from ranches in our community. Some of these animals, we sell to restaurants and grocery stores; others, we simply "cut and wrap" for farmers who sell their own meat. My work, as commander of this bandsaw brigade, gives me a front-row seat to the food system. From discussing weather and watersheds with producers to hanging out in the kitchens of my customers while the stock fortifies, I see the whole parade. I have the privilege, or thankless mandate, depending on the day, of being a collaborator with everyone.

I want so much to share with you the great creativity and commitment of these butchers as much as I want to share their delicious recipes. I hope you get even a fraction of the inspiration that I did from their stories and knowledge. I have taken a bellows to the definition of a butcher. These are not all men who work behind a counter in a shop, cutting meat all day. Some of them are. A new meat system is cropping up outside the centralized infrastructure and the butchers in *Primal Cuts* have found all sorts of deeply particular and inspired solutions to bring great meat to you. There are butchers in this book whom you might only find at a farmer's market, or on their farm, or in the kitchen of a café. It is my hope that this expanded view of the role of the butcher will urge you to keep your eyes peeled for those hidden meat mavens in your own community.

The recipes in this book are of one spirit but not of one kitchen. Some are simple home-cooking favorites from meat cutters and others are the work of Michelin star chefs. I have taken care to give you recipes from every primal of beef, lamb, goat, venison, and chicken, and to offer varied cooking techniques for every season and mood. Whatever is in your fridge or takes your fancy, I think you will find a recipe in these pages.

I spent my day with Joel walking his property under the spring sun. It was the day after Easter and no one was missing the metaphor. Every blade of grass was in ascension. Polyface Farm pastures were starkly greener and more abundant than their neighbors, the property lines defying another old saw. We sat at Joel's kitchen table and he shared his story, as so many other butchers had and would on my trip around the country to make this book.

"Have a glass of water. We have good water here."

He had been a journalist and had come back to the farm. He writes, still, books of protest and testimony and blueprints of a world in his image.

Writing about meat is, for me, about as sweet as it gets. I have been a writer since I've been anything, really, and I've never met a subject that talked back to me nearly so much as meat. I love meat. I love it in that uncomplicated, bacon-in-a-pan-on-Sunday-morning kind of way. But much more, I love the way weaving through an animal's life takes us through so many homes and habits and ecosystems. I love the traditions and the ceremony. I love the metaphors and the moral dignity it requires to eat meat in good faith, with a full heart.

—MARISSA GUGGIANA

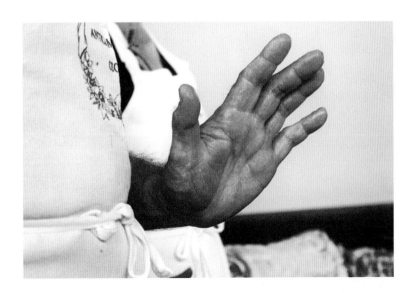

JOSH APPLESTONE

FLEISHER'S GRASS-FED & ORGANIC MEATS, NY

Though Josh and his wife, Jessica, are idealistic and focused on changing the food system, they are the cornerstones of a new traditionalism, not relativist free spirits. Fleisher's has a rabbinical role in this values-based world of sustainable meat; it is a place of learning for other butchers. No revolution for revolution's sake, but merely peeling back corporatization to the fleshy truth, the sacred word, the right way of doing things.

We opened up a shop without knowing how to carve—that came later. With a butcher shop, you need to be a much stronger businessperson than a knife-dragger. The fact that I know how to carve makes me a *better* small-business owner. Every time you put your knife to something, you can make less money; every way you turn your wrist could be a dollar. It's this teeny little bleed that you may never see. Everything's rotting the second you get it. You've got to really understand what these pennies mean.

Before we started, we were looking around at farmers' markets for sustainable animals. Everything was poorly cut, frozen, and wrapped in plastic—it was junk. I was a vegetarian at that point so it was just the dogs and my wife eating it. So we came up with the concept of Fleisher's, strictly whole animals. If we did anything else, we would be like everybody else.

We created a true safe zone, no question whatsoever. When people come to our shop, they know whatever they buy, it's good. It's a big deal for a farmer to put two years into an animal. It took a long time for them to believe in me enough to increase their herds based on my promise that I'll take them a couple years later. There's a leap of faith there. We bite our nose off to save our face because we know being elitist is wrong, but we also know that in this type of situation if you do not do exactly what you're saying, you're part of the problem.

It's very Buddhist not to grow constantly. I would never want to see Fleisher's coast to coast. This is what corporate America does though, they wave a couple of dollars in your face and take a label that customers trust is clean and make twenty million on it before people catch on that it's changed.

I stopped being a vegan six months in. I was vegan because animals were not being processed correctly. If someone hadn't done something about it, it would have kept going. Jessica and I are idealist idiots. All we want is people to pause before they pick something up at Walmart. I think the butcher trend is just the meat part of simple living. I refuse to think that sustainability is going to fall out of fad.

People ask me what it takes to be a good butcher—it takes a masters in theology. You need to sense when someone's having a bad day, learn how to speak to farmers, and you've got to read people. Everything contributes to this image of trust and relaxation and professionalism, which is unbelievably important in a modern-day butcher shop. It's like Jessica says: *We don't sell meat, we sell trust.* It's important. It's like being a priest. Or a rabbi.

> "PEOPLE ASK ME WHAT IT TAKES TO BE A GOOD BUTCHER— IT TAKES A MASTERS IN THEOLOGY."

HORSERADISH-CRUSTED ROAST BEEF

We showcase our flavorful grass-fed beef with this recipe. The roast—deliciously crusted with horseradish and black peppercorns—is perfect hot out of the oven, but it's also great cold on a sandwich. Grass-fed meat will cook differently from conventional, fattier, meat. It is best to use a meat thermometer and go by the internal temperature. A general guide to cooking your roast is about 20 minutes per pound at 375°F.

6-pound sirloin tip roast or bottom round roast, preferably grass-fed, tied
½ cup freshly ground or prepared horseradish
2 tablespoons kosher salt
2 tablespoons Dijon mustard
2 tablespoons finely chopped parsley
1 tablespoon coarsely ground black pepper
1 tablespoon sugar
1 tablespoon sherry vinegar

Remove roast from refrigerator and allow to come to room temperature. Preheat oven to 375°F. Set rack in large, deep roasting pan and place roast on rack. Blend the remaining ingredients together to form a paste and spread on top and sides of roast. Roast in lower third of the oven for approximately 2 hours, until thermometer reads 125°F when inserted in thickest part of roast. Transfer to a cutting board and let rest for 20 minutes. Temperature will rise 5 to 10 degrees and you will have a rare to medium-rare roast. Discard string and thinly slice the beef across the grain to serve.

An unsliced roast can be refrigerated for up to 3 days. The sliced beef can be wrapped in plastic and refrigerated overnight. It makes a great sandwich the next day.

Serves 10 to 12

STIR-FRIED LIVER

WITH ONIONS AND CURRY

This recipe is a play on the classic liver and onions from one of our apprentices, Chichi Wang, who is also a Serious Eats columnist. Instead of getting a sear on a hot and heavy pan, the liver is sliced and stir-fried briefly along with sweet onions. The flavoring for the dish is classic Indian: use high-quality coarse curry-powder mix if you can't make your own.

½ pound calf, chicken, duck, or goose liver
4 tablespoons lard, duck fat, or coconut oil
½ medium sweet onion, Vidalia or Spanish, sliced to a ¼-inch thickness
2 teaspoons curry powder *

Pat the liver dry and cut into ½-inch slices. Heat a wok until it's smoking. Add 1 tablespoon of the fat and let it melt briefly. Add onion and stir-fry for 2 minutes, rapidly moving the pieces around so that they touch the entire surface area of the wok, until it begins to brown on the edges but is still crisp. In the last 20 seconds of stir-frying, add ½ teaspoon of the curry powder and toss evenly with the onion. Remove mixture from wok and set aside.

Add remaining fat and let it melt briefly. Stir-fry liver pieces for 1 to 2 minutes, rapidly moving them around so they touch entire surface, until they begin to brown on the edges but are still tender inside. In the last 20 seconds, add the remaining curry powder and toss evenly.

Reintroduce the onion to the wok and toss together with the liver, being careful not to break up the meat more than is necessary. Plate and serve immediately.

Serves 2 to 4

* To make curry powder: Heat a heavy pan until moderately hot. Place 2 tablespoons coriander, 1 teaspoon cumin, 3 cloves, 2 teaspoons black peppercorns, 1 tablespoon brown mustard seeds, 1 dried red chili, and 1 teaspoon fenugreek seeds in the pan, and toast for just 20 seconds, moving the spices around with a wooden spoon to prevent scorching. The mustard seeds will pop. Remove all spices from the heat and let cool. Grind spices in a spice grinder or use a mortar and pestle. Add 2 teaspoons ground turmeric powder and set aside. Curry powder can be saved in a sealed container; for maximum freshness, use within 2 weeks.

PETE BALISTRERI
TENDER GREENS, CA

My friend, Douglas Gayeton, author of Slow: Life in a Tuscan Town *and no stranger to cured meats, pulled me into the kitchen during a dinner party with Christmas-morning giddiness, "You have got to see this, you are going to love this." From a back corner of the fridge, ostensibly far enough back so that the rest of the family is not confronted by it daily, was half a pig face, cured and eyelashed and grinning. "Pete at Tender Greens sent me this; this guy's the real deal." Indeed. Tender Greens really lit a candle in my sustainability window. Most restaurant chefs will tell you that buying whole animals and working with farms is only possible on a small scale. Tender Greens has four locations, each serving at least 600 people a day. By keeping an agile menu with simple preparations, they are able to feed the masses, all under ten dollars a plate. The warm incandescence of the future.*

My grandparents came over from Sicily. Food was everything. Everybody in my family were tuna fishermen. They would bring home lobsters, oysters, clams, and octopus, and you don't realize until you get older how cool that is. The tuna fishing is done, but my grandfather, who's eighty, still sews swordfish nets at the docks five days a week. He's one of the last guys who knows how to do it. Two of his fingers don't move but he can still play bocce, sew nets, and drink wine.

I played college football. When I got hurt, I realized I didn't want to sit in a cubicle. I finished school and went to San Francisco to work in restaurants. I worked at Masa and was a sous chef at Rose Pistola. I went to my first farm, County Line. That experience changed it all for me. I learned so much seeing the farmers come right into the restaurant. I really wanted to work at Rose Pistola to learn butchery skills. Something in me knew that I needed those skills.

After culinary school, I worked for Erik at Pan Pacific Hotel. He became a mentor, and he is the original brain behind Tender Greens. All three of my partners were executive chefs of five-diamond hotel restaurants. We all wanted out. Now, I work in a T-shirt, shorts, and my Chicago Bears Crocs. You couldn't put a chef coat on me for a million dollars. Well, maybe for a million.

I spend a lot of time going to visit the farms and trying to actually help them grow. We have about fifteen farms that we support out of this restaurant. We're not interested in just buying twenty pounds, we'll take hundreds of pounds, which is great for the farmers.

We took away the waiters, the white tablecloth, the tipping, and the valet parking, We took the food from the farm and we serve it for ten dollars. The produce that we use here is no different from any of the top restaurants in San Diego. We just get amazing product, and then we season it and grill it or roast it. Using whole animals has always been something that I really like to do.

We wanted to take it up a notch, so we make our own bacon, salami, pâté, and pickles. I think pâté is a great way to start with charcuterie. People are scared of making salumi. Romans were curing meats two thousand years ago. It's not rocket science. I've thrown away a considerable amount, but that's how you learn. I could just make one amazing salami every time, but I want to keep trying new recipes. Pulling down something that's ready is like opening a birthday present. I don't really have anyone to talk to that makes salami, so I just experiment. I wish I could fill up this whole place with salumi. I'd be like a mad scientist. I'd be in my glory.

BUTCHER'S COBB SALAD

WITH FREE-RANGE GUINEA HEN AND HOUSE-CURED LAMB BACON

Here's a classic with a Tender Greens twist! If you are limited on time or have trouble finding quail eggs, feel free to substitute fresh organic eggs. You can also use artisan bacon from your local butcher if you prefer not to cure your own lamb bacon.

Lamb Bacon
1 pounds lamb belly
1 tablespoon kosher salt
1 teaspoon black peppercorn
2 juniper berries
1 teaspoon chili flakes
1 tablespoon fennel seed
2 cloves garlic, peeled and minced
1/6 cup red wine
1 teaspoon pink salt *

Vinaigrette
1 egg yolk
1 cup champagne vinegar
1 tablespoon Dijon mustard
1 tablespoon minced garlic

2 tablespoons tarragon
3 cups canola oil
Salt and pepper to taste
Juice of 1/2 lemon

1 free-range guinea hen
Kosher salt and cracked black pepper
1 tablespoon canola oil
1 tablespoon butter
Juice of 1/2 lemon
4 quail eggs
2 large heirloom tomatoes
1 Hass avocado
12 heads organic speckled romaine, washed and
    dried (or 3 heads regular romaine, chopped)
1 cup Point Reyes blue cheese

To cure the lamb bacon, combine all dry ingredients in a spice grinder. Blend garlic and wine together. Place lamb belly on a half sheet pan. Rub dry ingredients onto both sides of the belly, and sprinkle with wine and garlic mixture. Wrap sheet pan and belly together in plastic. Keep refrigerated below 40°F for 6 to 8 days.

Prepare the vinaigrette by mixing all the ingredients together in a blender or food processor.

To roast the guinea hen, preheat the oven to 475°F. Truss hen and season both inside and out with salt and pepper. Heat a cast-iron skillet over medium heat and when pan is hot, add canola oil. Place the hen breast side up in pan. Roast for 20 minutes, then check every 6 to 8 minutes. The chicken should reach 165°F. When hen is done remove from the oven; add butter and squeeze lemon into the natural juices. Using a cooking brush, baste top and sides of hen for 1 to 2 minutes. Let rest for approximately 8 minutes before carving.

To prepare the ingredients for the rest of the salad, cut 2 cups of the cured bacon into lardoons and sauté until golden brown over medium heat. Discard the grease and set bacon aside. Place the quail eggs in boiling water for 2½ minutes, then move immediately to an ice bath. Remove from water and peel. Cut eggs in half and set aside. Core and cut each tomato into 6 wedges. Cut avocado in half, remove pit, and slice.

To assemble the salad, in a large bowl, combine lettuce, tomato, avocado, bacon, and blue cheese. Add kosher salt and cracked black pepper to taste. Dress appropriately with tarragon vinaigrette and place on a family-style platter, or plate individually. Arrange slices of the hen meat on top of the salad and serve.

Serves 4

* Curing salt. Necessary to inhibit growth of bacteria. Use and store with caution. See page 288.

SALAD OF SLOW-COOKED POTTED LAMB SHANK

WITH FAVA-BEAN PUREE AND GRILLED CIABATTA

This is a Spring-loaded dish using braised lamb shanks, so often identified with hearty winter menus. Lamb is at it's meataphorical peak in the spring and every lamb comes with a shank (or four), so don't put braising into hibernation for the warmer seasons.

Lamb Terrine

1 cup tomato sauce
2 quarts lamb or beef stock
4 whole lamb shanks
Kosher salt and cracked black pepper
Canola oil
2 large carrots, cut into 2-inch pieces
1 yellow onion, quartered
4 celery ribs, cut into 2-inch pieces
4 sprigs sage
2 cups red wine
6 sprigs thyme
1 cup bruniose vegetables (carrots, celery,
    fennel, and chives in an ⅛-inch dice)

Fava-Bean Puree

1 pound fresh large fava beans in the pod
1 bunch basil, stemmed
1 clove garlic, peeled
5 tablespoons olive oil
Kosher salt and cracked black pepper
1 teaspoon lemon juice

2 large organic navel oranges
¼ cup olive oil, plus extra
2 tablespoons champagne vinegar
8 heads organic baby lettuce, washed and dried
1 pound hard pecorino cheese
6 slices fresh ciabatta bread

Preheat the oven to 350°F. To prepare the lamb terrine, combine tomato sauce and stock in a medium-size pot and bring to a simmer. Season lamb shanks with salt and pepper. In a large skillet over medium heat, brown the shanks and remove to a roasting pan. Add the carrots, onion, celery, and sage to the remaining oil in the same skillet and brown. Deglaze with the red wine. Pour vegetable mixture and simmering stock/puree over the lamb shanks. Toss in the thyme sprigs. Cover with foil and slow roast until fork tender, approximately 2 to 3 hours.

Let the lamb shanks cool, then remove from pan. Pull bone completely away from meat—it should come away very easily. Strain liquid into a small pot and reduce by half. Refrigerate until cold and then skim fat off top of liquid. Pick meat away from skin and fat and break into small pieces. Place in a mixing bowl with the bruniose and cooked vegetables. Mix together and season with salt and pepper. Spray the inside of a terrine with oil and line with plastic wrap, leaving enough plastic-wrap overhang to cover the top when the mold is filled. Fill the mold with the shank mixture and add some braising liquid as you go so that the meat is very moist thoughout. Once terrine is nearly full, pour over braising liquid to completely cover meat. Cover with the plastic overhang and the terrine lid. Refrigerate overnight.

To make the fava-bean puree, blanch the fava beans in boiling water for 1 minute and then transfer to an ice bath. Remove and discard skins. Place beans on a paper towel. Combine fava beans, basil, and garlic in food processor and blend. Slowly add the oil to the puree and blend again until smooth. Season with kosher salt, pepper, and lemon juice to taste. Place in a small bowl and refrigerate.

To prepare the vinaigrette, first segment and deseed the oranges. Squeeze the remaining juice from the oranges over the segments in a small bowl. Add ¼ cup olive oil and champagne vinegar and mix well. Scoop out the oranges from the vinaigrette and set aside for the salad.

To prepare and plate the salad, brush bread slices with olive oil and quickly grill. Remove lid from terrine, open plastic on top, and flip over. Slice terrine into half-inch pieces and fan on a platter. Spoon a long stripe of fava-bean puree along middle of terrine. Toss orange slices and lettuce in a mixing bowl and season with salt and pepper. Lightly drizzle with the vinaigrette. Arrange salad on the platter or individual plates. Using a potato peeler, shave wide, thin slices of pecorino cheese to place on top. Add the grilled bread and serve.

Serves 6

DAN BARBER

BLUE HILL AT STONE BARNS, NY

I shed a tear during my dinner at Blue Hill at Stone Barns. Something tugged at that sentimental space between my throat and my heart. The meal was exquisite and punctuated by earnest theatricality, such as the presentation of a block of earth perched on a silver tray to spark discussion on the effect of winter on the sugars in my carrot. My sweet, unadorned, tiny, perfect carrot. There's no pretension in that level of hospitality: "We made this for you, we grew it and we harvested it and we prepared it—for you." The wholeness of vision at Blue Hill at Stone Barns and its relationship with Stone Barns Center for Food and Agriculture is clearly the work of a man who thinks simultaneously in generations and seasons and seconds.

To be a foodie is to be an environmentalist. And to be a foodie is to be a nutritionist. And to be a foodie is to be a community activist.

We're all looking for great flavor and so the question is: What are the ecological conditions of your area telling you to do to produce the best flavors? Going after really delicious food, a really delicious leg of lamb—an herbivore that's fed grass and raised in the right way—is a statement not just about food. Change is bottom up, not top down. I think the more effective and, ultimately, longer-lasting change is going to come from the soldiers, the chefs and writers and home cooks.

You need a community around an animal to make the animal work. And I would argue it makes the community work, too. The specifications of animal butchery were a result of the specialization of menus. Specialization of taste mimics the specialization in agriculture. The Hudson Valley wasn't even appreciated for its great grassland. In fact, overwhelming opinion of this ecology used to be that it was the worst place to make money because of humidity—you couldn't grow fruit or vegetables, the soil was rocky. But, those factors conspired to produce exceptional grassland.

Jose butchers the carcasses at Blue Hill at Stone Barns. "I try to learn every day the way to butcher faster and more perfectly. But, I take my time to do it right."

Milk production and the pasturing of animals created these gorgeous, iconic, Upstate New York landscapes.

Our dedication to the whole animal has always been intense. In the early days, a farmer would come in during dinner service with an animal and we would spend the night dealing with it.

What I like about our meat program is that it's evolved very organically from a totally unsustainable use of this stuff to an organization that works. A traditional à la carte menu has a somewhat limited capacity to deal with a whole animal. So now we have no menu. You sit down, you get a list of ingredients. We get to divide the animal the way we want. I'm hesitant to talk this way because it presumes that every chef could do this, and they can't. They don't have that kind of space. So I don't like to speak too universally. For us, it became a total unshackling when we just got rid of the menus. Now we're like free free—freer than you and me. If we had started like that, it would never have worked because we didn't understand enough. We also have a café and a charcuterie program. Within that matrix we can find a really good home for everything. And now we have this added bang of carbonizing the bones. After we make the stocks, we take the bones and put them through this machine, which is essentially making charcoal out of the bones. Then we use that to grill the meat on.

The institutional end really needs to be worked out to thrive because you can't make money buying whole steers unless there's an outlet for it that makes a lot of sense. We have these outlets and our waste is very small. Is the labor more because of it? Absolutely. And do all restaurants have the luxury of affording a butcher? No. Chefs today aren't trained in butchery. We're looking at a lost tradition, which is very frightening. You've got to have technique.

We've lost the generation of people who just knew how to cook and butcher, just people at home. If you're not cooking your own food, somebody's cooking it for you. It really comes down to: Do you have the ability to put together a meal? It's the simplest thing and it has frankly been absent from the conversation. Chefs play a huge role as educators and as arbiters of good taste. None of these political issues, health issues, or environmental issues matter unless you can cook. Unless the food tastes good.

Adam Kaye, Vice President of Culinary Affairs. Adam manages the curing program and brings with him experience in environmental policy, which is vivid in the decision-making of this restaurant.

CREPINETTES

The name "crepinette" comes from the French word for caul fat, which is a membrane that surrounds the internal organs of most four-legged creatures. Caul fat makes a lacey casing for this sausage, each crepinette a little package.

2¼ pounds pork offal (liver, spleen, heart and kidney, trimmed)
2¼ pounds fatty pork scraps and trimmings (about a 1:1 lean-to-fat ratio)
2¼ teaspoons salt
2¼ teaspoons sugar

½ teaspoon finely ground black pepper
¼ teaspoon ground nutmeg
½ cup finely chopped shallots
½ cup chopped parsley
½ cup sherry or Madeira
Caul fat

Grind the offal and fatty scraps through the fine plate of a meat grinder. Mix thoroughly with the remaining ingredients, except the caul fat. Form mixture into balls roughly 2 inches in diameter.

Cut small pieces of caul fat, just large enough to wrap around the balls in a single layer with very little overlap. Wrap the forcemeat in the caul fat and set on a sheet tray lined with parchment paper. Allow to sit in the refrigerator overnight.

Sauté in a little oil in a cast-iron pan over a medium flame, about 1½ minutes per side.

Makes about 24 3-ounce crepinettes

Craig Haney, Livestock Manager at Stone Barns Center for Food and Agriculture. Craig raises animals for Stone Barns, many of which end up in the Blue Hill kitchen.

SAGE AND RED-WINE PORK SAUSAGE

A classic and elegant pork sausage, which you could use without casings for a pasta al sugo *in the winter or alongside a pea-shoot salad for a spring lunch.*

4 pounds lean pork shoulder
1 pound fatback
1 tablespoon salt
½ tablespoon finely ground black pepper
3 cloves garlic, minced
1 bunch fresh sage, chopped
½ cup red wine
About 12 feet hog casings, 32 to 35 mm diameter

A few tips to get going: *
- Use very fresh pork.
- Partially freezing the meat and fat is essential to a good forcemeat.
- Mix the pork with the spices quickly by hand so as to keep the forcemeat as cool as possible.

Cut pork and fat into ½-inch cubes; spread on a tray and freeze for about 1 hour. Pass the lean and fat through the ¼-inch plate of a grinder into a large mixing bowl. Mix together all the dry spice ingredients in a small bowl until well blended. Add to ground pork along with the red wine, and mix thoroughly by hand.

Prepare the hog casings by rinsing in cool water and flushing with water. Load sausage stuffer with forcemeat and attach an appropriate-size stuffing tube. Slide casings onto stuffer and tie off at the end. Stuff forcemeat into casings. Twist off sausage into 5-inch links and prick links to remove any air pockets. If possible, hang sausages on hooks in the fridge or lay out on a rack in the fridge and allow to dry for 24 hours before using.

These links are best pan-fried in a little oil over a medium-low flame, and ideally should be served a little pink inside for maximum juiciness.

Makes about 25 5-inch sausages

* See also Sausage Basics, page 32.

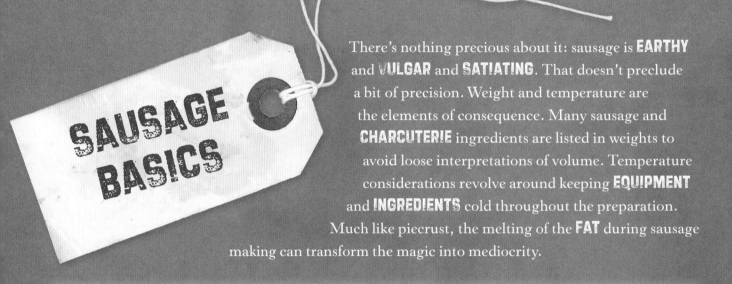

SAUSAGE BASICS

There's nothing precious about it: sausage is **EARTHY** and **VULGAR** and **SATIATING**. That doesn't preclude a bit of precision. Weight and temperature are the elements of consequence. Many sausage and **CHARCUTERIE** ingredients are listed in weights to avoid loose interpretations of volume. Temperature considerations revolve around keeping **EQUIPMENT** and **INGREDIENTS** cold throughout the preparation. Much like piecrust, the melting of the **FAT** during sausage making can transform the magic into mediocrity.

The recipe below is emblematic of any good sausage: lots of fat (20 percent, at the very least), some liquid to bind, and a balanced cohort of spices.

My great-grandpa Ritz moved from a small Alpine village in Italy in 1921 and brought this recipe, among others, with him. The recipes remain in active use in our family. From time to time, a package of cool, heavy sausages will appear, like napping babies, in a shady spot on my front porch.

GRANDPA RITZ'S SAUSAGE

4 pounds beef brisket, trimmed of fat and diced
1 pound pork butt, diced
½ pound pork fatback, diced
½ head of garlic (pureed)
2 cups red or white wine, chilled
5 tablespoons salt
1 tablespoon sugar
2 tablespoons black pepper
1 teaspoon nutmeg
1 teaspoon ground cloves
2 teaspoons ground allspice
2 teaspoons ground cinnamon
12 feet hog casings, 32 mm diameter, stored in
   water, then soaked in hot water prior to use
Cooking string

Keep your meats and fat as cold as possible through the sausage-making process. Combine first 3 ingredients and keep in refrigerator until you are ready to grind. (1) Using the small die of a commercial or countertop grinder or standing mixer with a grinder attachment, grind meat and fat into a mixing bowl set over a bowl of ice. Put mixture in freezer for a half hour, along with the mixing bowl. Mix the garlic with the wine and let sit in refrigerator.

(2) Add salt, sugar, pepper, spices, and garlic-and-wine concoction to the meat mixture. Blend thoroughly by hand.

(3) Slide an entire casing onto the nozzle of your stuffer. Clamp the loose end or tie it with string. (4) Fill your stuffer with meat mixture and stuff it into the casing, holding the casing on

(1)

(2)

(3)

(4)

(5)

(6)

the nozzle with your fingers. Every six inches, twist the casing four times to create a link. (5) When you run out of meat or casing, make an incision lengthwise in the casing and knot the two halves together, or tie with string. If needed, add a bit of water to help casings feed freely off nozzle. Air pockets in sausage may be removed by pricking with a pin or tip of a knife.

(6) These sausages were stuffed individually to hang and cure, so each was tied instead of twisted.

Cover and refrigerate or freeze until ready to use. You can sauté, roast, grill, or poach your sausage to internal temperature of 150°F. Let rest for 5 to 10 minutes and sausage will continue cooking another 5° to 10°F.

Yields 20 6-inch sausages

We've had issues with some of the processing plants here—new staff or new inspectors. I'll order a pig with the head on from a farm and it will come in with no skin, or no ears or tongue. The inspector will tell me I can't have that stuff. *But you gave me a skull with eyeballs in it! What am I going to do with that?* Seriously. The farms mostly blame the processors, and I can kind of see that, but I don't have time for people to be working out their systems on us. I need them to just have it figured out. I would love to see smaller processing places, but I know it's hard for them to exist. A few restaurant orders are not going to sustain a plant. That's got to be frustrating.

Eli is our salumist. He's a one-man operation and he can produce a hundred pounds

JASON BARWIKOWSKI
OLYMPIC PROVISIONS, OR

There's a practicality to Jason Barwikowski that I find as comforting as a cool hand on a hot cheek. It is the practicality that I have come to associate with butchers. A butcher works within the very predictable context of a carcass and seeks to most efficiently dispatch its parts. Chefs can (and perhaps should) deal more in artistic impossibilities. Simply put, a butcher will very rarely be heard to yell, "Make it happen!" into the phone at some hapless purveyor. A chef, on the other hand . . . Jason has worked at some of the more boundary-pushing restaurants in Portland, and Olympic Provisions is no exception. He has the soul of a butcher. A man acquainted with deftly managing the natural order.

of meat a day. Everyone in Portland makes charcuterie, but as far as I know this in the only USDA aging, dry-curing plant in Oregon, which is pretty exciting. We just started selling our first batch of charcuterie this week.

I used to absolutely loathe the idea of cooking. My mom was a great home cook. We were one of those families that always ate together: 6:30 pm, the four of us around the table. But I remember being asked to clean the stringbeans or help make the salad and I just hated it, it was drudgery. That feeling started to change when I had my first real girlfriend in high school. Her father just loved to cook. He was a cop in Detroit and cooking was his therapy. We'd go to her parents' for dinner and he'd make pesto using a mortar with herbs from his garden, listening to opera really loud, drinking rosé. I could see him decompressing. It almost reminded me of the scene in *Silence of the Lambs* when Hannibal Lector spits the key back up and he's in this Zen state.

I signed up for cooking school, and did better than I had ever done in school my whole life. My mom sent me an article about Brian Polcyn, who wrote *Charcuterie*. He had opened up a restaurant in the town next to the one where I grew up. I got a job by begging him, and telling him I would peel potatoes. And my education started over. He taught me more things than my classes ever could.

Buying whole animals, you can actually make the most money. The way food used to be, if you wanted a blade steak, you had to cut it yourself and then you had to utilize everything that came with it. The whole art of cellaring and rotating through product has disappeared. Charcuterie and salting and pickling are about long-term utilization. I'm not doing whole-animal cooking and charcuterie because it's the cool thing to do. I do things that fascinate me. I think the reason it's a trend is because more people are realizing they need to step back and look at the big picture instead of blasting into the future with the newest radical convenience. We're educating the public. It's a full-circle, symbiotic relationship between the community, the restaurants and the farms. It's very different being an owner; it changes your whole perspective. I'm pretty obsessed and compulsive anyway, very fanatical about stuff. When you're a chef someplace, you'll say, *Hey guys, linen isn't free, try to conserve.* But now I'm like going through the laundry basket pulling things out, just freaking out.

BUNUELOS DE CHORIZO

This recipe was created by our salumist, Eli Cairo. He says, "Everyone should know how to make a chorizo doughnut!"

1 chorizo sausage (about ¼ pound), finely diced
2 tablespoons olive oil
Salt
1 cup flour
3 eggs
1 bunch scallions, finely chopped
Piment d'Espelette, finely chopped
Vegetable oil for deep-frying

Sauté the chorizo in the olive oil until it gives up some of its oil but does not burn or get too crisp, about 30 seconds on low to medium heat. Put a cup of water in a saucepan. Once the chorizo pan has cooled down to room temperature, strain off the oil directly into the water. Set aside the rendered chorizo. Add a generous pinch of salt to the water and bring to a boil.

Once the water is boiling, add the flour all at once and reduce heat immediately to low, stirring continuously with a wooden spoon to create a dough. Just as you feel the dough begin to stick to the bottom of the pan, transfer to a stand mixer with paddle attachment in place. Mix on low speed and add eggs, one at a time, waiting until each one is fully incorporated. This should form a nice, smooth dough that is slightly runny. Fold in chorizo and scallion. Fold in piment d'Espelette, to taste.

Heat a deep pot of unused vegetable oil to 385°F. Fry teaspoon-size balls of dough until very light gold and cooked through, approximately 2 to 3 minutes. Remove fried dough to paper towel or cloth and serve warm. These should pull apart very easily and the centers should be light and airy. Season with salt, if necessary.

Makes 20 to 24 Bunuelos

CHICKEN LIVER RAGU

The richness of chicken liver and bacon with a little bit of tomato and vinegar for kick . . . Comfort food to gobble and peck by the bowl.

1 pound chicken livers	1 tablespoon minced fresh thyme
Salt and black pepper	3 tablespoons tomato paste
½ pound butter, room temperature	¾ cup red wine (barbera d'Alba preferred)
½ pound bacon, finely diced	2 tablespoons red wine vinegar
3 to 5 cloves garlic, minced	2 tablespoons balsamic vinegar
1 medium-size red onion, minced	Pinch chili flakes (optional)
1 tablespoon minced fresh rosemary	Chicken stock

Trim the livers of any fat and sinew. Separate the 2 lobes of each and lay them on a plate lined with a paper towel. Season well with salt and pepper; reserve.

Heat a large, heavy skillet over a medium-high flame. Add a generous 2 tablespoons of butter, allowing it to melt and foam, and then add one-third of the livers. Sear well on both sides, but do not cook all the way through. Imagine them being at perfect medium doneness. Remove the livers as they finish to another plate lined with a paper towel. Drain off the burnt butter, lightly wipe out the pan with a cloth, and repeat this process until all the livers have been cooked.

Place the pan back on the flame and add a smallish bit of butter. Toss in the bacon and cook, draining off the fat as it renders. When it crisps, about 5 minutes or longer, turn down the heat a bit and add the minced garlic. Let this bloom out for a minute or two, gaining very little color and releasing some aroma.

Add the onion and cook for about 8 minutes, seasoning with salt, which will release the moisture in the vegetable and help to convert the starches to sugars. Stir often, but try to let some fond build up on the bottom of the pan as the bacon, garlic, and onion meld. When the onion starts to wilt and soften, gains a little color, and is fragrant, stir in the minced rosemary and thyme. Let the mixture cook for several minutes.

Stir in the tomato paste. Let it cook and catch on the bottom of the pan. The heat should be persistent, not nagging. Let the flavors come out and transform slowly over time; do not force them out quickly. When the tomato paste starts to darken and the mixture is soft and homogenous, add the wine and turn the heat up a bit. Reduce the wine until there is barely any left in the pan.

Pour the red wine vinegar into the mix and reduce again till fairly dry. Follow with the balsamic. When the balsamic has reduced slightly, add the chicken livers and toss them well. There should be a bit of liquid in the pan, enough to coat the livers and keep everything slightly saucy. Add chili flakes, if desired.

Pour this mixture into a food processor and pulse it a few or many times, depending on the texture you desire. This can also be done by hand with a knife on a cutting board.

Slowly reheat the ragu in a pan, adding chicken stock and a little butter to get desired consistency. It is delicious slathered on grilled bread with a fried egg on top, or over polenta or taglietelle pasta.

Serves 8 to 10 as an appetizer with bread or 4 to 6 as a main course with pasta

BRINED ROAST CHICKEN

Brining adds an extra layer of flavor and tenderness: do it once, and you will be sure to do so again. I usually cut the keel bone and the backbone of my chicken, leaving a uniform, flat, and more even cooking bird. The English call this "spatch-cocking." This recipe is excellent on the grill or in the oven.

1 cup salt
¾ cup sugar
12 bay leaves
1 tablespoon peppercorns
1 teaspoon chili flakes
1 head garlic, cut in half around the equator
1 whole chicken, 3½ pounds
Olive oil
Garlic, minced
Fennel seed, crushed
Pepper
2 or 3 lemons, halved (optional)

Toss the first 6 ingredients into a pot with about a gallon of water and give the mixture a good stir. Put on a high heat and bring to a boil, making sure the salt and sugar dissolve. Cool completely. Remove the keel bone and the backbone of the chicken. Halve or quarter the bird, place it in a large nonreactive container, and add brine. Refrigerate 4 hours for quartered chicken, 8 hours for halves. Remove chicken from brine and pat dry with paper towels. Rub with olive oil and reseason with garlic, fennel seed, pepper, and lemon juice to taste. Add halved lemons to the roasting pan, if desired.

One hour before cooking, preheat the oven to 425°F; you want a lot of heat to start the roasting process. Make sure the seasoned chicken is fairly close to room temperature before it goes into the oven.

Roast chicken skin side up for about 20 minutes. Lower the heat to 325°F and continue to roast for another 20 minutes. Let the bird rest under foil on the stovetop for 10 minutes before cutting into it.

Before serving, I usually squeeze the super-soft, gooey roasted lemon halves over the chicken—and the rapini and potatoes that I invariably make alongside.

Serves 4

JAMIE BISSONNETTE
COPPA AND TORO, MA

Jamie's punk rock. We both came up in the punk scene, which meant being militantly vegetarian or vegan. I had always thought of my return to being an omnivore as a total left turn. Talking to Jamie about the camaraderie among his fellow chefs, playing with pig heads, and the conviction and creativity in each food choice, made it as clear as a power chord: whether you are a vegetarian or a supporter of sustainable farming and cooking, living your values without apologies is the real spirit of punk. Jamie puts the "oi" in oink.

The punk-rock community was mostly straight-edge and vegan. I became a vegetarian and toured in bands. I would still cook. We'd stay at somebody's house and not sleep in the van for a few days. We'd have these potlucks with other bands. By the time I was seventeen I was ready to give up being a punk rocker, so I went to culinary school.

I went to Paris for a while, kicked around, and was told by a friend that I had to start eating meat again if I was serious about this craft. I came back to Boston and kind of worked my way up in the community here.

After running Eastern Standard, I realized I wanted to open restaurants where cooks want to go on their days off. That's why we have Toro and Coppa. That's why we've got pig ear terrine, we've got headcheese, coppa di testa on the menu. We make all of our own salumi. At Toro, I took down a seventeen-month-old ham yesterday. It tastes like buttery cheese. And knowing the farmer that raised the animal made it even better. Right now we have about a thousand dollars worth of pork curing into hams. That's a lot of money sitting in pig escrow. Our Tamworth pig farmer always says, *I'm a papa for six months and then I give them to you and then you're a papa to the hams.* I'm still passionate about pigs.

For me, it's about the relationships. If people have all-natural, outdoor pigs to sell, my answer is always *Yes*. There's a lot of salt in the world. There's plenty of ceiling space. I'm sure that the electric company's wondering why our bill for air-conditioning is so insanely high. It is like growing pot. You could buy the Michael Ruhlman book, follow the exact recipe and hopefully make something formidable, but it's always going to taste the same. Every time I touch it, it tastes more like how I want it to taste.

If you have someone like me to butcher it, then absolutely, it makes financial sense to buy whole animals. If you don't have a solid meat cutter, it probably doesn't. A lot of people make stupid mistakes, like wasting stuff, trying to cure things. If you can't make a good *coppa*, don't. Turn it into a sausage. You make money with meatballs.

A lot of the guys of my generation, like Will Gilson, Louie DiBicarri, Robert Grant, are really committed to banding together into a culture of not just food but learning. We're not competing. There are three million people who are going to go out to eat sometime this week in Boston and I can't feed them all.

"RIGHT NOW WE HAVE ABOUT A THOUSAND DOLLARS WORTH OF PORK CURING INTO HAMS. THAT'S A LOT OF MONEY SITTING IN PIG ESCROW."

TRIPE À LA COLLINSVILLE

Tripe is one of my favorite foods, to eat and to cook. This recipe, from Toro, is fresh and light and very approachable—a gateway tripe dish.

2 pounds honeycomb tripe (pork or beef)
3 cups white wine
1 cup salt
1 quart chicken stock
1 teaspoon caraway
1 teaspoon coriander
1 teaspoon fennel seed
1 teaspoon mustard seed
1 cup diced onion
½ cup diced carrots
½ cup diced celery

Stew

4 shallots, julienned
2 tablespoons live oil
2 cloves, garlic sliced
1 Anaheim pepper, julienned
1 poblano pepper, julienned
1 red jalapeño, julienned
1 fennel bulb, finely diced
1 cup applejack whiskey
1 (10-ounce) can peeled plum tomatoes, crushed
  (alternately, if in season, 4 pounds mixed
  heirloom tomatoes, diced, skin on)
1 piment d'Espelette
¼ cup fines herbes (blended basil, chervil,
  tarragon, marjoram, and chives)
Lemon wedges

Soak tripe in the refrigerator in a pot of water with 1 cup of wine for 3 to 12 hours. Remove tripe, scrub with the blunt side of a large kitchen knife, and rinse. In a pot, cover tripe in cold water with rest of wine and salt. Bring to a simmer. Turn off immediately and strain. Return tripe to pot and cover with chicken stock. Make a spice sachet with the caraway, coriander, fennel, and mustard seeds, and add to the pot. Add onion, carrots, and celery. Bring to the boil, reduce to low simmer, cover, and cook for 5 to 6 hours. Cool tripe and let it sit in its liquid overnight in the refrigerator. The next day, bring the tripe and liquid back to a boil, strain, and reserve the braising liquid.

In a tall stockpot, sweat shallots in olive oil over medium-high heat until tender. Add garlic and cook until translucent. Add peppers and fennel and cook until tender. Add the tripe, sachet, and whiskey, and cook till reduced by half, about 3 minutes. Strain the tomatoes, add to the pot, and reduce to simmer. Cook for 45 minutes, rewetting with braising liquid as needed.

Thin to desired consistency with liquid. A salt and piment d'Espelette to taste. Serve with herbs and lemon as accompaniments. Cooled and refrigerated, tripe stew will keep for a week.

Serves 4 to 6

PIG EAR TERRINE

My sous chef, Josh Buehler, created this silky and tender terrine, which is a favorite at Coppa. The layers of ear make it a very visual and impressive dish. Season with fleur de sel, fried garlic, and snipped chives. We serve ours with a Yuzu aioli, though any creamy and sour sauce would pair fine. Garnish with mini red shiso leaves and ground sumac.

24 pig ears	**Sachet**
Kosher salt	1 stalk lemon grass, chopped
3 quarts chicken or pork stock	2 pieces crystallized ginger
3 cups soy sauce	1 fresno chili, chopped
2 cups mirin	1 tablespoon coriander seed, toasted
1 cup sake	1 tablespon grains of paradise
1 cup lemon or meyer lemon simple syrup *	1 tablespon fennel seed
	4 cloves garlic

Clean ears of any hair. Place in a pan with the spice sachet. Season lightly with salt.

In a saucepot, bring the stock, soy, mirin, sake, and simple syrup to a simmer. Pour the hot liquid over the ears, being sure that the liquid covers by the ears by ½ inch. Meat not covered by liquid will get charred and can't be used in the terrine. Cover tightly with aluminum foil. Cook at 200°F for 36 hours. Check periodically that it does not boil. When the meat falls to pieces but does not shred, it is done.

Cool the ears in the liquid to room temperature, then remove from the liquid. Reduce the liquid in the pot by one third. Line a terrine mold or loaf pan with plastic wrap, leaving enough overhang to cover the top when the mold is filled. Layer the ears to ⅛ inch from the top. Pour the reduced liquid and shake the mold to cover the ears. Fold plastic wrap over the top to seal. Press with 2-pound weight in the refrigerator overnight.

Remove the terrine from the pan, change the plastic wrap, and store in cool place until ready to serve. Slice with a very sharp knife ¼ inch thick. The terrine will keep for up to 10 days in the refrigerator.

Makes 1 mold

* Heat ½ cup sugar and ½ cup water over medium heat, stirring until the sugar dissolves. Add juice of 1 lemon and stir.

PRIMAL CUTS: PORK

The **PIG** is an efficient **BEAST**. Most everything can be redolently transformed. Here is a field **GUIDE** to your choices and general cooking suggestions:

BOSTON BUTT

The pork shoulder is usually called the butt. Pork butt is divided into two parts, the top part being the Boston butt. It is usually cooked very slowly, on a stove, oven, or barbecue, because it is ribboned with fat and connective tissue. It is often singed a bit at the end—if the sauce has any sugar in it—which caramelizes the fat and creates the wondrousness of carnitas and pulled pork and el pastor.

Cuts: bone-in or boneless roast (smoked or fresh), blade steaks, stew meat; excellent ground for sausage or cured meats because of the high fat content

PICNIC SHOULDER

Picnic shoulder can be treated in the same way as Boston butt, though it is a bit tougher, and is sometimes cured to make hams.

Cuts: bone-in or boneless roast (smoked or fresh, either whole or divided into the pectoral and cushion muscles to make four roasts per animal); hocks; also ideal for sausage

LOIN

This is where pork chops are made (though you can cut a chop from the shoulder, and steaks from the legs as well). The tenderloin nestles on the back of the loin and can be removed to prepare separately. If the tenderloin is left in, your chops will look more like T-bones and porterhouses.

The loin can be boned and served as a roast or medallions. Though there is a spectrum of fattiness in this primal (fattier toward the shoulder, bonier toward the rump), overall it is very lean and less forgiving than other primals. Roasting the roast is best, seared beforehand. For chops, I toss them in a pan that is very hot with a bit of oil and let them get all brown and crusty on both sides and then put them in the oven for a few minutes.

Cuts: tenderloin, rib chops, loin chops (T-bone or porterhouse), and cutlets; baby back ribs, pork rack, rib roast, (bone-in or boneless), loin roast (bone-in or boneless, 8 to 11 ribs)

BELLY

The belly, when cured and probably smoked, is bacon. This can be done rather easily. You can also leave the skin on and roast the belly. When you peel off the crust of thick skin, the belly lies as tender and vulnerable to attack as any underside should be. Alternatively, belly meat can be diced for stir fry.

Spareribs are fatty and bony, so cheap and delicious. If they are squared (sternum and rib tips removed), they are St Louis-style ribs. There are many different iterations of ribs that a butcher can toss at you: baby back ribs (from the loin), button ribs (from the lower spine), country-style ribs (from the shoulder blades), but they all want slow, long cooking.

Cuts: bone-in or boneless belly (bacon or fresh side pork; also specify skin-on or skinless); spareribs, and riblets

LEGS

Often referred to by their most popular outcome, hams, legs have plenty of uses even when not set aside for curing, smoking, and aging. They are, after all, one quarter of the carcass. You can roast a leg whole or as separate muscles, as with the leg of any animal. Grind it or make stew or sausage (with the help of some fatback or belly to avoid dryness). You can make steaks that are sliced very thin, and pan-fry them to serve with red-eye gravy.

Cuts: whole ham or ham steaks, cutlets, or scallops; hindshanks; rear hocks; bone-in or boneless roasts, whole or divided into inside,

outside, and knuckle roasts; strips and cubes

OFFAL

If you buy a whole pig, you must ask for the following things or you may not receive them. If your butcher buys whole animals, they can save these items for you. You have to be very clear with the slaughterhouse that you would like the head, ears, feet, caul fat, fatback, hocks, and trotters. Have them remove and save the cheeks and jowls for you. The cheek of most any animal is a silky and tender muscle that is best cooked slow and wet. The jowls are often cured and sometimes cured and smoked into what the Italians call guanciale, a sort of "face bacon." You can also make head cheese by cooking the whole head in a giant stockpot, resulting in morsels and gelatin (see Headcheese, page 150). Fatback, the strip of unadulterated fat on the top of the pig, is a treasure trove for sausage and charcuterie. The fatty skin becomes pork rinds and the fat itself is seasoned and cured to make lardo, which can be spread upon anything. It can also be rendered for cooking fat. Usually hocks are smoked and tossed into soups as a flavor pill, adding bass notes of smoke and salt. Trotters and hocks can also make a nutrient-dense, gelatinous stock.

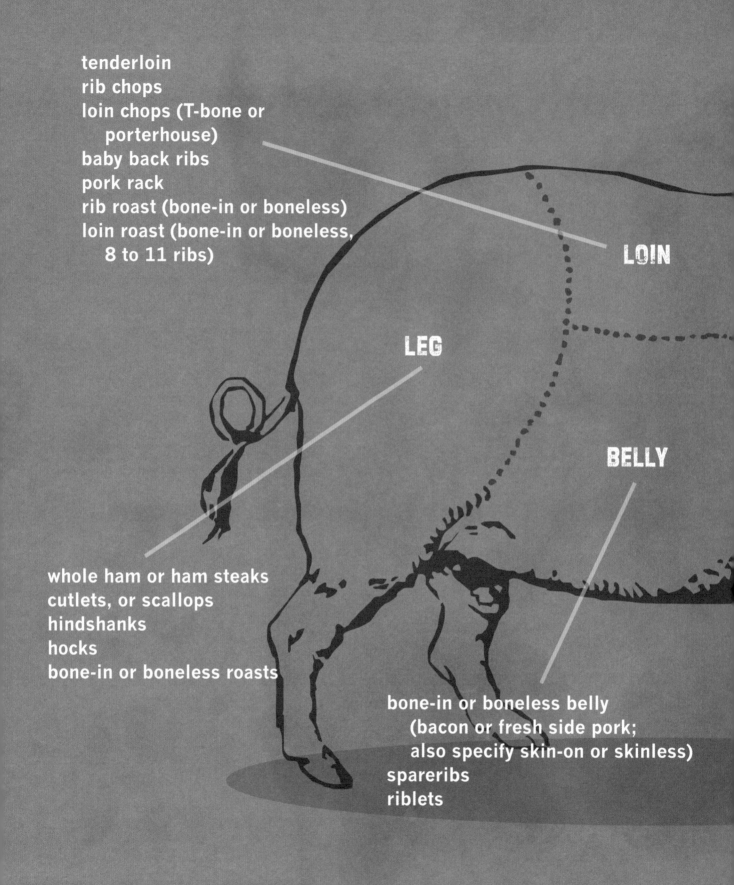

tenderloin
rib chops
loin chops (T-bone or
    porterhouse)
baby back ribs
pork rack
rib roast (bone-in or boneless)
loin roast (bone-in or boneless,
    8 to 11 ribs)

LOIN

LEG

BELLY

whole ham or ham steaks
cutlets, or scallops
hindshanks
hocks
bone-in or boneless roasts

bone-in or boneless belly
    (bacon or fresh side pork;
    also specify skin-on or skinless)
spareribs
riblets

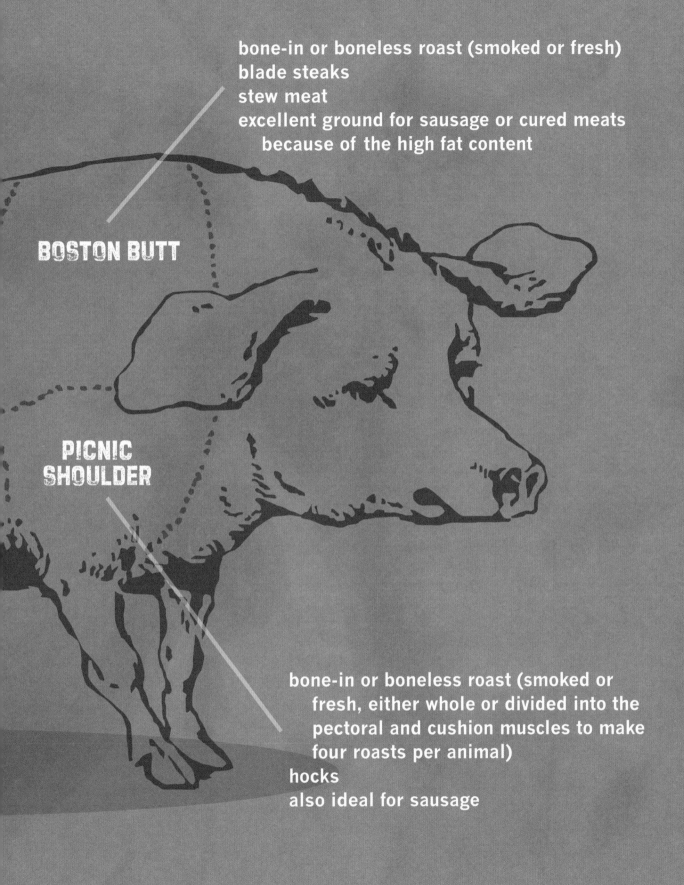

bone-in or boneless roast (smoked or fresh)
blade steaks
stew meat
excellent ground for sausage or cured meats
because of the high fat content

BOSTON BUTT

PICNIC SHOULDER

bone-in or boneless roast (smoked or
fresh, either whole or divided into the
pectoral and cushion muscles to make
four roasts per animal)
hocks
also ideal for sausage

TAYLOR BOETTICHER
FATTED CALF, CA

The Fatted Calf is like the charcuterie workshop at the North Pole. Taylor and his wife, Toponia, are possibly the most adorable couple in all of Meatdom and you always leave with gifts—smoked, cured, and aged—bundled up with red-and-white butcher string. The counter is a phantasmagoria of treats, carefully crafted by hand in the happily humming kitchen.

You haven't lived until you've had bacon warm out of a smoker. It is one of life's great pleasures. There are so many different styles of bacon. It's like barbecue—you just can't get into what's better or worse. Our selection is a mile wide and an inch deep. We don't make big batches but we make a lot of stuff. We have forty sausages, a dozen pâtés, ten or twelve cooked salamis, ten or twelve dry-cured salamis, jerky, bacon, hams, turkey. Headcheese is one of those things we don't make very often because people get kind of spoiled. If you just make it now and again, people who like that kind of thing will search you out. Our prosciuttos take two years. We take one down every three or four months. Our chef, Bailey, just took down her first prosciutto. That was a big milestone.

I got started with all this because Marsha at Café Rouge needed somebody to work the meat counter. My only real experience with meat was at school, a week-long meat program, and their charcuterie classes, which were old-school French, stuff laid out on mirrors, lots of gelées. At Café Rouge, I learned about forcemeats and making sausages and true pâté de campagne, things like that. We made a lot of awesome food together.

Then, I went to Italy on my honeymoon and I learned different ways of cutting things, especially big prime cuts, because the style of cutting varies from region to region. I worked with Dario Cecchini at his place in Tuscany for a bit. He's got this cadre of little Italian ladies in heels who are making all this stuff in the back. His shop has been in the

family for hundreds of years, just the kind of history that does not exist here. The whole time we were there we were talking about opening our own place, what it would be like.

Toponia and I started working out of a commissary kitchen and selling at farmers' markets. We had one worktable, a shitty little hand grinder, and a tiny stuffer. We never took out a loan, never bit off more than we could chew. After a while we were able to hire somebody so that we could concentrate on recipe development and growing the business.

We opened the Napa shop in January of '08. The hardest part for somebody who comes to work here from the restaurant business is the amount of planning. We're always looking ahead at the month and the quarter, rather than the next day.

BRASATO AL MIDOLO
(BRAISED BEEF SHANK)

This little number ups the richness quotient from a so-so braise into the stratosphere by employing that friend to Real Butchers worldwide: marrow. We remove the bone from a beef shank and replace it with the bone's marrow, fresh rosemary and black pepper to create the pot roast of your dreams.

1 whole beef shank, about 8 pounds, seamed open, left in one piece, with the shank bone removed and split lengthwise (you can ask your butcher to do this)
Sea salt
Freshly ground pepper
1/3 to 1/2 cup chopped fresh rosemary

2 tablespoons extra-virgin olive oil
2 pounds shallots or cipollini onions, peeled
6 cups beef stock (page 73)
1 bottle of Vin Santo or medium-dry sherry
Prepared cream-style horseradish (optional)

Remove the marrow from the shank bone using a sharp knife. Save the bone for your next batch of broth. Season the shank liberally on both sides with salt and pepper. Sprinkle the rosemary on the inside of the shank and lay the bone marrow down the center of the roast. Fold the sides of the roast around the marrow to mimic the original shape of the shank and secure with several loops of cooking string.

Preheat oven to 300°F. Heat the oil in a heavy-bottomed pot or deep casserole over medium heat. Brown the shank roast on all sides. Add the shallots, broth, and wine. The roast should be nearly covered with liquid.

Place the pot in the oven and simmer, uncovered, for 5 to 6 hours, until fork tender. Turn the meat occasionally. You can serve the roast at this point or reserve in refrigerator for up to 2 days in its braising liquid. (Brasato is even more delicious when it is allowed to sit for at least a day.) The refrigeration also makes it easy to skim off and discard the layer of fat that forms at the top.

To serve, remove the brasato from its liquid and slice to desired thickness. Serve over polenta or mashed root vegetables topped with the braised shallots and a generous ladleful of the braising liquid. You can also accompany with creamed horseradish.

Serves 6 to 8

FATTED CALF MEATLOAF

A really tasty and easy recipe. You can hardly go wrong, with sausage and bacon in it! Our tip for a perfect loaf is to fry up a little patty first and make sure it tastes just right.

2 large eggs
½ cup plain bread crumbs
1 onion, diced
2 tablespoons olive oil
1½ pounds freshly ground beef
1½ teaspoons sea salt
½ teaspoon freshly ground black pepper
1½ pounds loose sweet pork sausage
3 slices bacon, diced to about ¼ inch
½ cup ketchup
½ teaspoon Tabasco sauce
½ teaspoon Worcestershire sauce
1 tablespoon freshly grated horseradish or 1½ tablespoons prepared cream-style horseradish

Glaze
½ cup ketchup
1 teaspoon Tabasco sauce
1 teaspoon Worcestershire sauce
2 tablespoons freshly grated horseradish or 3 tablespoons prepared cream-style horseradish

Preheat oven to 325°F. Beat the eggs and add to them the bread crumbs. Sauté onion gently in olive oil until soft and translucent. Place the ground beef in a large mixing bowl and season with salt and pepper. Add the sausage, bacon, and onion. Mix lightly. Add to the meat the egg-and-bread-crumb mixture, ketchup, Tabasco, Worcestershire, and horseradish. Knead the mixture by hand until it begins to hold together. Test for seasoning by cooking a quarter-size patty of the mixture in a small frying pan on the stove. Taste, and adjust seasoning if necessary.

On a parchment-lined baking sheet, shape meatloaf by hand into an oval approximately 3 inches high by 9 inches long, smoothing the edges and cracks. Place in middle of oven.

To make the glaze, combine all ingredients.

Insert a thermometer into the center of the meatloaf after about 30 minutes. When it reaches 100°F, begin basting with a thin layer of the glaze every 10 minutes, until the loaf reaches 145°F. The glaze will darken to a rich molasses color at the edges. Remove the meatloaf from the oven and let it rest for 10 minutes. Slice and enjoy. This meatloaf is best served with mashed potatoes and a butter lettuce salad. Leftovers make excellent sandwiches with pickled onions and homemade mayonnaise.

Serves 6

SCOTT BOGGS
HUDSON RANCH, CA

Scott Boggs is the rancher and farmer at Hudson Ranch, the acclaimed Hudson Winery run by ex-oilman Lee Hudson. Scott runs a CSA [Community-Supported Agriculture], selling restaurant chefs and civilians meat from animals that roam through the carefully cultivated chaos of the ranch. Scott left his position at French Laundry, perhaps the most famous restaurant in the world, to monitor the seasonal catharses of birth, growth, and butchery in Hudsonia.

Lee wanted to show people that you can have a very diverse poly culture here in Napa Valley because it's one huge monoculture of grapes.

We have pigs, chickens for eggs and meat, guinea fowl, turkey poults, and then we do some beef. The pigs are foraging acorns. We give them free reign on about thirty-two acres. It's interesting when you read books about hog farming and they say to sanitize everything, but then what happens when the pig finally goes outside?

I don't name animals anymore. Slaughter is an intense procedure, especially the bigger the animal is. I am definitely okay with it. I know the animals have had a phenomenal life. And I know they are going to people who understand the whole process.

We invite people to come watch us slaughter. It gives you perspective. We do the major butchery the same day we slaughter. We have lunch, which is usually pork liver and onions, and then the next day is the sausage making, meat sausage and blood sausage. People are fascinated by the whole thing—especially the ones who have never been exposed to it before. We don't eat that much meat, because for one thing it's expensive to get really good meat, and for another I know the whole backstory of the animals.

At French Laundry, I was hired to be the butcher and that position is so complicated. Almost everything was coming in whole animal. We got a lot of wild game from Scotland, whole pigs, and Devil's Gulch rabbits, milk-fed poulards from Four Story Hill Farm. You never knew what you were going to get.

On the tasting menu, there's always a first fish, a second fish, a first meat, and a second meat, which are based on what is on hand. Then you come up with the dish itself, and it's fascinating because a vegetable won't be repeated. So if there are peaches in one course, you won't see any other stone fruit anywhere on the menu. It gets difficult when you're the last person to decide what you're going to use. You're like, *Uh . . . kohlrabi?* So I would try to get my dish set before I even sat down.

Selling cuts would be so easy for us, but selling whole animals is difficult. So many people don't know what to do with everything. Even when I explain it to them, it doesn't mean that they're willing to take on something new. I remember once when I was at French Laundry, we shot a bunch of squirrels that were eating all of our acorns and cooked them up different ways. I took it to some of the chefs in the kitchen and they're like, *I'm not eating that!*

LAPIN À LA MOUTARDE

(MUSTARD-CRUSTED RABBIT)

This is a recipe I used to serve at Fringale Restaurant in San Francisco. Search out a very high quality mustard from Dijon, versus the "Dijon-style" mustard found in supermarkets. Rabbits don't slum.

1 whole rabbit, cut into 8 pieces
½ cup Dijon mustard
Salt
Freshly ground black pepper
5 tablespoons unsalted butter
1 small onion, finely chopped
½ cup French Chablis or other dry white wine
1 bouquet garni (rosemary, thyme, bay leaf)
¼ cup crème fraîche
2 tablespoon finely chopped flat-leaf parsley

Smear rabbit pieces with mustard and season with salt and pepper to taste. Heat 2 tablespoons of the butter in a large, heavy skillet over medium-high heat. Sear rabbit pieces, turning frequently, until crisp and golden brown, about 12 to 14 minutes. Transfer to a platter.

Reduce heat to medium and melt remaining butter in skillet. Add onion and cook until softened, stirring occasionally, 8 to 10 minutes. Add wine to skillet and scrape up any browned bits. Return rabbit pieces to skillet, along with bouquet garni. Cover and cook until rabbit is tender, about 25 minutes. Turn off heat and remove rabbit to a warmed platter. Stir crème fraîche and parsley into skillet. Spoon sauce under the rabbit to maintain the crisp crust.

Serves 4 to 6

CORNED VEAL TONGUE

We developed this corned tongue while I was the butcher at the French Laundry. We used veal tongues, which are my favorite, but most any type of tongue would work great with this recipe.

Brine
2½ quarts water
6 tablespoons salt
3 tablespoons pink salt *
1 tablespoon whole peppercorns
5 allspice berries
½ teaspoon mustard seed
¼ teaspoon coriander seed
5 tablespoons sugar
4 cloves garlic
½ teaspoon chili flakes
1 bay leaf
¼ teaspoon ginger powder

2 veal tongues or 1 beef tongue
1 carrot, chopped
1 medium onion, cut in half
1 bouquet garni

Sauce Gribiche
1 large hard-boiled egg
½ tablespoon Dijon mustard
3 tablespoons olive oil
1 tablespoon white wine vinegar
1 tablespoon chopped parsley
1 tablespoon capers, chopped
2 tablespoons cornichons, finely chopped
Salt and pepper

Heat the water to dissolve the salts. Toast the peppercorns, berries, and mustard and coriander seeds in a small sauté pan. Add all brine ingredients to the pot and let cool. Add the veal tongue and brine in the refrigerator for 7 days. You can weigh down the tongue with a small plate so it is completely submerged and flip it every 2 days. If film appears on the surface simply skim it off before flipping, and wash the plate.

Remove tongue from brine and rinse thoroughly under cold water. Place tongue in a saucepan, cover with water, and add carrot, onion, and bouquet garni. Bring to a boil and reduce to a light simmer. Cook for 3 hours or until tender, and let cool in the liquid.

Meanwhile, prepare the sauce. Extract the yolk from the egg and mash with the mustard until smooth. Add the oil a little at a time, whisking to make an emulsion. Finely chop the egg white and add to emulsion with the rest of the sauce ingredients. Mix well. Add more olive oil, if desired, to adjust consistency. Add salt and pepper to taste.

Peel skin off tongue. Cut across the meat on a 45-degree angle into ¼-inch-thick slices. Serve cold with sauce. You can also reheat and serve with pickled onions and simple boiled potatoes, or coarsely chop and cook with chopped potatoes for a corned tongue hash, served with poached eggs.

Serves 4 to 6

* Curing salt necessary to inhibit growth of bacteria. Use and store with caution. See page 288.

DAVID BUDWORTH

DAVE THE BUTCHER
AND MARINA MEATS, CA

David invited me to Sunday supper with his friends, a weekly tradition that involves eating for many hours, Belgian beer, and a rooftop view of Coit Tower and Sts. Peter and Paul Church in San Francisco's North Beach neighborhood. The other guests included his ex-wife/best friend, his roommate who runs the Belgian beer bar on the ground floor of the building, and his roommate's father, a 78-year-old retired baker who now navigates the world on Rollerblades, which he wore the entire evening.

David keeps his butcher knives in their scabbard in his bedroom (which I halfheartedly assured him wasn't strange in the slightest), smokes hand-rolled cigarettes, and thinks poorly of organized religion even though he went to Catholic school. Classic bad boy. But then he invites skating old men to dinner. And talks about butchering. You wouldn't think butchering would be the tender inside of anything but you would be wrong.

In the young meat-obsessed culinary crowd I run into in the Bay Area, most find butchery a satisfying means to an end. Dave is most sincerely a butcher. His passion lies primarily in the pursuit of a perfect cut.

I'm not a chef, I'm a butcher. I've been cutting meat for more than twenty years—long before the whole rock-star butcher trend started. Butchering is part of my heritage. My grandfather came over from Germany just before the turn of the century and opened up a butcher shop here. I still use his knives—they're over a hundred years old.

I love the educational part of my work. I'm at Avedano's a few days a week right now, teaching some of the girls how to break down carcass. They're getting really good. The rest of the time I'm at Marina Meats. We have a good counter and I've got a lot of regulars who trust me. They come back all the time and tell me how their dinner turned out.

I enjoy creating events that bring together people from the local meat and food world to share ideas and opinions. I've also been going to Cochon 555, which is a great pig party where different butcher-chefs break down and cook whole pigs to raise awareness for heritage breed hogs. It's a total bonding experience and such hard work to prepare the pig from start to finish.

I came up in the early nineties at Ver Brugge Meats in Oakland, that was my boot camp. I had been a manager at another place before, so my resume looked good, but after a few days they realized I didn't really know anything. The father of my boss who opened their first shop grew up during the Depression, so he could barely even feed his family until the place was paid off.

We would work for twelve hours a day, six days a week, and then if there was still work to do, my boss would give us cash to stay. There was something about the way he looked at me. Even if I was exhausted, if he asked me if I had anything to do, I just couldn't lie to him. I'd be filleting until midnight and then back at 6 am.

At Ver Brugge, I learned to just keep working. You cut your finger—check it to make sure too much didn't come off, tape it up, and keep going. I think I was the youngest butcher there by twenty-five years. For the first time in my life, I had a title. I was really proud.

GRILLED GOAT RIB CHOPS

These are magnificent when cooked over a grill on a rooftop, preferably with a view of steeples, but they will taste just as good anywhere you can prop your grill. If you cook them stovetop, make sure the surface is good and hot, so you only have to flip them once. Don't worry about losing the raisins to the grill—they'll add a sweet, smoky, subtle flavor to the finished chop.

1 cup Dijon mustard
1 cup raisins
½ cup olive oil
1 bunch Italian parsley, chopped
6 cloves garlic, chopped

2 tablespoons curry powder
Coarse cracked pepper
Chili flakes
8 goat rib chops, about 2 pounds *

For the marinade, mix the mustard, raisins, olive oil, parsley, garlic, and curry. Add pepper and chili flakes, to taste. Blend well. On a sheet pan, lay out chops. Cover with marinade. Let stand at room temperature up to 3 hours, or marinate in fridge overnight.

Grill chops over hot flame about 2 to 3 minutes per side so they are still pink inside.

Serves 4

* The chops in this recipe are from the rack, but you can also use goat loin chops. If using lamb rib chops or loin chops, tone down the curry just a bit. For pork loin chops, I would take out the curry altogether.

BABY BACK RIBS

I never cook with recipes. I tend to look at a recipe for an idea, and then have fun creating the idea in my head. So here is my baby back ribs for you to try and experiment with!

3 racks of pork baby back ribs, about 3 to 4 pounds
Olive oil
Garlic cloves, chopped
Red onion, chopped
Pinch of salt
Freshly cracked black pepper
2 (28-ounce) cans whole peeled tomatoes
Honey, about 3 tablespoons
Mustard, about 2 tablespoons, any favorite
Red chili flakes or Spanish smoked paprika
Cilantro, chopped

Preheat oven to 325°F. Split ribs in half, creating 6 half racks. Lay ribs in a baking dish.

Barely cover the bottom of a sauce pot with olive oil. Heat over medium flame for 2 minutes, then add some chopped garlic, onion, salt, and cracked pepper. Sauté until onion starts to sweat, about 5 minutes. Add tomatoes, reserving liquid for later. Stir and smash tomatoes in pot. Simmer for 10 minutes or so. Stir a tablespoon each of honey and mustard into sauce. Taste and add more honey and mustard as desired. Sprinkle in chili flakes to taste. Continue to stir slowly until blended. I like my sauce chunky, but you can process the sauce, adding reserved tomato liquid as needed, to desired consistency.

Pour sauce over ribs and spread evenly. Cover with foil and bake in oven for 1½ hours. To crisp, cook for about 15 minutes on medium-hot grill, place under the broiler for a few minutes, or leave in oven for another half hour. Cut into individual ribs and serve with a sprinkling of chopped cilantro on top for color.

Serves 8 to 10 as an appetizer or 4 to 6 as a main dish

SCOTT BUER

BOLZANO ARTISAN MEATS, WI

Bolzano is a Germanic town in northern Italy that Scott visited. The name is fitting, as Bolzano Meats is a pastiche of a Milwaukee boy's Germanic surroundings and his Italian culinary curiosity. It is also the town where they found a man from the Bronze Age frozen in the Alps. I like this parallel even more. Out of a turgid food culture of factory farming and low-grade lagers melts a man of ancient knowledge and old-fashioned ideals. Mustachioed and fastidiously sincere, he is both of Milwaukee and apart from it, like a man just emerged from a glacier.

I'm a big food-science geek, so I was curing at home for a long time. And I had previous experience in quality control at a rat poison company. So, between those two things, I thought I could do this.

I bought an armoire from Home Depot and controlled the humidity with a pan of salt water. If it was too humid, I put the dehumidifier in the basement. That worked pretty well. I used a fan from inside a computer because they're free and they never break. I used the plug from an old broken cell phone charger, stripped the wires and tied them together. That provided airflow.

We have eight products. We're basically making prosciutto out of all the cuts. Yes, prosciutto is a ham, but I call it that because we're curing whole muscles until they're ready to eat, shelf stable. Prosciutto you don't need to cook or refrigerate. We use the whole hog except for the front hock, but I'm working on that. We're not doing sausage, we are only aging whole muscles. So any bits left over are waste, as far as the company is concerned. Restaurants can always wing what they're doing. But I've got to know exactly what I'm making. I had to go through so many more regulations than any restaurant, that I think it's a good thing to leave plants to do it. I'm not really cool with the illegal curing.

I don't add any cultures. There's good mold and bad

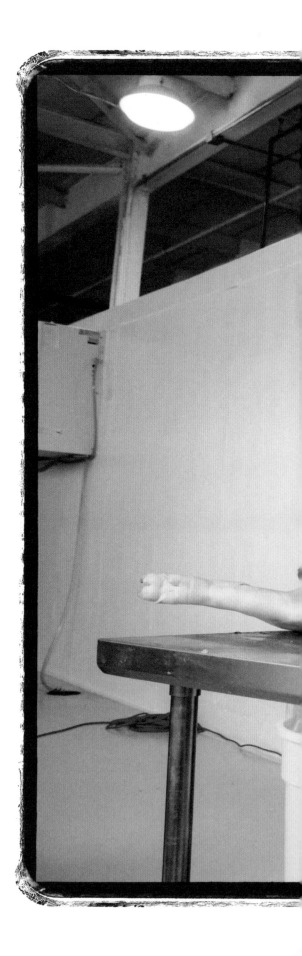

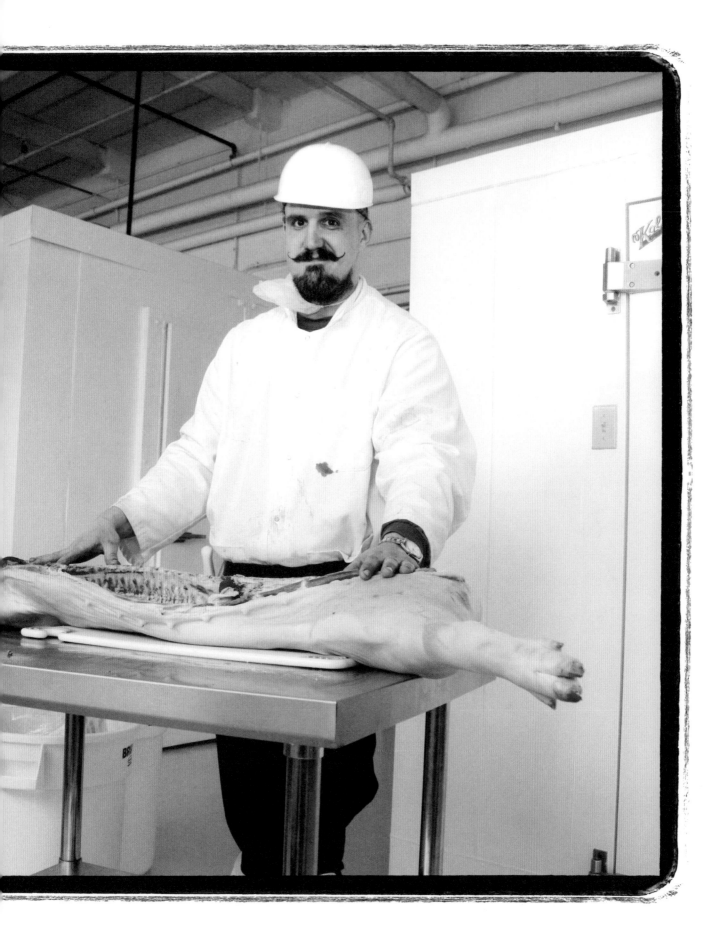

molds that develop but we just watch it. The airflow really controls it. If bad mold happens, we just get vinegar and wipe it down. We use nitrates on everything but the Speck Prosciutto. Nitrates have been used for a thousand years. If you have a big serving of dark, leafy greens, you're getting the same amount of nitrates as a serving of cured meat. You shouldn't be eating cured meat at every meal anyway.

I think the people who like our stuff understand why it costs so much. You could say cognac is grape juice and it's only fifty cents for grape juice, right? It's perspective. This is like a triumph over Wisconsin food.

Growing up in Wisconsin, at Christmas you would have raw beef sandwiches. No one does that anymore. Everyone's afraid it. Ground beef with salt and pepper on rye bread; and it was pretty awesome. Now that I am an amateur food scientist, I feel safe enough to try it on my own. I just give the beef a dunk in vodka.

RED-COOKED PORK HOCKS

For a while, this was the only part of the hog I wasn't using, so it was my little take-home treat. This "red-cooked" or casserole method of cooking is a classic but under-represented Chinese technique. These intense dishes are great with tough and fatty cuts. They are meant to be almost a little too intense and tempered with lots of rice.

1 cup dried shiitake mushrooms
1 cup dried woodear mushrooms
  (if unavailable, double the shitake)
6 to 8 pork hocks, to yield 3 pounds
  of skinless uncooked meat
1 tablespoon lard or oil
1 large onion, cut into large slices

2 tablespoons minced garlic
2 tablespoons minced ginger
1/3 cup shaoxing rice wine (substitute
  pale dry sherry)
5 tablespoons mushroom-flavored soy sauce
  (substitute dark soy sauce)

Preheat the oven to 300°F. Soak the mushrooms in about 2 cups of boiled water to cover. Slice mushrooms when softened and set aside, reserving the mushroom liquid.

Skin the hocks, remove the meat, and cut into 1-inch pieces. Brown the meat in lard in a heavy cast-iron pot with a lid. Add the onion and lightly brown. Add garlic and ginger and sauté for a minute or two. Add the rice wine; scrape bottom of pan to get any browned bits. Add the mushrooms and mushroom water and the soy sauce. Cover pot and transfer to oven. Cook for 1½ to 2 hours, until the meat is tender. Check mushrooms to make sure they are softened as well.

Serve with plenty of white rice.

Serves 4

PORK KIDNEY AND LIVER PIE
(OR PÂTÉ BRISÉE)

Even for someone who cuts up hogs, this one was a little intimidating, like something out of a Dickens novel. But this utterly delicious pie comes out as dense pâté in a delicate, savory crust. Very decadent and very rich.

Piecrust
2 cups all-purpose flour
½ teaspoon baking powder
¾ teaspoon fine sea salt
¾ cup (4½ ounces) chilled leaf
   lard, diced
4 to 8 tablespoons ice-cold water

Pie Filling
2 pork kidneys
1 pound pork liver
½ pound pork lean trimmings
⅛ cup pork fat trimmings
2 tablespoons milk
½ tablespoon salt

2 teaspoons nutmeg, grated
2 teaspoons black pepper
½ cup onion, minced

To make the piecrust, blend flour, baking powder, and salt in a medium-size mixing bowl. Add the lard, and use a pastry blender in an up-and-down motion until mixture resembles coarse crumbs with some small pea-sized pieces. Or, pulse in a food processor until the lard is reduced to pea-sized pieces, about 15 seconds. Turn the mixture into a bowl.

Sprinkle half the water over the flour-and-lard mixture and mix with a fork. Add more water and squeeze a bit of the mixture between your fingers. If it holds together, transfer the dough to a lightly floured surface; if not, add another couple of teaspoons of ice water and test again. It should form a smooth ball when pressed together. Gently knead the dough into a ball. Divide in two (one part slightly larger than the other) and flatten into 2½-inch-thick round discs. Wrap each disc in plastic wrap and refrigerate for at least 30 minutes before using. On a lightly floured surface (or between two sheets of wax or parchment paper), roll larger half first, with steady pressure from center outward, into a circle 2 inches wider than pie plate for the bottom crust. Transfer dough to pie plate by loosely rolling dough around rolling pin. Center the rolling pin over the pie plate and then unroll, easing dough into plate. Roll out smaller dough disk for top crust and refrigerate.

To prebake the bottom crust, first prick bottom and sides of unbaked dough with fork (50 times) to prevent it from blistering or rising. Bake crust in lower third of oven at 425°F for 10 to 12 minutes, or until edges and bottom are golden brown.

To prepare the pie, preheat oven to 325°F. Grind all the kidney, liver, and lean and fat trimmings. You want to make an emulsion, so don't worry if the fat is too warm and smears as you grind. You can use a sausage grinder followed by an immersion blender, or a food processor. Add milk and salt, nutmeg, and pepper, and mix into the emulsion. Then mix in onion. Pour the mixture into the prebaked piecrust bottom. Cover with the refrigerated top crust and trim edges of dough, leaving a ¾-inch overhang. Fold top edge over bottom crust. Press edges together to seal, and flute as desired. Cut slits in top crust or prick with fork to vent steam.

Bake for about 45 minutes. Test for doneness with a toothpick. It should come out dry, not wet, when pie is ready. Remove from oven, let cool until warm to set up. To serve, slice into thin pieces. This pie is very rich!

Serves 6 to 8

HOW TO SHARE A COW

Purchasing a **COW** from a farmer is a commitment beyond the filling of a freezer. This is hundreds of pounds of **MEAT**. You can try to buy a section. If the farmer doesn't have a program to sell quarters or halves, then find some cohorts. You now have a co-op, a CSA, a buying group, a sacred fraternity of **CARNIVORES**—however you prefer to think of yourselves.

Sharing a carcass is art and science, relying on principles of discovery both deductive and intuitive. The science of sharing an animal involves procuring a chart of ratios, provided on page 66. Once you have the weights, you can begin the work of parceling out the meat. The art of sharing comes in valuing the parts in relation to one another, and in service to people's taste and sense of fairness. The chart provided on page 67 is one version of fairness. You may have your own.

The first step is to facilitate the safe and humane slaughter from grazer to carcass, and from carcass to chop, cheek, and shank. When you have found an animal, ask the farmer where they normally have their livestock slaughtered. It is legal to have the animal killed on the ranch, if you are buying it whole.

Once your noble beast has been killed and eviscerated, it must be aged. It really would be a shame to go to all this trouble and not age the beef. The best option is to find a butcher with an aging room and ask them to hang your carcass for around three weeks. If no one has room to hang the carcass, the second-best option is to

have the butcher age the beef after it has been cut into primals (while many butchers no longer have rails to hang carcasses, they can break down the animal into primals and stack it somewhere). The final option is to wet age the beef. To properly wet age, the cuts must be vacuum-sealed and kept at a consistent temperature until you freeze them. Wet aging increases tenderness but it does not have the flavor-concentrating effect that dry aging does, because it traps the moisture in the bag, where dry aging allows the moisture to slowly evaporate.

Your great hulk of meat is ready to be butchered once it has been properly aged. This is where you get the chance to form a relationship with your butcher—because you must be clear about what you want, in the correct proportion to your deference for their greater experience. Many butchers will not have shared an animal amongst one, two, or twelve people. They may find this either charming or extremely irritating. It will require not only a good butcher but the right butcher. They may charge you a bit more because each cut will be wrapped and identified. Some butchers will be open to the idea of

divvying up your shares and will have a pretty good idea of what is fair, based on market value (plus you can blame them if your neighbor gets bent out of shape about not getting a tenderloin). If they will not divvy, or if you prefer to do this part yourself, you can use the guide that follows as a key to sharing. It was developed from resources created by the Bay Area Meat CSA—a Slow Food Berkeley project that facilitates the purchase of whole animals by offering resources, advice, and community—and from the Sonoma County Meat Buying Club, a pilot project I developed with the University of California Cooperative Extension.

BREAKING IT DOWN!

These are weights from a cow that originally weighed 880 pounds "on the hoof." After slaughter and evisceration, the carcass weighed 474 pounds. The total amount of meat shared was 380.93 pounds, while the balance of 93.07 pounds were made up of fat and bones (which can also shared but are not generally given a value in a CSA). The opposite chart gives an example of sharing.

GRILL (tender meats that benefit from high heat and quick cooking)

	LBS	LBS PER CUT	NO. OF CUTS
filet *	9.39	1.17	8
rib eye *	13.89	0.87	16
new york strip *	12.56	0.52	24
TOTAL:	35.84	0.86 (average)	48

ROAST (medium tenderness meats that can be served rare to medium rare)

	LBS	LBS PER CUT	NO. OF CUTS
top sirloin	16.68	0.70	24
eye of round	7.63	3.82	2
sirloin tip	5.50	5.50	1
flank	2.80	1.40	2
skirt steak	4.50	0.64	7
flat iron	4.50	0.64	7
cross rib roast	26.50	4.42	6
tri tip	3.41	1.71	2
TOTAL:	71.52	2.35 (average)	51

BRAISE (meats slow cooked in wet heat)

	LBS	LBS PER CUT	NO. OF CUTS
chuck roast (boneless)	26.12	3.27	8
brisket *	13.37	3.34	4
rump roast	7.69	1.28	6
short ribs	13.27	1.11	12
cross cut shanks (osso buco)	14.00	1.75	8
back ribs	6.63	3.32	2
TOTAL:	81.08	2.34 (average)	40

GROUND (burgers, bolognese, bourguignon)

	LBS	LBS PER CUT	NO. OF CUTS
stew meat (bottom round)	25.12	1.05	24
ground beef (flap meat, top round, and trim)	167.37	2.62	64
TOTAL:	192.49	1.83 (average)	88

	LBS		NO. OF CUTS
GRAND TOTAL:	380.93		227

* These muscles can be left whole, if you want to let one person have a whole piece, in lieu of other cuts.

SHARING IT!

Shared amongst eight people, everyone gets a little under 50 pounds of our sample cow. It's not exact, but exactitude is not the spirit of the matter. In the roast section, the shares look uneven, but I have balanced the weight, since some of the roasts are heavier than others. I have left them out of the shares, but the kidneys, tongue, liver, heart, and bones can also be shared with those who are interested.

	GRILL	ROAST	BRAISE	GROUND
1	1 filet 2 rib eyes 3 New York strips	3 top sirloin 1 eye of round 1 flank 2 skirt steaks	1 chuck roast 1 brisket 1 rump roast 2 short ribs	8 ground 3 stew
2	1 filet 2 rib eyes 3 New York strips	3 top sirloin 1 eye of round 1 flank 3 skirt steaks	1 chuck roast 1 brisket 1 rump roast 2 short ribs	8 ground 3 stew
3	1 filet 2 rib eyes 3 New York strips	1 sirloin tip 1 cross rib roast	1 chuck roast 1 brisket 1 rump roast 2 short ribs	8 ground 3 stew
4	1 filet 2 rib eyes 3 New York strips	3 top sirloin 1 cross rib roast 2 flat irons	1 chuck roast 1 brisket 1 rump roast 2 short ribs	8 ground 3 stew
5	1 filet 2 rib eyes 3 New York strips	3 top sirloin 1 cross rib roast 1 tri tip 1 flat iron	1 chuck roast 1 rump roast 1 short ribs 1 shank 1 back ribs	8 ground 3 stew
6	1 filet 2 rib eyes 3 New York strips	4 top sirloin 1 cross rib roast 1 tri tip	1 chuck roast 1 rump roast 1 short ribs 1 shank 1 back ribs	8 ground 3 stew
7	1 filet 2 rib eyes 3 New York strips	4 top sirloin 1 cross rib roast 1 skirt steak 2 flat irons	1 chuck roast 3 shanks 1 short ribs	8 ground 3 stew
8	1 filet 2 rib eyes 3 New York strips	4 top sirloin 1 cross rib roast 1 skirt steak 2 flat irons	1 chuck roast 3 shanks 1 short ribs	8 ground 3 stew

CHRISTIAN CAIAZZO
OSTERIA STELLINA, CA

In Mexico, there are cities that have been decreed magical by the state. If we did that in America, Point Reyes would be a magical city. It is fecund with creatives and the electricity of ocean air. And Christian is its native son. He may not have been born here, but Osteria Stellina's "Point Reyes Italian" has rooted him in this agriculturally blessed corner of the earth. Having a beer at Stellina in mid-afternoon, I met a fisherman who supplies the restaurant, the lady who runs the coffee stand Christian also owns, and a cheese maker. Ruddy from the coastal sun, we all talked about the weather and the local lager. Magic.

I have wanted to be a chef for as long as I can remember. As a kid, I was always curious about how and why things were made. The mysteries of mustard, bread, and cheese were much more interesting to me than the Loch Ness monster and Bigfoot.

I'm mainly self-educated as a cook. The information isn't there by instinct, but I've always learned the most by giving myself the freedom to make mistakes, and then figuring out what I did wrong. Frying a cheeseburger in a pan on the stove wasn't the first thing I ever made, but I remember it being one of the greatest cooking lessons I've ever given myself. I was eleven years old and accidentally let the oiled pan get hotter than usual. The burger turned out much juicier and more flavorful than it usually did. It was an "aha" moment. I was a gangly, sports-obsessed kid, and I'd just taught myself searing. I felt as though I'd uncovered one of life's great secrets. This was a forgotten memory until more than a decade later when I was searing the lamb appetizer at Postrio. I was twenty-five years old and completely in over my head, waking up nights with worry from the stress of being a line cook at top-rated restaurant in San Francisco; and it hit me: *I know how to do this.* I did it when I was kid, and I really learned it. It wasn't described to me in a cooking class at some money-grubbing culinary school. I lived it.

Postrio was an incredible experience for me—a second

education. All these trends that are going on now in restaurants were happening there twenty years ago: buying and butchering whole animals, homemade charcuterie, sausages, breads, mustards, everything. It was intense. After Postrio, I spent a year at Union Square Café in New York City, and that's where I really became a market-to-table cook. I would go shop the green market in the morning a block away, and design that night's specials menu using what I'd bought. Once I started cooking that way, it was hard to do it differently ever again.

I moved to Point Reyes about ten years ago. I was at the height of my cooking career, when I had a terrible car accident that left me paralyzed for four days. I underwent major surgery and it was a long recuperation. That slowed me down; I met a girl and moved to the country. Osteria Stellina, which is named after my daughter, is the third business I opened in Point Reyes—after the coffee bar and the grilled cheese stand. With all the great produce, grass-fed beef, and fresh seafood around here, I felt the region was very locally underrepresented.

The farmers' market is where I still get my creativity. I go at least once a week, twice in the summer when the Point Reyes market gets underway. Stellina's menu is ever changing. There are things we can't get locally, and that's hard. But do we give up our ideals just to make sure people have what they expect? We're not really trying to reinvent the wheel. We're just trying to make delicious food out of the best possible ingredients.

People ask me a lot if I miss the pace and excitement, the glamour of the city—but I really don't. I did a radio show recently in San Francisco and at one point the host said to me, "You really do live in a fantasy, don't you?" The truth is, most days it really does feel that way.

VEAL BREAST

STUFFED WITH SOURDOUGH BREAD AND SAUSAGE

The preparation of this impressive dish is a 2-day process, but deliciousness is in direct proportion to time and effort. The veal is mild and the sausage stuffing intense. The superb sauce ties everything together.

½ split breast of veal (5 ribs, about 10 pounds)
1 teaspoon salt
1 teaspoon pepper
2 tablespoons olive oil
2 quarts filtered water
2 cups homemade beef stock (page 73)
½ bottle red wine

Stuffing
3 to 3½ cups mixed ground veal, pork, and beef
2 tablespoons ground mace
2 tablespoons whole fennel seeds
2 tablespoons ground fennel seeds

1 tablespoon paprika
3 tablespoons olive oil
2 tablespoons chopped garlic
1 pinch dry, crushed chili flakes
2 large onions, ¼-inch dice
8 ribs of celery, ¼-inch dice
Salt and pepper
1 tablespoon chopped fresh thyme
4 tablespoons chopped Italian flat leaf parsley
1 loaf stale good sourdough bread, hand ripped into 1½-inch chunks and dried in a 200°F oven for 30 to 40 minutes
2 tablespoons chiffonade of sage

The day before: preheat oven to 325°F. Using a small sharp knife, separate the flap of meat above the bones of the veal breast, but do not cut through the ends of the breast, creating a pocket for stuffing. Season the veal breast with salt and pepper inside and outside the pocket and let sit while preparing the stuffing.

In a small bowl, mix the meats and the ground mace, whole and ground fennel seeds, and the paprika by hand until thoroughly blended. Heat a large thick-bottomed sauté pan over medium-high heat for a minute or two and add the olive oil. Stir in garlic and then chili flakes. Working quickly to insure garlic does not burn, add the onions and celery. Season with salt and pepper to taste, and sauté until vegetables are soft. Stir in the thyme and half the parsley; remove from heat and let cool in pan.

In a large bowl, begin to combine bread and meat. Do not overmix; be careful not to break up bread. Add the sage, the rest of the parsley, and the celery/onion mixture. Season with more salt and pepper as needed. This should be a very intensely flavored dish.

Stuff the veal breast evenly with the bread-and-sausage mixture. Tie the entire stuffed breast with butcher twine or other trussing method so that when the stuffing expands during cooking, it's contained. Rub the outside of the veal breast with a tablespoon of olive oil. Put the veal breast in a large thick-bottomed roasting pan. Dry roast at approximately 325°F degrees for 3 hours, checking now and then to make sure it's browning slowly and evenly. Adjust heat as needed. When roast is nearly finished browning, warm the filtered water and heat the beef broth to just below boiling.

Remove roast from oven and deglaze the pan with the wine. You may need to shift the roast from side to side to accomplish this. Pour the hot beef stock and warm filtered water over the roast. Return pan to oven and wet roast, for another 3 hours. This extra moisture will help soften the meat's texture as it cooks.

Check the tenderness of the meat with the tip of a sharp paring knife. It should enter and exit the roast with ease. Pull the roast out of the oven when done and let sit until it has cooled enough to handle. Carefully transfer the whole roast, without breaking it, to a sheet pan. Cover and refrigerate until the next day. Strain the remaining roasting/cooking liquid into a container and refrigerate. You will have around 5 cups.

The day of: preheat the oven to 375°F. Skim off the layer of fat on top of the reserved cooking liquid. Reduce the liquid by one-fourth over low heat. Season to taste and set sauce aside. While reducing the sauce, remove the trussing string from the veal and cut the whole veal breast into large chops, so that with each slice you can see the layers of bones, stuffing, and meat. Heat a large thick-bottomed sauté pan and add one tablespoon of olive oil. Sear the chops well on one side, then turn and sear on the other side. Do the chops in batches if they don't all fit in the pan. When both sides are seared, carefully pour off any cooking oil and transfer the chops to a large roasting pan. Add ½ cup of the sauce to the sauté pan you seared the chops in. Bring to a boil, scraping up all the little bits. Pour sauce over the chops and put in the oven for about 8 minutes to heat through. Remove and arrange on a large platter. Add the juices from the roasting pan to the reserved remaining sauce and serve with the chops. Accompany with a good local green vegetable—like broc-colini, asparagus, or brussels sprouts—and mashed potatoes and a green salad.

Serves 8 to 10

STELLINA BEEF STEW

This hearty beef stew is the definition of the term "comfort food." Serve with side dishes that will provide a foil for the stew's richness, such as soft herbed polenta or mashed potatoes, and some sautéed bitter greens.

7 cups homemade beef stock (page 73)
3 pounds beef or veal shoulder, cut into 1 to 1½-inch cubes
Salt and pepper
Olive oil
2 or 3 cloves garlic, chopped
Small pinch chili flakes
2 whole cloves
1 large whole cinnamon stick
2 carrots, chopped into ¾-inch pieces

1 Spanish onion, chopped into ¾-inch pieces
4 celery stalks, chopped into ½-inch pieces
2 tablespoons chopped Italian flat-leaf parsley
1 tablespoon chopped fresh thyme (stems removed)
1 tablespoon coarsely chopped winter or summer savory (stems removed)
1 fresh bay leaf (or 2 dried)
1 cup good quality red wine for cooking

Put stock in a large pot and heat over low flame while you prepare the rest of the ingredients. Keep an eye on the stock throughout to be sure it stays just below a boil, and adjust flame as necessary.

Up to 1 hour before cooking but no less than ½ hour, season cubed beef chunks very generously with salt and pepper. Let sit in a colander in a large bowl to drain any liquids that come out due to salting. Pat dry with paper towels. Warm a large, thick-bottomed roasting pan in the oven at 450°F for 5 minutes. Add a few tablespoons of olive oil to pan, and as soon as the oil begins to smoke, remove pan from oven and add the meat. Shake the pan or use a wooden spoon to spread meat out evenly. Return pan to oven. Stir meat every 5 minutes for 20 to 30 minutes, or until evenly browned. Be careful not to over stir: stirring releases internal juices and if done too frequently will inhibit browning. Once meat chunks have a bit of color around their edges, remove pan from oven.

Using a slotted spoon, remove meat from pan, and place the pan on the stovetop over medium heat. Working quickly, add garlic to pan, stirring with a wooden spoon. Stir in chili flakes, cloves, and cinnamon stick. Once the garlic and dried spices have infused the meaty oil, but before they've started to burn, add the carrots, onion, and celery, and continue stirring. Add half the parsley and season vegetables with salt and pepper, to taste. Stir in half the thyme and savory. When the vegetables are sweating and the onion bends toward translucent, add bay and remaining fresh herbs, and deglaze the pan with the wine.

Put beef chunks back in pan and carefully pour hot beef stock over meat. Adjust seasoning, keeping in mind that the broth will increase in saltiness as it reduces. Stir mixture and return pan to oven. Once the stew begins to bubble (5 to 10 minutes) turn oven down to 375° to 400°F, just below simmer. Cook for approximately 1½ hours, depending on the tenderness of the beef, stirring about halfway through. Check to be sure that liquid is reducing and meat is softening at about the same rate. Add broth and adjust seasoning if necessary. To determine when the meat is ready, pierce with a paring knife to check tenderness. Once beef is fork tender and liquid has reduced by about half and thickened, remove stew from oven and let sit for 5 minutes before serving.

Serves 6

MAKING STOCK

Every **CHEF** I know takes an enormous amount of pride in his or her ability to produce a broth of clarity and concentration. It is a **ZEN** skill of preparation, practice, and patience. I never realized how much I needed stock until I started making it religiously from any left-over **BONES** I had. When there is a jar of homemade stock in the fridge, I use it to make soup, stew, or in lieu of water for **ENRICHING** risotto or vegetables. Or I might just boil it, plunk in a few tortellini, tiny dices of vegetables, and some herbs, and call it **LUNCH**.

Here's a stock recipe that Morgan Maki uses at Bi-Rite Market to process all bones from each day's meat fabrication. Ask your butcher in advance to set some bones aside for you. Morgan uses the stock to make his Glace de Viande (page 197). It is a good lesson that with time, technique, and discipline you can make something special and delicious out of vegetables, bones, and water.

5 pounds bones (beef, lamb, pork, poultry, or mixed)
3 pounds yellow onions
1½ pounds celery
1½ pounds carrots
3 bay leaves
1 teaspoon black peppercorns
½ cup dry white wine

Roast bones at 450°F for about 30 minutes, for even browning and liquefaction of excess fat. While bones are in the oven, wash, peel, and coarsely dice mirepoix (onions, celery, carrots).

Remove bones from oven, and carefully drain fat from roasting tray.

Place bones, trim, vegetables, bay leaves, and peppercorns into a stockpot and cover with cold water. Heat the stock over medium-high flame. Meanwhile, use the wine to deglaze the fond left on the roasting tray. When the wine has reduced by half and all of the little bits of caramelized protein are scraped from the bottom of the tray, pour into stock and give it a swirl.

Leave the stock alone until you notice a bit of foam and scum accumulating on its surface. Then reduce heat to low and carefully skim stock at 1-hour intervals. This stock should run about 170°F for 6 to 8 hours.

Scoop and discard spent bones and vegetables and strain your stock through a fine sieve or cheesecloth. Cool in an ice bath until the temperature hits 50°F, then refrigerate overnight. Now the stock is ready for use in soups, braises, and other moist-heat cooking applications.

Yields 20 to 22 cups

TANYA CAUTHEN

BELMONT BUTCHERY, VA

On my breakneck butcher tour, I had scheduled my visit to Richmond for a Sunday, not noticing that that it was Easter. Tanya didn't bat an eye, inviting me to Easter dinner with her fiancé and his family. Within five minutes of reaching the house, I was on the front porch with a gin and tonic, sharing stories. You can run restaurants, cooking schools, and a butcher shop that has been featured in Food & Wine *and* Gourmet, *but if you can't still soak up a spring dusk on the front porch, you're no Tanya Cauthen.*

I did a year as a Swiss journeyman, which was where I first saw a carcass. I didn't speak German and they didn't speak English, but they would let me stand in the corner and watch. Eventually, one of these old, gnarled German butchers put a knife in my hand. I just knew that I loved it.

If my dad were here, he would tell the story of when I was five and we went to the Officers Club in Rhode Island (my dad was Navy) and I would order the Hanging Steamship—a whole leg of beef, roasted with the bone in and weighing about 100 pounds. And I would ask for rare. They'd give me medium and I would say, *Rare is red, please.* My dad is not really surprised that I'm a butcher. I was pretty much a meat girl growing up.

I traveled through Europe and Russia for seven months. I ate everything. I stayed with Anne Willan at LaVarenne Cooking School, she was a protégé of Julia Child. I met her at a convention where she was speaking and told her she reminded me of my mother, and she invited me to stay at her chateau. I slept in the guesthouse they were renovating for Julia's visit, so I warmed up Julia's bed.

I moved from Switzerland to Richmond, CA, on Anne Willan's recommendation to work at the Frog & the Redneck. I opened up the Red Oak Café as chef at the ripe old age of twenty-two. I learned what I didn't know, like how to work with people. I was a stick in the mud as a young person—way too serious. My sister, Karen, and I opened a very high end, small catering company, Capers Catering. We would become seven-year-olds when we didn't get along. My parents said, *You bought yourself a job and you hate each other.* So I became a food writer for a local magazine. Food gossip. I had great style but my grammar sucked. My tendency has always been to say what I think.

I was working on a deadline at 3 am and I had the Food Network on in the background and Alton Brown said, *Ask your local butcher to . . .* I said out loud, *Screw you, Alton Brown, we don't have one!* I had an epiphany and immediately wrote a business plan.

When I walked into this space, I immediately saw the butcher shop. I went to the beach for four days with Julia Child's *My Life in France,* realizing it was going to be my last vacation ever. I was the same age as Julia when she learned to cook. At first, a lot of chef friends came in to help out and I hired some kitchen rats part-time. The first year was just about doing as best as we could. And just talking to people, asking our customers: *What do you want us to be?* I realized very quickly that it was about the team. In the first year we would put things out there and no one would buy them—they didn't understand what we were trying to do. By year three, the same thing would sell like wildfire. It just took a while for it to catch on. Somewhere along the way we realized that we were butchers, not meat cutters. It was an evolution.

There are builders and sustainers. I'm a builder. I've structured the business so that I don't get bored. I can keep working on new projects. I like comfortable for a little while and then I think, *What's next?*

ROASTED SQUAB

WITH VEGETABLES

I created this dish for my husband, Henry, on his birthday. Henry loves squab! Perfectly glistening roasted birds on a bed of vegetables makes for a gorgeous presentation. Be careful not to overcook squab: cook medium rare for a rich, tender, and juicy bird. Leftover squab is delicious cold the next day.

4 squab, 1 pound each, cleaned
Kosher salt
Freshly ground black pepper
2 tablespoons duck fat (or other cooking fat)
½ pound carrots, cut into 1-inch chunks
½ pound turnips, quartered
½ pound ramps, trimmed, or substitute leeks and spring onions
White wine
Butter

Preheat oven to 450°F. Pat squab dry and season inside and out with salt and pepper. Heat duck fat in a large ovenproof pan over medium-high heat. Brown all sides of the squab. Once browned, set aside, backs down.

In same pan, add carrots and turnips. Toss in hot duck fat, adding salt and pepper to taste. Top with a layer of ramps (if bulbs are well developed, split lengthwise in half up to the green). Set squab on top of veggies. Transfer to oven and roast uncovered until the thigh temperature registers 140°F, about 25 minutes. The juices will run a rosy color. Remove pan from oven and transfer squab to a plate to rest about 10 minutes. Transfer ramps and veggies to a platter.

Drain off excess oil and juices from pan to a heatproof cup and allow to separate. Deglaze roasting pan with a splash of white wine. Scrape up all the brown bits. Return separated pan juices to roasting pan. Add 1 or 2 pats of butter to pan and stir. Taste sauce and adjust for salt and pepper.

To serve, make a bed of ramps on the plate, top with the squab (can be cut in half if desired), side dress with veggies, and drizzle the whole thing with sauce.

Serves 4

PAN-SEARED HANGER STEAK

WITH PAN SAUCE

At the Belmont Butchery, we call this "Tuesday night" steak. Hanger is inexpensive and easy to cook, and the variations on the pan sauce are limitless. Use high-quality ingredients and keep it simple. Pair it with an everyday red wine, and big salad, and in less 30 minutes you have dinner.

1 teaspoon oil or rendered fat (duck, lard, etc.)	**Sauce**
1 hanger steak (about 1 pound) *	¼ cup red wine
Salt and freshly ground black pepper	¼ cup beef stock or veal demi-glace
	1 teaspoon unsalted butter, cold

Heat a large heavy-bottomed sauté pan or skillet over high heat and add oil. When the oil is hot, season the steak with salt and pepper, and brown evenly, turning as needed, until it is done to your taste—6 to 8 minutes for medium-rare hanger steak (remember, the steak will continue cooking while it rests); a minute longer for medium; 2 to 3 minutes longer for well done. You can also use a meat thermometer and the table of suggested cooking temperatures on page 287. Transfer the steak to a plate and set aside in a warm place while you make the pan sauce.

Deglaze the pan with wine: simmer while stirring and scraping up brown bits until liquid is reduced by half, about 1 minute. Add stock and simmer, stirring, until sauce is slightly thickened, about 1 minute. Remove from heat and whisk in cold butter. This will thicken your sauce slightly. Adjust salt to taste.

To serve, slice steaks on the bias (across the grain) into finger-width pieces, fan out a half steak per person, and drizzle with pan sauce.

Sauce variations: After cooking the meat, sauté onions, mushrooms, or anything that you think would go great on your steak. Then deglaze and proceed. This sauce is limited only by your imagination!

Serves 2

* If hanger steak is not available, you can substitute with flatiron or skirt steak instead, and adjust cook times. For 1-pound flatiron: cook about 3 to 4 minutes per side for medium rare. For 1-pound skirt steak: cook about 2 minutes per side for medium rare

HAMBURGER BASICS

A hamburger is one of the most **STRAIGHTFORWARD** meat preparations in the American culinary canon. That doesn't mean there's not a right way to do it. **PAT LAFRIEDA** is a butcher, a meat consultant to Martha Stewart, the New York Yankees beef **PURVEYOR**, and a burger **IMPRESARIO**. Pat LaFrieda Meats creates burger blends for New York City's **TONIEST** joints. Consultations can stretch out over months, debating **NUANCES** of grind, muscles, and fat ratio.

Here are the keys to an excellent burger at home.

THE MEAT

Ask your butcher to grind a whole muscle, not trimmings

"I understand people want to do what's most economical, but trimmings have almost no flavor. Brisket is a favorite of mine. You can't use it alone because the [meat-to-]fat ratio is sixty to forty. When you prepare it, you usually have to slow cook it, but if it's ground, you can eat it right away. It has the great flavor of a brisket sandwich.

"Two-piece chuck is also good, but you have to have the flat iron [steak] on the [shoulder] clod; the flat iron has most of the flavor.

"We always say that the chopped-beef machines hide no sins. What you put in is really what you're going to get out of them."

Try aged meat as part of your blend

"I've played around with putting aged strip loin in the burger meat and people are loving it. It's an ingredient in the Black Label Burger at Minetta Tavern. The strip has the most flavor when it's aged. When you grind that, it just smells heavenly. I have four or five different aged mixes because people like differing degrees of that aged flavor. Some people just want a fresh taste."

Add some lamb

"I never add pork because that is getting more into meatloaf. To me, veal doesn't add anything. Lamb adds a lot. A lamb burger even on its own is great. I would add some lamb to beef to set the beef flavor apart. We've made some great lamb burgers with provolone cheese and salt and pepper."

THE GRIND

Fresher is better

"To get a fresh, crisp, roast-beefy flavor, you need to make it fresh that day. Once you Cryovac ground beef, it's like fresh bread, you

lose some of the specialness. If you're in a place where you don't have a nice butcher shop, I think to buy a piece of chuck, chill it, cut it into cubes and grind it yourself is wonderful. I think it's worth it. You do have to keep the blades and plates sharp; otherwise you've got a pasty burger. Don't put the equipment in the freezer: it will chip. Put the meat in the freezer. We grind the meat at 27°F, quickly."

THE GRILL

The Platonic Burger

"Six ounces makes the perfect size, four inches in diameter, about an inch thick. If you want more, eat two."

High heat, short cooking time

"Always leave the burgers in the fridge until the last minute and get the grill very hot, four hundred degrees or better. The first flip, your meat has to be cooked to the point where it comes clean off the grill. If it sticks, it's not very forgiving at that point. Flip it four times, about thirty seconds each. Then the last flip, you put on the cheese. People think because I'm a meat guy, I want it black and blue. That's going a little overboard. I like it cooked, but I want it to still have color on the inside."

Season judiciously

"If you put seasoning or any kind of herb in the meat, you may as well put tomato sauce and mozzarella cheese on it, because it tastes like meatloaf. You can put salt in—I've heard it breaks down the meat. Not true. On the exterior, I put fresh-ground black pepper, salt—and I like cayenne."

Fixings

"Fresh baby arugula instead of lettuce has twenty times the flavor. Slicing cherry and grape tomatoes instead of those mushy things that taste like watermelon is wonderful. Ketchup is fine in moderation. I even put on a little mayo."

NICK CHASET

BULLMOOSE HUNTING SOCIETY
WASHINGTON, DC

BMHS takes their name from Teddy Roosevelt's political party. That makes perfect sense. There's the flush of American royalty about Nick, some rough-hewn glamour. Of course he hunts—and I wouldn't bat an eye if he also played polo and could sail solo around the Cape of Good Hope.

Roosevelt's sort of a hero for us. He really understood that there was a value to hunting, especially the role it plays in the preservation of natural space.

I went hunting for the first time with a friend of mine from Holland, sort of a Hunter S. Thompson type, always wanted to do something related to shooting. Being this is America, you really can just go buy a gun.

I walked into a gun store in the Mission in San Francisco. I was kind of nervous. My father wasn't a rifle guy. They actually tried to sell me a pistol at first. But I stood my ground. It turns out that wild boar is a year-round open season because they're an invasive species. You can kill as many of them as you want, as long as you have a fifty-dollar tag and your Hunter Safety certificate.

We found a guy on the Internet who would take us wild boar hunting. He seemed pretty legit. He had a handlebar moustache. He gave us a five-minute overview. Within forty-five minutes I saw my first pig and I drew on it. There was so much adrenaline pumping through my veins that I had no hesitation. It was a powerful moment. I'd never killed anything before.

Then we gutted and quartered it. Boars are strong, mean critters. They're so bacteria ridden that if you get cut by them, you should go to the hospital immediately. We put the meat in a cooler and drove home. We had tentatively organized a barbecue for the next day but we hadn't thought through the butchering.

I walked into a carnicería on Mission Street. The butcher didn't speak much English, and I speak very minimal Spanish. I showed him what we had. He had this big smile

and said, *Absolutely, I'll butcher it for you*. We tried to pay him, offered him some meat, he didn't want anything. He thought it was fun. We gave him a tip.

At that "boar-b-que" we had about a hundred people over. That's where I met Nick, my BMHS cofounder. Nick had started hunting as a way to commune with his food. We decided we should start going together. Every couple of months we'd take a trip. We'd call it hiking with guns, not hunting, because we rarely saw anything. Nick and I decided to start a club. There are chapters now in Austin, Phoenix, and DC with their own leaders.

We really want to expand further, build a critical mass with active, self-sustaining groups in multiple cities. Once you have that, the growth is limitless. This weekend a big group is going out turkey hunting, another group is going out pheasant hunting. And there are some of us now who are into fishing.

You want to know that when the time comes you could pull the trigger. I felt like I needed to be able to kill the animal, so when I look at a steak I know it's not just a unit of protein, it actually comes from somewhere. I eat a lot less meat than I used to do.

SLOW-ROAST PIG

The guest of honor: a beautiful, nakedly pink, entire pig or boar. You: an undaunted, hungry horde salivating for a whole-animal adventure. For the piggy pinnacle, consider a heritage-breed animal, such as Red Wattles or Ossabaws, which grow slower and develop more intense flavors.

BUILD A PIG ROAST HOUSE

48 to 60 cinder blocks from a builder's supply
Roll of heavy foil
40 to 80 pounds mesquite charcoal for a 60- to 100-pound pig or boar (have extra on hand)
6 to 7-foot length (or longer) of heavy-gauge rebar with no galvanizing or plastic coating, scrubbed well, or buy a mechanized spit with a wheel for easier turning
Nongalvanized wire or heavy twine for tying pig to spit

For the roaster site: Never build a grill house on asphalt (the heat will melt it), or on grass (unless you want strange, grass-flavored pork). Do tear up the underlying turf or cover it with sand before beginning.

Our preference is for a rectangular shape. Depending on animal size, walls should be 3 or 4 rows high, with inside enclosure width 2 blocks or more (see diagram on opposite page). Lay the first 2 rows, then line the bottom area and sides with heavy foil, extending it over the top of the block wall. The next row or two will sit on top of the foil, holding it in place. There you have it!

ROASTING THE PIG

A 60- to 100-pound heritage-breed pig or boar	10 to 15 sprigs each of fresh thyme and rosemary
	20 or more cloves of garlic
Marinade	1 to 2 handfuls of sea salt
1 to 2 3-liter bottles of wine (Carlo Rossi)	

Your porcine guest has arrived! What to do with it? If frozen, you will have thawed it slowly in a cool spot with very cold water running over it (the bathtub is excellent). The pig must not be allowed to get warm.

Combine all marinade ingredients and refrigerate for an hour or two. You can inject very thick areas of the meat with this briny brew, if you're of a mind, to tenderize and guard against dryness. Slather the pig generously and allow it to marinate in a cool place for 6 to 8 hours or overnight. Reserve the marinade.

In the center of the roaster, douse about 20 pounds of charcoal (to start) with lighter fluid and fire it up. After a half hour, rake the glowing coals over to the four corners of the grill house so that no coals will be directly under the pig. Added coals should be dropped only into the corners.

Getting the large-diameter spit through the pig is not easy, so make sure you have help prying the piggy's jaws open. Getting the whole thing to stay on the spit while it's roasting requires strong wire or twine. Especially tie the rib cage, head, and shoulders to the spit, or splitting and loosening can become a problem, and tie the feet together. *

Spit grill a smaller pig for a minimum of 6 hours, and an 80 pounder 8 to 10 hours. Larger animals can take 12 or even 24 hours, so plan accordingly. Have two people per team to baste and several people to turn the spit, in "shifts." A large animal ideally should be turned every minute or two, while a small, young pig every 30 minutes. Baste with marinade at least every half hour.

When the internal temperature reaches 160°F, it's time to transfer the pig to a table, a step that is as much about the theatrics of whole-animal roasting as it is necessary to the cooking process. Once it has rested beneath a tent of foil for at least 20 minutes, you can start carving. Cut it how you will, but don't be afraid to get dirty. And save the cheeks for yourself!

Roast pork goes great with Southern Barbecue sauce, Asian-style sauce such as terriyaki, or tacos and salsa.

Serves the neighborhood

* An alternative to spit roasting is to split the animal end to end, spread it flat, and sandwich it between two sheets of heavy nongalvanized steel mesh wired together tightly, with lengths of rebar sticking out beyond the length, and running crosswise where needed for added support. The team flips this "piggy stretcher" at the halfway point using the long rebars. An advantage to this is that you can check the doneness of the hams with a fork from the underside without splitting the skin.

GABRIEL CLAYCAMP
THE SWINERY, WA

I met Gabe in a carnivorous, David Lynchian dreamscape. I ascended the stairs of the Sanctuary, a Tiffany-windowed church that is being transformed into twelve posh condos. In the center, on a table that one cannot escape thinking of as an altar, under a stained-glass eyeball—presumably God's—stands Gabriel. I am offered communion—a glass of bubbly and a plate of prosciutto, sliced thinner than a sinner's excuses. The ceremony was a six-course reunion of Claycamp's Gypsy, a former underground restaurant that roved from illegal venue to illegal venue until it was shut down. Tonight was a repentant chef, born again into butchery.

The prosciutto that you tried was the beginning of the downfall. I did this *Sacrificio* two years ago. I took people to a farm, where we killed a pig, Hector, and ate the meat. There were at least seven people there who had been at the slaughter and had blood on their hands. Almost every person at the dinner was or had been a student of mine. When I started out the talk I was totally emotional. The Hector dinner turned out to be this watershed moment, the first negative thing that had ever been written about us in the press.

I got into a lot of trouble doing charcuterie. In Seattle, I was on the vanguard of illegality. At the cooking school, I was getting in whole pigs and we were doing pig breakdown classes. We had 140 different classes but the charcuterie classes became ridiculous, they would always sell out. So they became more and more elaborate. We had a cave with a dirt floor that we lined with hazelnut shells. If students are making it, it isn't illegal.

But we wanted to sell at the farmers' market, so we started the Swinery as a side business. The health department had just instituted that you needed an HACCP plan to sell charcuterie and then, literally, within a few weeks, they were like, *We're going to arrest you.* They didn't actually arrest me but they talked about it. About two months ago, everyone started to get pinched and the health department issued three-week warnings to a dozen restaurants, big names.

So Gypsy got big, especially after we were on Anthony Bourdain's show, *No Reservations.* It was a lot of fun. We started flying chefs around the country. It was like the worst/best kept secret in Seattle. We were doing four dinners a month. It was so cloak-and-dagger. You submitted an email to get on the list and then you got an application and then we reviewed your application. We had 2,600 members. I started to take it relatively seriously and I hired a coordinator. But she and I did not get along, and I fired her. A week later, the control board, the health department, everybody's at our door. It was all over the papers and it created this whole situation. The state politicians had to get involved and force the control board to give us a license, because they wouldn't do it.

They allowed us to become a restaurant, but we were a school, which means we had to build a commercial kitchen. We sank about $30,000 into the kitchen that we didn't have and then the economy started tanking. We had to sell everything we owned in order to pay the employees their final checks. There were 450 people that came to the sale. People were fighting over their favorite knife.

The Swinery had already existed but it didn't have any debts. It also didn't have any assets besides a meat grinder. So, we could restart that. I found an investor. But it was within about three months, so blogs and newspapers were like, *Obviously they stole all that money,* because no one can start a business that quick.

Our goal for all of this is transparency. After everything that happened, people told me, "If we know the whole story, there won't be any judgment." So we're telling people everything, like the real cost of buying local. We're paying $6.71 a pound for beef. Then there's bone loss and any dry aging and thirty percent of the animal is ground. So we decided we are going to get one steer a month. The price to the farmer is the best we can do, I don't feel like we're being gouged. I do sell about twenty gallons of stock a month. But if I buy more steers each month, that's a lot more bones than I can get rid of.

You should try our bacon hot dogs. We're actually having a problem with them because all of our close friends don't want to buy them anymore. They'll say, *If you made crappy hot dogs I'd buy a couple dozen of them but with one of these, I'm done.* Now if only I could create a dog that's delicious and you could eat more than one.

"I GOT INTO A LOT OF TROUBLE DOING CHARCUTERIE. IN SEATTLE, I WAS ON THE VANGUARD OF ILLEGALITY."

CINNAMON OXTAIL STEW

WITH SLIPPERY NOODLES

This luscious dish is enhanced by the garnishes . . . everyone can get in on flavoring their own. If you prefer your stew to have more liquid, try adding an extra ½ quart of stock.

4 pounds oxtail, cut into 1-inch pieces
Salt and pepper
3 tablespoons vegetable oil
½ cup sugar
6 cloves garlic, smashed
4 slices ginger, smashed
6 scallions, trimmed, cut into 1½-inch sections
1½ teaspoons hot chili paste
2 cinnamon sticks

1 teaspoon aniseed or star anise
½ cup soy sauce
1 quart veal stock *
½ pound flat Chinese wheat-flour noodles
½ cup Thai basil leaves, picked
¼ cup minced cilantro
1 cup bean sprouts
3 tablespoon scallions, thinly sliced

Preheat oven to 325°F. Season oxtail with salt and pepper. In a large, heavy pan heat the oil over medium heat. Add the sugar and cook until a light caramel. Add the oxtail and brown on all sides. Remove oxtail from the pan and add the garlic, ginger, scallions, chili paste, cinnamon, and aniseed. Sauté until soft, about 3 minutes. Add soy sauce and veal stock. Bring to a boil and season to taste. Return oxtail to the pan, cover, and slide into the oven. Braise for 4 hours or until falling-apart tender. Remove from oven and cool slightly.

Strain liquid, degrease, and reserve. Pick the meat off the bones and return to the liquid. Bring liquid and meat to a boil. Bring a large pot of salted water to a boil. Cook noodles according to package directions and drain.

To serve, divide noodles, meat, and broth into individual bowls. Top each bowl with basil leaves, cilantro, bean sprouts, and scallions. Serve immediately.

Serves 4 to 6

* Veal stock can be hard to come by. If your local butcher cannot provide you with any, you may find online retailers who sell frozen stock.

GIGOT FARCI

(STUFFED LEG OF LAMB)

Gigot farci, or stuffed leg of lamb, is a traditional, deliciously aromatic roast. Lamb is naturally tender, so you don't want to overcook it. Around 140° to 150°F on a meat thermometer will give you a medium-rare to medium leg.

Stuffing
1 tablespoon butter
2 ounces bacon, minced
1 fennel bulb, minced
8 ounces wild mushrooms, chopped
2 tablespoons chopped parsley
2 tablespoons chopped chervil
4 sprigs thyme, minced
½ tablespoon nutmeg

Kosher salt
Freshly ground black pepper
¼ cup bread crumbs
5 cloves garlic

1 boned and trimmed leg of lamb, 3 to 4 pounds
1 tablespoon olive oil
1 tablespoon chopped rosemary

Preheat oven to 450°F. Melt butter in a large sauté pan over medium heat and lightly brown the bacon. Add the fennel, mushrooms, parsley, chervil, thyme, and nutmeg, and salt and pepper to taste. Cook until everything is very tender and liquid has evaporated. Mix in the bread crumbs and garlic, allow to cook slightly. Let stuffing cool.

Stuff the leg with the mixture and make shallow crisscross cuts into top of lamb. Truss well with kitchen twine. Rub olive oil and rosemary over top and season well with salt and pepper, to taste. Roast for 30 minutes. Turn over and roast 25 minutes further. Depending on the weight of your leg, you may wish to adjust time by internal temperature.

If meat is up to temperature, remove and let rest 10 minutes on a counter, covered in foil. Otherwise, turn off oven and let lamb rest inside for 10 minutes before serving.

Serves 8

CHRIS COSENTINO
INCANTO AND BOCCOLONE, CA

The first time I saw Chris was at the annual Slow Food turkey slaughter. He came to bear witness. And get his hands on testicles, lungs, combs, and all those other parts you might forget turkeys even have. Chris is madly vigilant, like a general. Talking to him is ferocious and exciting because he is engaged in a battle with the forces that keep food from being grown fairly and freely. Slashing through the brush of PETA-philes and pedantry, he has defined a new kind of animal welfare: eat it to protect it.

People come here looking for the more unusual stuff. I'll get ears and snouts. I buy trotters like nobody's business, all the organ meats. I think for a lot of these ranchers, I'm kind of heaven-sent. I'm the guy who will take everything that nobody wants.

The motto is "no status quo." The moment you're uncomfortable is the moment you're learning. We're never ever as good as we can be. If you think you know everything, you might as well f'ing quit. You're just stupid at that point.

Buying local and seasonal is natural. The catch phrase almost becomes a curse because people that don't say it on their menu are chastised for not publicizing it. What I ultimately want to do is give the guest the best experience with what's in season. It's February now, so in five weeks we're going to start seeing asparagus. New York, the Midwest, they won't see anything for another three months. We live in a very unique place, which allows us to have things quicker and a lot easier.

I have relationships with every farmer that I buy from. I look at some of them as family. When I found out I was going to be a dad, Andy at Mariquita Farms came up here every single week just to give me advice, help me through. I was really nervous. There's no way I can put any dollar sign on that.

We try to do a lot of things here that are as organic as possible. When I say organic, I'm not talking about growing vegetables. I'm talking about just what's right. We carbonate and filter our water and we give it away. Because going out to eat is about hospitality. We grow specialty herbs on the roof. We work with a local charity that collects our cardboard and our bottles and cans for San Francisco Conservation Corps. We get all our grease picked up for biodiesel, we save all of our wax boxes, rubber bands, twist ties, plastic bags, to give back to the farmers so they don't have to pay for them again. We're really trying to make sure that every component of what we do is thought through.

Boccolone, our full USDA processing facility, is an offshoot of an Incanto. When I came here seven years ago, one of the goals was curing meat. Boccolone branched out of that. We had no more room to cure in house. Now we make twenty-plus cured pork items. If you talk to an Italian, our stuff's not traditional. I make Mortadella hot dogs during baseball season.

My goal is always to make sure that Incanto and Boccolone are at the top of their game and that's the most important thing. I'm here so much these guys get tired of looking at me. When I'm not filming, I'm here. And when I'm here, I'm here. Like this morning, I got here at 9 am and I'll leave here tonight probably at 1 am. Whoever thought being a cook would get you on television? Going home smelling like a goat has been glorified. But, you know, opinions are like assholes, everybody's got one or two.

ROASTED LAMB NECKS

Long, slow cooking in a low oven creates an incredibly flavorful dish from this less-familiar cut.

2 lemons
¼ cup garlic cloves, about 1 head's worth
2 cups fennel fronds
1 cup extra-virgin olive oil
1 tablespoon coarsely ground black pepper
6 lamb necks, about 2 pounds each
Salt and pepper

Gremolata
1 cup picked parsley
1 cup picked mint
1 cup picked chervil
1 cup picked tarragon
Zest of 2 lemons
1 tablespoon fresh grated horseradish
Salt and pepper
¼ cup extra-virgin olive oil

In a food processor, combine the lemon juice, garlic, and fennel fronds with the olive oil and black pepper and grind together to make a marinade. Season the necks with salt and pepper to taste, rub with the marinade, and refrigerate overnight.

Preheat the oven to 200°F. Place necks on a roasting pan and bake for 8 to 11 hours, until meat is very tender.

For the gremolata, mix the herbs, lemon, and horseradish. Season with salt and pepper, to taste, then add the olive oil. Serve with the lamb necks.

Serves 6

GRILLED BEEF HEART

WITH ROASTED GOLDEN BEETS

Preparing a beef heart is not for the faint of heart! Grilled to medium rare and sliced thinly though, tasters kept in the dark could mistake the heart for a lean piece of meat.

1 beef heart, about 2 to 3 pounds
Salt and pepper

Marinade
1 cup orange juice
1½ cups white wine
12 sprigs fresh thyme, crushed
3 cloves garlic, crushed, skin on
Splash of extra-virgin olive oil

Beets
3 bunches baby golden beets, leaves and stems
    removed and washed
1 bunch thyme
1 bunch flat-leaf parsley, leaves picked and
    washed
1 cup orange juice
1 cup water
2 heads garlic, split in half
Extra-virgin olive oil
Ground fennel seeds

Horseradish Vinaigrette
¼ cup Champagne vinegar
1½ cups extra-virgin olive oil
2 tablespoons orange juice
¼ cup finely grated horseradish

Remove sinew and gristle from heart; quarter or cut into 2 by 6-inch pieces. Mix orange juice, wine, thyme, garlic, and olive oil in a bowl; let the flavors blend for 1 hour before use. Pour mixture over beef heart and marinate for 2 hours in the refrigerator.

Preheat the oven to 325°F. Place the beets, thyme, parsley, orange juice, water, garlic, and enough olive oil to coat in a roasting pan. Season with fennel seeds, salt, and pepper to taste. Cover the pan with aluminum foil and bake until knife tender, about 45 minutes. Carefully remove foil and let cool. Remove the beet skins by rubbing with a cloth. Cut beets into rounds and quarters. Whisk together the vinaigrette ingredients. In a bowl, toss beets with enough vinaigrette to coat, or to taste.

Remove heart from marinade and season with salt and pepper to taste. Grill the heart to medium-rare, about 3 minutes on each side, depending on thickness.

To serve, divide the beets among individual plates or place on one large serving platter. Top with thinly sliced beef heart. For garnish, grate fresh horseradish over heart and drizzle with a bit of extra-virgin olive oil, if desired.

Serves 8 as an appetizer or 4 as a main dish

COOKING METHODS

DRY HEAT

BARBECUING — cooking slowly on a grill over indirect heat, which tenderizes tougher cuts and imbues the meat with a smoke flavor

Suitable for beef brisket and chuck; pork loin and butt (you can barbecue an entire animal, but because of the slower cooking, it has special appeal for fattier cuts with lots of connective tissue)

Technique:

Like grilling, barbecuing is a technique of cooking meat over charcoal and/or hard wood; but in this case, the meat is not directly over the heat. This allows it to cook slower and, generally, absorb more flavor from the smoke than with grilling.

Setting up the grill is the same as char-grilling, but when the coals are white-hot, they are distributed to the sides of the grill. There are many variations on barbecue apparatus, including smokers that allow the meat to cook very slowly. You can also barbecue underground or in a caja China ("Chinese box"), which cooks the meat by trapping the smoke and steam.

BROILING — fast cooking directly under radiant heat, which seals in juices on tender cuts and imparts a flavorful outer surface

Suitable for tender, well-marbled beef cuts from the loin and rib, sirloin, ground meat, and marinated skirt steaks; chicken; lamb leg steaks and loin and rib chops; thick pork chops

Technique:

Preheat broiler. Season meat before broiling. The thicker the cut, the farther away from the heat it should be positioned, to avoid burning the outside before the center is cooked. Turn the meat halfway through the cooking process so both sides get direct exposure to the heat.

BROWNING/SEARING — cooking the outside surface in oil on high heat, which adds flavor to meat before slow-cooking

Suitable for anything you are going to stew or braise

Technique:

Allow meat to reach room temperature, and then season with salt and pepper. Heat the pan and add oil (if the meat isn't fatty), warming until it is almost to the smoking point. Sear meat on all sides, removing when the entire surface has changed color. This will happen very quickly. After searing or browning, use a slower method to cook the meat through.

CHAR-GRILLING — fast cooking on a grill over very high heat, which seals in juices of tender cuts and adds a smoke flavor

Suitable for: tender, well-marbled beef cuts from the loin and rib, sirloin, ground meat, and marinated skirt steaks; chicken; lamb leg steaks and loin and rib chops; thick pork chops

Technique:

Marinate meat or season generously with salt, pepper, olive oil, and any desired herbs or spices. Marinating overnight is helpful for tougher cuts, like the skirt steak.

Hardwood, charcoal, or a combination can be used as grill fuel. Different woods imbue meat with different flavors, and serious grillers get religious about their preferences. You can also use a gas grill.

When the coals are white-hot, push them to the side or cook right above them, depending on the heat you want. At this point, you can add water-soaked wood chips for flavor.

Put the meat on the grill at the desired temperature, which you can check with a thermometer or with the hand test: Squeeze the fatty section on the edge of your palm between the thumb and forefinger—that is what rare meat feels like. Medium meat gives about the same as the center of your palm and well-done meat has the solidity of the outside of the palm near the pinkie. As with roasting, you want to take the meat off the heat a hair before it is done because it will continue to cook while it rests.

FRYING — cooking in oil to add flavor to tender cuts

Suitable for tender, fine-grained beef fillet cuts, rib-eye, sirloin, T-bone, rump and seamed rump; also cutlets, short-loin and middle-loin chops, and eye of short loin; lamb fillets; rump chops and steaks, and thick flank and topside steaks.

Technique:

Evenly cut meat pieces to a bite size. Pat dry. You can coat with flour or a batter to keep especially thin cuts moist. Meat cooks quickly in this method, so prepare everything before you begin cooking and do not cook until you are ready to eat. Heat oil to just before smoke point. Do not crowd the pan; cook in batches if necessary. Drain excess oil on absorbent paper.

ROASTING — slow cooking under dry heat, sometimes with added fat to keep large, tender cuts juicy

Suitable for tender whole muscles such as rib, loin, and leg muscles, if they are aged and/or have some intramuscular fat

Technique:

Season a room-temperature roast and place in a shallow roasting pan. Cook either at a consistent temperature or at a higher heat to start. Doneness is measured by internal temperature, which is, of course, most accurately monitored with a food thermometer. Federal guidelines recommend cooking all pork to a safe minimum internal temperature of 160°F and all poultry (chicken and duck) until 165°F throughout. Check the Table of Suggested Cooking Temperatures on page 287. The roast will continue to cook as much as 5°F to 10°F after you take it out of the oven, so take that into account. Always let your meat rest for 15 minutes.

SPIT ROASTING — open-fire rotisserie of a whole animal while basting to evenly cook an "uneven" carcass

Suitable for whole-carcass pig, poultry, or even a steer, if you have a large-enough rig

Technique:

Buying a whole carcass will require some planning ahead. The carcass will usually yield a bit less than 50 percent meat (the rest fat and bones), so carcass size should be twice as much as your desired amount of meat.

You will need at least as much weight in coals as the weight of the animal, and because of the long cooking time, you will be adding to the fire, so stock up.

Concentrate the coals under the thickest parts of the animal: the shoulders and legs.

Baste continually, even if it requires assembling a team of basters and bribing them with beer; you can use a brush of fresh herbs for flavor. As with a roast, the meat is done when the juices run clear. A 100-pound hog can take 8 hours (or 160°F internal temperature) and a steer can take a whole day (or 140°F internal temperature), unless you break it down into primals or sub-primals.

STIR-FRYING — fast, high-heat cooking of lean cuts in shallow oil while continuously stirring

Suitable for lean beef cuts such as flank and skirt steak (cut across the grain to increase tenderness); chicken; pork leg cuts

Technique:

Cut meat ahead of time into bite-sized pieces and pat them dry. Add oil to the pan or wok, coating the entire cooking surface, and heat to almost smoking. Cook meat in batches to avoid crowding the pan. Let the meat sit in the oil for a few seconds and then begin stirring. If you use a sauce, heat it in the middle of the pan and then stir it into the meat. Take the meat off the heat just before you think it is done and serve immediately.

WET HEAT

BRAISING/POT ROASTING — covered, slow cooking in fat and small amounts of liquid, which tenderizes cuts with a lot of fat and connective tissue

Suitable for lamb shanks and shoulder; beef brisket, chuck, round top blade roasts, shanks, and short ribs; and pork shoulder and butt

Technique:

Season the room temperature meat with salt and pepper. Sear the outside surfaces of the meat in the braising pot. Deglaze the pot with liquid. Fill braising pot with liquid to halfway point of meat. Cook until the meat is fork-tender, either on the stove or in a 350°F oven. Strain the meat from the liquid. Remove excess fat from the cooking liquid and reduce to desired thickness. A pressure cooker can stimulate the effects of braising in a shorter period of time.

POACHING — cooking in simmering liquid, which seals in flavors of lean meats

Suitable for chicken without skin; beef tenderloin; duck; leg of lamb

Technique:

Bring liquid, such as stock, to a boil and reduce to a simmer. Add small pieces of meat, ensuring there is enough liquid to completely cover it. Add stock vegetables and herbs to add flavor (onion, carrot, celery, etc.). The meat is done when it is cooked through and is firm.

STEWING — slow-cooking small chunks of meat completely immersed in liquid to tenderize tough cuts

Suitable for stew meat cut from shoulder or leg, sometimes with fat added

Technique:

Season the room-temperature meat with salt and pepper. Sear the outside surfaces of the meat in a pot. Deglaze the pot with liquid. Fill pot with liquid to completely cover meat. Cook until the meat is fork tender, either on the stove or in a 350°F oven. Vegetables or starch should be added near the end of the stewing process to prevent overcooking. Remove excess fat from the cooking liquid before serving.

MIKE DEBACH

LEONA MEAT PLANT, PA

The Debachs are just good people. I slept in their home and ate loin chops from a lamb they had raised and killed, we said grace and finished a bottle of wine. Or two. And sitting at that table sat the whole story. Almost everything I want to tell you, sitting right there: Mike and his brother Chick, who grew up boning out beef carcasses, and Mike's daughter, Lindsay, a smart, pretty girl who finds herself in the enviable position of happily accepting her birthright. Leona Meats is a small slaughter and butcher plant that keeps coming back to the same truth—the skill is the thing.

I was boning whole carcasses at eight or nine years old. If you learn how to cut meat that way, then you know every joint, every cut, all the seams. It's like learning a language. You just can't teach that at twenty-five or thirty.

Chick and I have been there since day one. I was fired once. I don't think Chick was ever fired. Back in his day, it was Dad's way or no way. He was pretty hard on us. We were supposed to be down there at six o'clock in the morning and I was having a tough time getting up. I'm running down at five after six. He says, *I want you in this goddamn meat plant at ten to six and your knife sharp and ready to go. If my other people were like you, this f'ing place wouldn't even run.* He'd go through a whole thing. I heard it hundreds of times. He'd always close with, *You haven't even combed your hair yet this morning.*

Dad came from a real poor family. He started butchering in 1963. He had a smokehouse. He made sausages. It was just two rooms. Then he started a little distribution. But he never grew with the business, because if he couldn't control it, he wouldn't let it grow. I'm probably sort of like that. He enjoyed himself. All those old butchers were the same way. They were a unique group, just like they are today. They all made a good profit. It's all changed since then. Dad used to send a truckload of beef down the road and he'd make five thousand dollars. That was huge money in the sixties. He made more money back then than we'd ever make now. I've watched farmers go broke year after year because they bought bigger tractors and more cows and all they're doing is producing more milk for less money. The price of milk is ten dollars. That's where it was back in the sixties, and everything else is going up.

We did meat distribution for awhile, but the Sysco Foods of the world had so much money behind them, we couldn't compete. We'd always be so busy but we could never make a buck. You'd open the door and you go for ten, twelve hours a day and when you're all said and done, you have nothing to show for it. Before, we were doing five to six million dollars of sales and we couldn't make a living. Now we're doing one and a half million and doing great. There's more money in service than there is in selling a product.

"I WAS BONING WHOLE CARCASSES AT EIGHT OR NINE YEARS OLD. IF YOU LEARN HOW TO CUT MEAT THAT WAY, THEN YOU KNOW EVERY JOINT, EVERY CUT, ALL THE SEAMS. IT'S LIKE LEARNING A LANGUAGE."

GRILLED LAMB CHOPS

A tried-and-true family recipe that taught me to love lamb! If you don't have a grill, broil the chops 3 inches from heat in the oven.

4 lamb loin chops, about 1 inch thick (you can use thinner ones, but adjust the cooking time)
2 tablespoons red wine vinegar
2 tablespoons chopped fresh rosemary
1 tablespoon chopped fresh thyme
2 cloves garlic, minced
2 tablespoons olive oil
Pinch of freshly ground black pepper
Sea salt

Trim most of the visible fat from lamb chops. Combine rest of ingredients except salt in a large sealable plastic food storage bag. Add lamb chops and marinate 1 to 4 hours in refrigerator.

Preheat gas or charcoal barbecue grill to high heat (you can hold your hand above it for only 1 or 2 seconds). Grill lamb chops about 5 minutes per side for medium rare. Cooking time will depend on the thickness of the chops and how hot your grill is. Season with salt, to taste.

Serves 2

ARMENIAN LAMB SHISH KEBABS

The unusual flavors of this recipe are subtle and well balanced. These kebabs will please the less adventurous while satisfying more sophisticated tastes.

½ cup dry red wine
1 teaspoon dried marjoram
¼ cup tomato paste
1 teaspoon ground sumac or lemon-pepper seasoning
¼ cup olive oil
1 teaspoon coarse salt
2 tablespoons red wine vinegar
1 teaspoon ground black pepper
1 large onion, coarsely chopped
½ teaspoon chili flakes
3 cloves garlic, chopped
¼ teaspoon ground allspice
1½ pounds boneless lamb (shoulder, sirloin chops, or leg)

Process all ingredients except the lamb in a blender or food processor. Cut the lamb into 1¼-inch cubes, then butterfly each cube by slicing down the center about three-quarters of the way through. This allows the marinade to better penetrate the meat and impart a more intense flavor. Transfer lamb pieces to a bowl; pour marinade over meat and toss until well coated. Cover and marinate in the refrigerator for 8 hours or overnight.

When you are ready to cook, remove cubes and thread them on metal skewers. Grill over hot coals, rotating each kebab one-quarter turn every 1½ minutes until browned (about 6 minutes). You can also cook lamb under the broiler. Broil each side until well seared. Serve with plain yogurt and pita bread.

Serves 4

EMILE DeFELICE
CAW CAW CREEK, SC

Emile has the gift of epic, focused impatience. Impatience is a deeply undervalued quality. Impatience sees problems and will not wait for the tectonic shifts of bureaucracy. Caw Caw Creek is a farm that raises pigs, letting them loose in acorn-rich environs. Besides fresh meat, they also make exquisite aged hams. Emile has run for ag commissioner because no one adequate was running. He has created a farmers' market to compete with the commodity markets in sheep's clothing. He has become a voice for small-scale farming because it is clearly the right thing to do—tapping his fingers, fidgeting in his seat, and volunteering for duty before most people even hear the cannon.

We could take a photo at the farm. But do you really want to have another photo of a guy next to a pig? Let's do something more creative. Like a paper route with bacon. I'll hop on my bike.

I decided to divide my life into Work, Personal, and Civic. I went to Terra Madre in 2004, which just completely blew my mind. When I came home, I changed everything. Everything. I lost weight, got healthy. And I ran for ag commissioner. I talked about food safety in terms of creating local food systems. A cow that eats grain is a thousand times more likely to carry E. coli than a grass-fed cow. Cows are supposed to eat grass.

I've been working for and with Glenn Roberts for almost twenty years. He owns Anson Mills, which is the building across the parking lot. We're both out in that parking lot, both running our Priuses just to keep the juice in the phone. Two eco-dudes charging our friggin' telephones. He underwrites our market. We have a good thing right here.

I need to be surrounded by a lot of people who are smarter than I am; I want new ideas. The All-Local Farmers' Market is in this little building here every Saturday. The other markets around here are run by the state and it's just wholesale crap trucked in from wherever. That's just despicable. I had no choice but to offer an alternative.

MILE
COMMISSIONER OF
RICULTURE
4ag.com

Test Bag
not For sell

EMILE'S FAMOUS COLD-SMOKED PORK TENDERLOIN

This is absurdly easy, inexpensive, and delicious, once you have your piece of oak. Leftovers make great sandwiches with coleslaw or slices of Swiss cheese.

4 pounds pork tenderloin
1 cup olive oil
Kosher salt and pepper

Soak a wine-bottle-size piece of oak in water for an hour.

Bring tenderloin to room temperature. Rub with olive oil and salt and pepper. On one side of a grill with a lid, start a bed of coals. When half the coals are white, place the oak on top. Place meat on other side of the grill, away from direct heat, and lower the lid. Smoke for 4 hours.

Remove meat and cool slightly. Slice into medallions. Serve chilled with a caprese salad or your favorite salad greens, and a loaf of fresh crusty bread.

Serves 6 to 8

SUCCULENT BLADE STEAKS

These affordable cuts are utterly delicious and require no prep time. You don't even have to be home. All you need is the ability to think ahead—because the longer you marinate, the better they are.

4 1-inch-thick pork blade steaks, about ⅓ to ½ pound per steak

Marinade
4 tablespoons sesame oil
4 tablespoons soy sauce
4 tablespoons minced ginger
honey (optional)

Tenderize meat by jabbing all over with a fork. Mix together marinade and spread on steaks. Marinate in a covered container or plastic sealable bag for 1 to 3 days in the refrigerator.

Remove meat and put in Crock-Pot on low for approximately 6 hours (or slow cook in oven at 250°F). Remove and do a quick char on the grill, or sear on a hot skillet.

Serves 4

MARK M. DeNITTIS

IL MONDO VECCHIO SALUMI, CO

Mark is a slightly different animal from most butchers. He comes from the meat industry angle. He knows food safety, trend predictions, and productivity metrics as well as anyone. I think this is tremendous. Technical knowledge is often missing and the meat business is extremely tough. I know a butcher who got frustrated with a demanding customer he'd had for ten years, and he dropped a sack of pennies in front of him and said, "This is how much money I've made off you, all right?"

It is heartening that someone with his industry savvy thinks sustainability is a viable business model. IMV buys from local ranchers and develops products for ranches to sell under their own label. And he's got soul. You can't fake soul. While I was visiting with him, a Florentine ex-pat came in to buy some guanciale. Within moments, he was invoking his mamma and gushing with gratitude. "I can't believe it, it tastes just like home."

I won't say our USDA inspector put us through the wringer, because that would denote that it was negative, and it wasn't at all. When we met with our inspector, his first question was, *You guys know what you're doing, right?* Yes. *You sure?* Yep.

He basically said, *A dry cure facility is going to be a learning experience for us, too, so we'll work with you.* Half of it is your approach. If you're a jerk about it, you're not going to achieve much.

The health department shows up at a hotel, restaurant, or institutional food service operation maybe twice a year. I see my USDA inspector every day.

Besides our own products, we're creating products for ranchers. Everybody uses the old Uncle Bemis sausage mixes by the bag, dumps it in. So people want something a little different. We work with them to create custom flavor profiles. We've got bresaola, salumi, and sausages, including a fresh hot-dog-style sausage called The Ranch Link.

I've got two partners. I'm the butchering instructor at Johnson & Wales University in Denver and Adam teaches sports nutrition. He was the track and field Olympic chef in Beijing. When I met our other partner, he was experimenting with making prosciutto in his basement. And I said, *well, interestingly enough, I have a company set up to do that.* We were going to do a *salumeria* wine bar, but the fact that the cost of outsourcing fifteen hundred pounds was the same as three months rent here—this ended up being the thing to do.

I had just done some lamb jerky for the American Lamb Board that they were using as a PR thing. They were going to start revising the lamb section of the Meat Buyer's Guide, which is the US industry standard for meat cuts. I ended up being the chair of that committee, which included Niman Ranch Reps, Superior Farms, and a couple of the other major lamb producers.

It was just throwing out there what's been selling and what's not been selling. For me, it was about capturing a chef's perspective of what would do well in wholesale, how chefs were thinking now. We had been already working on promoting the value cuts from the educational sector. From retail sector to food-service sector, there's a lot more opportunity for chefs now to go into R & D for processors. And that's huge. Because the ideas that get developed for things like the Meat Buyer's Guide dictate what ends up on our plate.

GRAMMY'S SAUCE WITH MEATBALLS AND BRACIOLE

Growing up in an Italian neighborhood in Worcester, Massachusetts, you could get into a fistfight over whose grandmother's meatballs were the best. And of course those would be my Grammy Emma Ferraiuolo's. I was her chef assistant for Sunday dinner, in charge of quality control. This Calabrese-American red-sauce recipe serves a bunch of family, with enough for leftovers.

Meatballs
2 pounds ground "butcher's blend trinity"
  (equal parts beef, pork, veal, 85% lean)
¼ cup bread crumbs (no crusts)
¼ cup grated Parmesan/pecorino cheese blend
¼ cup parsley, finely chopped
1 tablespoon minced garlic
1 large egg, beaten
½ tablespoon sea salt
1 tablespoon fresh cracked black pepper
Olive oil for cooking

Braciole
1 pound beef top round, thinly sliced against
  the grain and pounded lightly
Sea salt and cracked black pepper
¼ cup minced garlic
¼ cup chopped parsley

Sauce
2 cups finely diced onions
6 to 10 cloves garlic
1 cup red wine (burgundy)—got to be the
  Gallo jug!
1 (28-ounce) can whole peeled tomatoes
1 (28-ounce) can crushed tomatoes
1 (28-ounce) can tomato puree

2 to 4 pounds cavatelli pasta, cooked

Prepare meatballs by mixing all ingredients and incorporating well in a bowl. Portion into 2-inch balls. Set aside in refrigerator. Season both sides of the braciole with salt and pepper to taste, and mix together garlic and parsley. Lay beef slices on a flat surface and place a thin layer of the parsley-and-garlic mixture on top. Roll slices over themselves once, with mixture on the inside, and tuck each with toothpick or tie with twine.

Heat a small amount of oil in a pan over medium heat. Sear meatballs until all sides have browned, remove, and set aside. Using same pan, sear small batches of braciole until browned. Remove. Add onions and garlic, and cook until translucent; do not brown. Deglaze the pan with red wine, and simmer, stirring, for 5 minutes. Add tomato products and bring to a boil, then reduce to very low simmer. Add meatballs and braciole, and let simmer for 4 to 5 hours, skimming off any fat that rises to the top. Transfer meatballs and braciole to serving dish and remove any toothpicks or twine. Toss one-fourth of the sauce with cavatelli or other favorite pasta. Reserve the rest to serve on the side. Mangia!

Serves 6 to 8

ANDREW DORSEY
MARLOW & DAUGHTERS, NY

Marlow & Daughters is part of a gloriously chaotic collaboration of restaurants, namely Diner, Marlow & Sons, and Roman's, as well as Diner Journal, one of the loveliest food publications in existance. They define the esprit de corps of beliefs above technique and systems above rules in Brooklyn. My memories of these locations include a gluttonous rabbit feast in the backyard Airstream dining room and dancing on the bar after hours.

Andrew Tarlow, one of the owners/ringmasters

describes the Marlow & Daughters origins: "We opened the butcher shop to streamline the local, organic, grass-fed, whole-animal meat program that we developed to supply the restaurants. We had been butchering and storing whole animals in a miniscule walk-in in the backyard of Diner. We also wanted to offer our high-quality meat to our community so they could cook it themselves at home and have access to information about the farmers, the animals, and how to best cook it."

Andrew Dorsey fits in perfectly here. I was leaving the shop, about a block away, and he caught up to me. "One of our pigs is being delivered, you can't miss this."

My friend called me and said they needed a warm body to throw pizzas and make jalapeño poppers at a movie theater. Just shy of a year later, I went to culinary school in Dallas.

I moved to New York and worked for David Chang at Noodle Bar. I got really bored of making ramen. It was an amazing company but anyone can get into a rut. On my days off, I'd hang out at Marlow & Daughters. I was working for beer and slowly learning to cut things up. They extended a job offer when my teacher, Brent, put in his notice to work at the Meat Hook. I didn't get a classic apprenticeship, it was very spontaneous. Whatever they needed help with, I would learn how to do it. I'm good and I can always get better, faster, and more precise. You need to teach your hands how to do things.

Right now I'm really happy. In the summer, when it's even hotter in the kitchen than it is outside, it's great to be in a nice, cool butcher shop. There are three restaurants and we do the majority of meat buying for them—all the beef and pork with the exception of dry-cured salamis. We have a guy now whose primary focus is to do the terrines and charcuterie for the restaurants.

We walk a fine line between being prep cooks and being butchers. When we do things for the restaurant, we cut the meat down into portions, trimmed and ready to go on a tray. They take the tray and put it straight on the grill. We get in earlier than the chefs at the restaurants, so we go through their walk-ins and make estimates about what they need and start cutting. They come in and double-check on what we're doing.

As a restaurant group, we really stress the importance of being a creative, impromptu cook. Like you can go in a walk-in and cook with what's there. We rely so heavily on seasonality with our ingredients that you really have to be able to swing if something goes in or out of season. That translates into the chefs all being very flexible with the meat they get. It's not all tenderloin and rib eyes. We brainstorm with the chefs. *We've only got one pork loin for you today. So I can cut you fifteen pork chops or twenty orders of scaloppini if I bone it out.*

The beef and pork are exclusively local. All the beef is grass-fed and finished, hormone- and antibiotic-free, and humanely raised. Good meat. We age the rib and strip loin. We shoot for four weeks because that strikes a nice balance among flavor, limitations of space, and profitability. At sixty days, you have a much smaller product and at three weeks you just begin to see changes in flavor. It has to have some good fat or it will turn into a raisin.

We had one piece of beef that came in and had great marbling and huge fat cover and we decided to age it as long as we could. We went ninety days. I shared a porterhouse with all the butchers and it was very flavorful, cheesy. It was right there on the edge.

Part of our concept is transparency. Our walk-in has a huge window, where anyone can take a look at what we are doing. We aren't hiding anything and we want people to know it's a wholesome operation and eating meat isn't evil.

Everyone at Marlow & Daughters right now has at least seven years' experience in the kitchen. We each have our specialties, our different backgrounds. You have to break people out of the mold of only wanting boneless skinless chicken breasts. It's not like were forcing beef kidneys down people's throats, but like an oyster steak or a shoulder tender, something they haven't tried before.

MARINATED BEEF SKEWERS
WITH CHILLED SOMEN NOODLES

This recipe uses chuck flap, which is a cut from the chuck that has a similar texture to short ribs. The meat is cut against the grain, threaded on skewers, and then marinated. These are great grilled but could also work seared in a cast-iron pan. Somen are thin, quick-cooking Japanese noodles that are sold in packs of single-serving bundles.

1½ pounds chuck flap
4 servings somen noodles
4 eggs, optional
Sesame oil
Soy sauce
2 tablespoons sesame seeds, toasted
2 radishes, thinly sliced
2 spring onions, thinly sliced

Marinade
¾ cup thinly sliced spring onions
2 tablespoons finely chopped ginger
¼ cup soy sauce
3 tablespoons neutral-flavored oil, grapeseed or an olive-oil blend
1 tablespoon sesame oil
1 teaspoon sherry vinegar
1 teaspoon lemon juice
1 teaspoon red chili flakes

Combine marinade ingredients in a mixing bowl. Slice meat against the grain into ¼-inch strips or cut into small cubes and toss with marinade. Cover and refrigerate at least 2 hours or overnight.

Soak 8 skewers 30 minutes ahead of time. Thread marinated meat onto skewers. Grill the skewers on high heat, turning every couple of minutes until done, about ten minutes. These are best well done.

Cook noodles in boiling water until tender. Immediately put noodles under cold water to stop cooking. Fry the eggs, if using, while noodles are cooking. Drain noodles and toss with a drizzle of sesame oil and soy sauce. Divide noodles and skewers among 4 bowls and garnish with sesame seeds, radishes, and spring onions. Top each bowl with a fried egg, if desired.

Serves 4

PRIMAL CUTS: BEEF

The **STEER** is a complicated **CREATURE** in its generous **MUSCULATURE**. The primals are separated by cooking styles, while the cuts within each primal tell **TALES** of cultures, history, and lifestyle.

CHUCK

The burly bundle of muscle on which rests the weight of the world. The chuck is, like the shoulder on all animals, full of fat and connective tissue. From a good steer, however, the chuck can also be ground or used for roasts.

Cuts: chuck roast (bone-in or boneless, or square cut), cross rib roast, clod roast, arm roast, mock tender, shoulder tender medallions, chuck roll, chuck eye roll, chuck tender steaks, chuck short ribs, flat iron, and stew meat

BRISKET

A barbecue staple, the brisket is festooned with fat garlands; it blossoms in a long, slow heat. It is also gorgeous as corned beef. The foreshank can be sliced into osso bucco.

RIB

The resting place of prime rib, this primal has the three graces of roasting: big eye (with marbling depending on the animal), a fat cap, and a bone for sweetness.

Cuts: short ribs (which extend to the plate), back ribs, rib roast, rib steak (aka cowboy steak), and rib eye (boneless rib steak)

PLATE

Here lie some of my favorite beef cuts: the short ribs, the hanger steak, and the skirt steak. Short ribs are stripes of fat, meat, and bone, chunky and longing to lounge in a warm, saucy bath. And then there are the skirt and the hanger steaks, lean strips of muscle, concentrated in flavor and eager for quick preparation: ground, made into tartare, or grilled.

Cuts: short plate, outside (extends into the flank) and inside skirt steaks, short ribs (extend up to the rib section), and hanger steak (aka butcher's steak)

SHORT LOIN

This is the priciest section of the steer, for all the big-ticket steaks, with marbling and, hopefully, some good age on them (21 days is the ballpark). Loins are lovely roasted, especially with the bone in, which gives them deeper flavors and better moisture retention.

The tenderloin is a nearly unused muscle, so there's very little resistance in the texture. Sear it but serve it rare.

Cuts: bone-in or boneless loin roast, strip loin (tenderloin, flank and chine removed), tenderloin roast; porterhouse, T-bone, strip steak, and tenderloin steak (aka filet mignon or fillet)

FLANK

Marinate, cook hot and quick, and cut on the bias. The flank is, like the hanger and skirt steaks, an individual muscle that is deep in flavor, thin, and grainy in texture. Used often for London broil.

SIRLOIN

The sirloin is the posterior of the loin, with some characteristics of the loin and some of the leg. Steaks are best cut thick and cooked on high heat to medium rare.

Cuts: bone-in or boneless sirloin roast, top sirloin butt roast (bone-in or boneless), top sirloin cap (see Tia's instruction on cutting into culotte steaks), bottom sirloin butt roast (bone-in or boneless), tri-tip roast and steaks (aka sirloin tip), beef loin tip or flap steak, ball tip roast, and round (bone) steak

ROUND

The leg of a steer is more manageable when divided into five muscles and the hindshank. The inside or top round provides excellent braising meat. The outside or bottom round is a tough muscle; accustomed to hard work, it takes a long time to relax, so stew it or grind it into burgers. The eye of round is also ideal for an elegant braise; put it in the Crock-Pot when you leave for work. The rump is a hardworking hump that should be braised or ground for a meat sauce. The hindshank, like the foreshank, can be sliced into osso bucco.

Cuts: top (inside) and bottom (outside) round roasts and steaks, eye of round roast, rump roast, heel roast, hindshank, and tip steak

OFFAL

These are extras you have to order ahead from your butcher or take extra care that you will receive them from the slaughterhouse. From the head, you can get silky beef cheeks that are seductive when braised. You will also get the tongue which you can boil and peel. Beef offal includes sweetbreads, liver, and brains. Oxtail can be prepared like osso buco, in a braise.

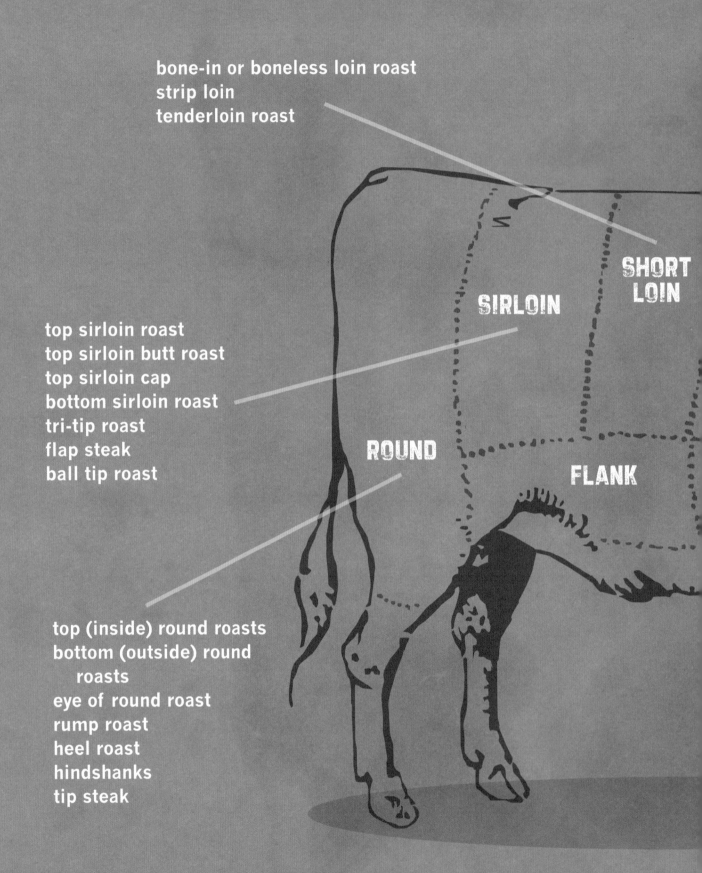

bone-in or boneless loin roast
strip loin
tenderloin roast

top sirloin roast
top sirloin butt roast
top sirloin cap
bottom sirloin roast
tri-tip roast
flap steak
ball tip roast

SIRLOIN

SHORT LOIN

ROUND

FLANK

top (inside) round roasts
bottom (outside) round
   roasts
eye of round roast
rump roast
heel roast
hindshanks
tip steak

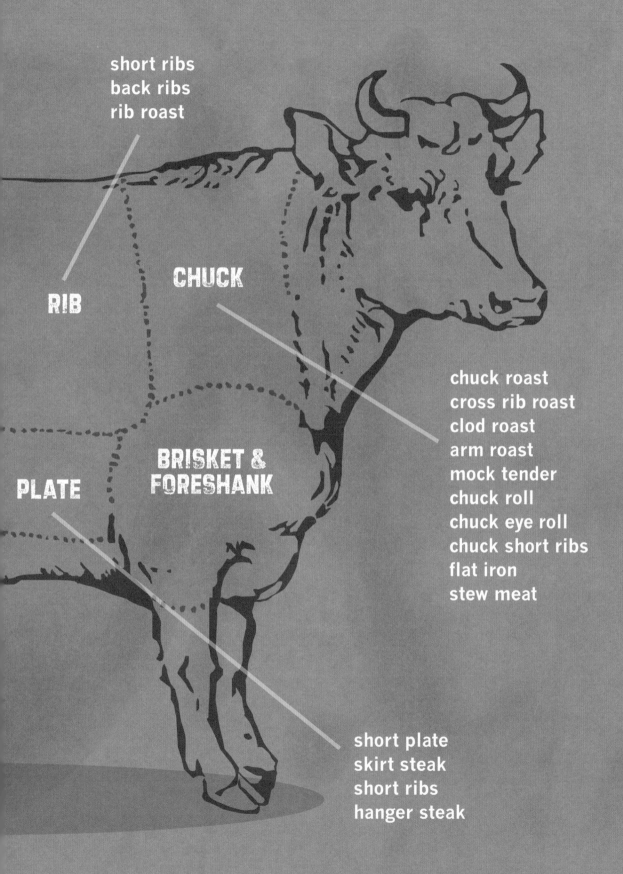

short ribs
back ribs
rib roast

CHUCK

RIB

chuck roast
cross rib roast
clod roast
arm roast
mock tender
chuck roll
chuck eye roll
chuck short ribs
flat iron
stew meat

BRISKET &
FORESHANK

PLATE

short plate
skirt steak
short ribs
hanger steak

VINNY DOTOLO & JON SHOOK

ANIMAL, CA

As a collaboration junkie, I have to say this partnership blows my mind. Vinny and Jon are best friends, business partners, and have traveled and lived together throughout their eleven years in cahoots. And they still crack each other up. Sitting in their typical restaurant office (part afterthought, part escape hatch) with an industrial-sized box of top-tier chocolate chips, I thought: Vinny and Jon are the heroes of a new age in the kitchen. Gone are the days of militaristic adherence to hierarchy; gone are the days of life-long ladder climbing. Hail the coming era of self-guided creativity in the kitchen, collaboration above boredom and bros before sous chefs!

Jon Shook: This bum told me one time, head west to the gold, west to the gold!

Vinny Dotolo: L.A.'s been good to us. People think everybody's fake in L.A. and I don't understand that. There's always been good food here. People just didn't talk about it.

Jon: We have other ideas, besides Animal.

Vinny: It's just the first thing we started. L.A. was kind of in the dark about the shit we're doing, it was missing here. It's amazing the difference in price between factory- farm product and sustainable product.

Jon: The inconsistency is crazy, too. If you get factory-farmed stuff, you're going to get the same cut every time. The free-range stuff's all over the place. We got this tiny belly the other day, like it snuck by the gate. *Come on, Bud, you're in the gate, you're getting slaughtered.* He's like, *What? I'm supposed to have seven more months.*

Vinny: It's always something. As a business owner you think, *Damn, I could serve the same stuff but not make it sustainable and make twice as much money.* But . . .

Jon: Money is not why we got into this. We could have cashed in a lot of other ways, besides just changing the meat.

Vinny: Like, we don't have a burger on the menu. We could sell burgers all night long.

Jon: What makes you feel good? Is it the extra hundred dollars a day, or is it knowing that you're serving somebody a product that they're not able to get up the road at the supermarket?

Vinny: We keep about half the menu the same, always. I definitely believe you have to have some base because change creates chaos. And chaos isn't always fun. We learned that early on. There are things that are just f'ing good and we're not going to take them off the menu.

Jon: They are f'ing good. If we took our pig-ear dish off, people would be really upset. We sell twenty pounds of pig ears every other day. It's crazy.

Vinny: We've been cooking together for eleven years. We met at the culinary school at the Art Institute in Fort Lauderdale.

Jon: We worked in a lot of restaurants together, did a lot of traveling together.

Vinny: We went to Colorado and then came to a restaurant in Beverly Hills. When it closed we ended up catering and that took off and led into the show and the book, *Two Dudes, One Pan*.

Jon: We didn't enjoy the show.

Vinny: It's natural for some people; we just still want to be in the kitchen. But we learn through our experiences. And you can get trapped in a restaurant, so you've got to force yourself to let go. It'll be fine, as long as it doesn't burn down.

Jon: You've got to trust your staff. It's great when you are out of town and somebody's like, *Oh, I had the best meal at Animal*, and you're like, *Yes! I wasn't even there*.

Vinny: People just walk down the street and come into our restaurant and they don't know what the heck this place is, so I feel responsible about what we're serving people.

Jon: There are very few rules here. The ones there are, you just can't break them. Vinny's somebody who thinks about what he wants to do. I'm the guy who picks up the scraps and figures something out. But we have very similar styles. It is really hard to work with someone this long but you make it to a level where you just understand each other's boundaries and we've already put in eleven years. Things are just getting good. Why the heck would we stop now? We're like family, me and him.

"PEOPLE THINK EVERYBODY'S FAKE IN L.A. AND I DON'T UNDERSTAND THAT. THERE'S ALWAYS BEEN GOOD FOOD HERE. PEOPLE JUST DIDN'T TALK ABOUT IT."

FRIED PIG EARS

This dish has become a perennial at Animal. We serve it with a fried egg on top and a sprinkle of kosher salt. Break the yolk and let the pig ears soak it up.

2 pounds pig ears
Frying oil
Kosher salt to taste
4 fried eggs

Vinaigrette
1½ cups lime juice, strained
1 cup chili garlic paste
1½ teaspoons kosher salt
¼ cup chopped green onion

Clean pig ears of any extra hair. In a large pot, cover the ears in plenty of water, bring to a boil and braise for 36 hours at a light simmer. Check occasionally to make sure ears stay submerged in water. Skim the surface of the water occasionally. After 36 hours take out the ears and lay them flat on sheet trays to cool.

Mix all vinaigrette ingredients and set aside. Julienne ears ⅛ of an inch thick.

Heat oil in a large deep skillet to 360°F. Fry ears for 3½ minutes, or until crispy. Place ears in a large bowl lined with paper towels. Season liberally with salt. Take out paper towels and toss in vinaigrette, coating the ears lightly. Serve with fried eggs.

Serves 4

As someone who owns a butcher shop I probably shouldn't be saying this, but people need to eat less meat. You need to eat a higher-quality product. And I know it's expensive, I know it's hard. But eat less, eat better, and make it a special thing.

I was born a vegetarian. My parents have been vegetarians since the 1970s. They eat fish, so I don't know if it's a health thing or a "fish don't have feelings" thing. But I rationalize it that if I am going to be playing with meat, at least I'm working with the best quality and working closely with the farmers.

As much as people despise the whole Food Network/celebrity chef thing, it has had a huge impact on the way that America thinks about food. Food is cool again, which is great because for a long time, meat was just something red, on a foam tray, wrapped in plastic. There was a real disconnect between what people were eating and where the food was coming from. I love how not only chefs have become celebrities but so have farmers. When we have special dinners at the restaurant, we bring in the farmers and everyone wants to talk to them; they're treated like stars. That's a great by product of the way the whole food movement has changed over the years.

I don't really consider myself a very artistic person but the closest I come to doing art is preparing food. It appeals to every sense—taste, smell, look, and even sometimes sound, depending. I love that. I got into charcuterie when I was working as a cook. My feeling was, anything that somebody had done before, I didn't see any reason why I couldn't do it myself. So when the opportunity to buy Viande Meats came up, it just seemed like it would be a lot of fun. We started smoking all of our own sausages, making all of our deli meats from scratch, brining and smoking hams, curing and smoking pastrami. Really, I'm just drawing on all those things that I loved to cook with before and producing them now myself.

Eventually, we missed cooking for people every night. You're definitely one step removed when you're selling raw meat that someone is going to take home and cook. We started doing these dinners around the city in odd places. It was all very word of mouth and sort of underground. Next thing we knew we were catering. We were working really closely with local farmers, using whatever produce came in that week. We're kind of purists, we don't believe in fusion food. I think that's just crap. I don't really feel like I need to reinvent anything. Classic food is classic for a reason, I love it for that.

At the end of 2008, I sold Viande to my employees, and a few months later we opened Laurelhurst Market. I still think of myself more as a guy who just owns a butcher shop, I guess by default that kind of makes me a butcher. I mean, I break down whole animals and cut meat all day, so I guess I am.

BEN DYER
LAURELHURST MARKET, OR

Ben Dyer owns Laurelhurst Market in Portland, which actually is not a market at all. It is a restaurant and a butcher shop. A restaurant where you can point to a diagram of beef primals and call out your steak order. And a butcher shop where you can pick up pickled sausages and house-made pâté. Ben initially seems quiet and reserved, and then feats of boldness unexpectedly tumble from his mouth. I like this, when people get more interesting the longer you talk to them. His contradictions aren't confusing at all, they just make you want to hear more.

SMOKED BRISKET

WITH OZARK-MOUNTAIN BARBECUE SAUCE

This is one of our signature dishes; it went on the menu soon after we opened, and we have no intention of taking it off anytime soon. At the restaurant, we use briskets from Wagyu cattle—this is the breed the Japanese raise for their Kobe Beef. It is especially well marbled and fatty, which makes for a very tender, rich, and delicious final product. We slather the smoked brisket with one of my favorite barbecue sauces of all time. The sauce has a nice balance of sweetness and tang, and is a perfect foil to the fatty, smoky brisket.

Sauce
¼ cup vegetable oil
1 cup finely chopped yellow onion
5 cloves garlic, minced
1 tablespoon ground black pepper
1 tablespoon kosher salt
1 tablespoon dry mustard
1 tablespoon paprika
1 tablespoon chili powder
2 teaspoons ground cumin
2 teaspoons crushed chili flakes
1¼ cup cider vinegar
4 cups ketchup
¼ cup worcestershire sauce
1½ cups beer (American Lager)

½ cup plus 2 tablespoons honey
½ cup brown sugar

Dry Rub
2 cups kosher salt
1 cup granulated sugar
½ cup ground black pepper
¼ cup paprika
¼ cup onion powder
⅛ cup garlic powder
1 teaspoon cayenne pepper

1 Wagyu brisket, 12 to 15 pounds, nose on
   (or highest grade meat available)

In a heavy-bottomed saucepan, heat the vegetable oil over medium heat. Add onions and garlic, stirring often with a wooden spoon. Cook until golden brown, being careful not to burn. Add all dry spices and continue to cook, stirring often and scraping as you go, until spices begin to stick to bottom of pot. Add cider vinegar. Bring to boil, being sure to scrape all spices from bottom of pot. Simmer until vinegar is reduced by half. Add rest of ingredients and stir to combine. Return to a simmer, then reduce heat to very low and cook for approximately 30 to 45 more minutes, stirring occasionally, until sauce has thickened. Remove from heat and pour into a nonreactive metal or glass dish and place in refrigerator to cool. Store in an airtight container in the refrigerator for up to two weeks.

Combine all of the dry rub spices in a bowl (can be stored in an airtight container for up to four weeks). Rub brisket with a generous amount of dry rub. Place on a rack or absorbent paper in the refrigerator, uncovered, for 24 to 48 hours. Smoke at 200°F for 12 hours over hardwoods, preferably pecan or apple. (Replace the chips when they are no longer smoking.) Over this amount of time, the brisket develops a dark, thick "bark," which is a large part of its final flavor.

To serve, cut the brisket into large chunks, then sear it or grill it to bring it back up to temperature and give it a nice crust on the outside. Slather brisket with the sauce.

Serves a crowd

LITTLE SMOKIES (HOT MAMAS)

PICKLED SAUSAGES

This is our take on the Hot Mama, those little red pickled sausages at gas stations and convenience-store countertops. They are pickled in a hot, vinegary brine and a little on the spicy side.

Brine
1 gallon cider vinegar
1 cup whole garlic cloves, peeled
½ cup red chili flakes, crushed
½ cup kosher salt

5 pounds boneless, skinless pork shoulder, 2-inch dice
3 tablespoons kosher salt
2 tablespoons paprika
2 tablespoons minced fresh garlic
2 tablespoons sugar
1 tablespoon freshly ground black pepper
1 tablespoon pink salt *
½ tablespoon cayenne pepper
½ teaspoon dried thyme
¼ teaspoon ground mace
About 10 feet hog casings, 32 to 35 mm diameter

Place all brine ingredients in a stainless-steel pot and bring to a boil. Remove from heat and allow to cool. Place in refrigerator to cool completely before adding sausages.

Mix rest of ingredients, except casings, in a large bowl. Place mixture in freezer for 10 minutes to chill. Grind once through the fine die of a meat grinder. Emulsify by hand by gradually adding ½ cup ice water, stirring well until meat is sticky and well combined. Immediately stuff into medium hog casings, tying into 4-ounce links, and allow to dry overnight in the refrigerator. **

Hot smoke at 180°F to an internal temperature of 150°F. Return to refrigerator, allow to cool, then place sausages in brine in a nonreactive (glass, plastic or stainless steel) container with a lid. Allow sausages to pickle in brine in refrigerator for 30 days. Sausages will keep in brine for up to three months. Keep refrigerated until ready to cook.

Makes 20 4-ounce links

* Curing salt. Necessary to inhibit growth of bacteria. Use and store with caution.
** See Sausage Basics, page 32.

CHRISTOPHER ELEY
GOOSE THE MARKET, IN

As a tall person, I have formed a lot of theories about how height affects someone's nature. Chris is a case study of one of my core concepts—the tall person becomes a caretaker. Maybe it is just that we always seem older than our peers or that we have some primal instinct to look to the largest for safety. There is empathy in all of Chris' efforts. His involvement with Slow Food Indianapolis is focused on creating food access for low-income residents; his market will uplift a neighborhood in transition and support farmers seeking markets; his restaurant work is a crusade to save flagging eateries.

If you goose something, you change the way you think about it, so that's how we got the name. Goose was also my wife's childhood nickname. The other connotation is Mother Goose, being a provider for the neighborhood. I grew up here, I moved back to do this market. I have a lot of roots here.

This neighborhood is nicknamed Dodge City. I'm not Italian. I don't have that connection. So, we name the salumi for different parts of this area. Like our Dodge City Salami is pork that's dry cured with peppercorn and fennel pollen. We have a Gin & Juice Salami, which is lamb that's cured with juniper and orange peel. We have a Delaware Fireball, named after the street, it's wrapped in caul fat, crepinette style, then dry cured with fresh chilis, garlic, and then cold smoked over bourbon barrels.

My passion has always been butchering and charcuterie. We would always do a charcuterie plate, but no one really went for it. I started to see that it was making a resurgence. So I based this concept around the old-world neighborhood butcher shop. I mean, I live upstairs with my wife.

I worked for the restaurant division of a hotel company and I was on their task force to help turn around restaurants that weren't doing well. I opened eight restaurants. I've seen so many people lose their hats, so I always told myself I'd never have my own place.

We work directly with all the producers, I don't go through any middlemen. Before we opened, I spent six months driving around, meeting farmers. A lot of them were very skeptical of me. I even had to show them a business plan. It takes going out there and building those relationships to succeed at this business. The farmers I work with are definitely seeing growth. One thing that I've promised is that I'd help to get them into other restaurants, so they're not traveling to Indianapolis just for me.

We have people that come from all over the state to buy here. But we also get a lot of foot traffic, people out walking their dog. What I love about this neighborhood is that it's pocketed. There can be a bad area and then just a few blocks away, it's completely different. I want what we do to reflect that uniqueness.

ROASTED GOOSE
WITH TANGERINE GLACÉ AND DUCK-LIVER STUFFING

If you have been trotting out the same old turkey year after year, give this goose a try. This preparation is rich and ceremonial and not nearly as difficult as people will think it is when they take in the complex layering of flavors.

½ teaspoon ground cinnamon
¼ teaspoon ground cloves
1 teaspoon ground black pepper
1 tablespoon kosher salt
1 tablespoon sugar
1 whole goose

Tangerine Glacé
½ cup apple-cider vinegar
1 cup honey
½ cup tangerine juice
½ cup orange juice

Duck-Liver Stuffing
4 ounces duck liver, cut into 4 equal slabs
4 tablespoon goose fat, rendered
1 yellow onion, diced
2 cups roasted smashed potatoes
3 red cooking apples
1 tablespoon roasted-garlic puree
1 cup chestnuts or walnuts, roasted, peeled, and chopped
1 cup poultry broth or stock
1 cup ½-inch baguette cubes, crust removed, left out to dry overnight
1 tablespoon fresh chopped rosemary
1 tablespoon fresh chopped sage
1 tablespoon chopped flat-leaf parsley
Salt and pepper

One day before: combine the cinnamon, cloves, black pepper, salt, and sugar. Mix well and evenly distribute it over the exterior and interior of your goose. Fill a roasting pan with a rack with about 2 to 3 inches of water. Place the roasting rack in so that it is just barely in the water. Place the goose on the rack breast side up. Tuck the wings close to the body. Place the excess fat from the cavity of the bird on the roasting rack. Tent the bird with aluminum foil.

Place the pan over a large burner on the stove on medium high until the pan starts to steam. Reduce the heat to low and steam for 45 minutes. This will render the skin so that it crisps during roasting. Remove the bird and rack from the pan and set aside. Drain the fat and water from the pan into a jar. Separate and reserve the fat to be used in the stuffing. Discard the water. Return the rack to the pan and allow the bird to cool and dry in the refrigerator overnight.

Heat the honey, vinegar, and juices to a boil and reduce to simmer. Cook until it thickens slightly. Remove from heat, cool, and cover. Set the glacé aside.

Preheat a heavy-bottomed pan until nearly smoking. Sear the duck liver for 10 seconds on each side. It should be a deep golden brown. Reserve the rendered fat. Chill the duck liver for 10 minutes. In the same pan, heat the rendered duck liver and reserved goose fat until nearly smoking. Then add the onions, potatoes, and apples. Cook until crisp and lightly browned. Reduce the heat and add the garlic, nuts, and broth. Heat to a simmer, then add the bread and all the herbs. Combine well, cool, and refrigerate.

Day of: preheat oven to 375°F. Fill the cavity of the goose with the stuffing. Brush exterior completely with glacé. Roast goose for 2 to 2½ hours. The leg bone should wiggle when done. Remove from oven and allow to rest 15 to 20 minutes before serving.

Serves 6 to 8

NICK FANTASMA

PARADISE LOCKER MEATS, MO

Generations ago, a baby boy was found on the doorstep of an Italian orphanage. The caretakers named him Fantasma, the Italian word for "ghost." The name stuck. Generations later, his descendents opened a meat plant in Paradise, Missouri. Ghosts in Paradise, gently ushering in four-legged creatures to the afterlife.

Getting a hog from piglet to pork chop means handing off the animal from one person to the next, each with a noble piece of responsibility. That sense of honor can transform a meat plant into a mission, as the relationship between Paradise Locker Meats and Heritage Foods USA has. Heritage aggregates traditional breeds of livestock, in order to promote biodiversity in the wholesale market. They can't get all the way to the plate without a processing partner, without the Fantasmas. Together they create a shadow of the centralized meat business. Ghosts in the Machine.

My whole family works here. Mom is doing clerical stuff. Dad runs everything. I'm managing the plant, twenty-five employees, six on the slaughter floor. I have been here off and on since I was thirteen. I started on the cleanup crew after school. During college, I didn't think this was what I really wanted to do. After we started working with Heritage, I got excited about coming back into the business.

We got a call from Heritage Foods about becoming USDA-inspected. There's only about twenty other USDA-inspected plants in Missouri. We started off doing ten or so pigs for Heritage but now we're their primary processor. I couldn't even begin to count how many specialty cuts we do for Heritage off the top of my head. We slaughter on Monday, Tuesday, process Wednesday and Thursday and everything ships out on Friday morning. It gets to the chefs about seven days from slaughter. They sell to Chez Panisse, Daniel Boulud, Edwards Hams, and Armandino Batali—Mario Batali's father. Heritage changed the face of where we were headed by a long shot.

We had Animal Welfare and Certified Humane up here and we've been approved by both of them. There's a lot to be said for treating the animals well prior to slaughter, both for the quality of the meat, and a simple respect for the animals that we're using to sustain our own health.

You have to make sure you're not stressing the animals with loud noises or physical abuse. Hogs and cattle are very, very stubborn animals, so if they're in an area that they're not used to, they don't want to move. That's where a lot of the larger slaughter houses can lessen the quality of the meat by pushing those animals through roughly or giving them hot shots. Also, it's important to make sure that the animals aren't overheated. We provide feed and water and comfortable spacious areas before they go into slaughter. When you pack fifty animals into a pen meant for thirty, they get stressed out. When an animal gets stressed, it releases toxins into the muscles; the acidity level rises while the pH balance drops, and it will start to lose moisture content and get tough.

We built new pens. We clean them twice a week and put misting fans inside for the summertime. It will get over 103°F. When I run that fan, it's usually about twenty to thirty degrees cooler in these pens than it is outside. Hogs don't sweat, they cool themselves by panting, like dogs. If they get overheated they can asphyxiate.

All the breeds have their distinguishing characteristics. DuRocs are leaner pigs with a bigger muscle structure, more meat in the bellies, which makes great bacon. The red wattles are exceptionally fat, creating extremely flavorful pork that many chefs prefer. A lot of chefs also like to use the thick back for curing and cooking. Berkshire is—I hate to call it a middle-of-the-road breed, but it doesn't have extreme characteristics. It's a good balance of fat content and meat content. If I did only white-haired hogs every week, I could probably go up another twenty to twenty-five percent on the number of hogs that we do every week. It just takes that much extra work to do the black- and red-haired hogs because there's so much to scrape and you can't miss any.

We're getting ready for an expansion. We're going to build out almost to the end of the parking lot, adding another 23,000 square feet. It's exciting and scary. We're trying to develop more wholesale markets in the Kansas City area and all of the Midwest. Organic feed and natural feed cost more than commercial feed. So, farmers need a premium price and it's worth it. But not a lot of them know how to market it well enough to get that premium. We can help them with that.

There are a lot of people my age who went away to college or culinary school and have moved back to the Midwest ready to start sustainable natural restaurants, supporting local products. Finally, people are starting to realize that naturally raised animals taste better. The food movement is coming to the Midwest.

BEEF STIR-FRY

This stir-fry is pretty forgiving: the beef is cooked quickly and removed to prevent overcooking, and these vegetables are more tolerant than most and not likely to loose color. The apple cider vinegar adds a nice kick to the thick sauce . . . Perfect for a bowl of steaming rice.

2 pounds flank or skirt steak
2 tablespoons peanut oil
3 tablespoons cornstarch
¼ cup water
1 medium onion, sliced
2 medium carrots, sliced on the diagonal, about ¼ inch wide
3 ribs celery, sliced on the diagonal, about ¼ inch wide
3 cloves garlic, minced
1 teaspoon ginger
½ cup white wine
1 cup chicken broth
¼ cup soy sauce
3 teaspoons apple cider vinegar

Put the steak in the freezer for 15 minutes for easier slicing. Slice the beef in half lengthwise (along the grain) and then cut into thin strips, 2 inches long and ¼ inch wide. Heat 1 tablespoon oil in wok over high heat. Stir-fry the beef quickly for 1 to 2 minutes until browned but still pink inside. Remove and set aside. In a small bowl, mix cornstarch with water and set aside.

Add 1 tablespoon oil to wok and allow to heat. Add the vegetables, garlic, and ginger, and stir-fry 1 to 2 minutes. Add the wine and let simmer for around 3 minutes so the alcohol cooks off. Add broth, soy, and vinegar, and stir-fry to mix well. Taste and continue to stir-fry if you like the vegetables more tender. Return the beef and any juices to the wok, add the cornstarch mixture, and stir-fry quickly until meat is at desired doneness and sauce is thickened. Serve immediately with rice.

Serves 4 to 6

FINDING A FARMER

You should be able get recommendations from a local **BUTCHER**, farmers' market, nearby **SLAUGHTERHOUSE**, your county's Farm Bureau chapter, or the University Cooperative Extension. You can also ask **CHEFS** that serve local meat, 4H or FFA clubs, or a hunting club. Once you find a farmer who can sell you a **WHOLE** animal, make sure it is an animal you want. Breed, feed, and **QUALITY** of life are the most important things. Ask your farmer what breeds they choose and why. Most farmers **CROSSBREED** to get the right combination of qualities for their farm. When it comes to breed choice, for me it is more a matter of education than preference.

Good fat sets great pigs apart from the rest of the herd. While breed has say-so on this, feed also has an "opinion." Acorns and peanuts are classic fatteners, but pig farmers are ingenious at using the nutritious detritus available from brewers, dairymen, and bakers—almost as clever as are the pigs themselves at rooting about for nutrition, if given the opportunity. I prefer lamb, goat, and beef to be solely fed on grass, but some ranchers finish with grain: you have to decide what suits you.

Antibiotics or hormones are the top concerns, the banning of which forms the cornerstone of organic certification. Ask about the beast's life. A good farmer will usually enjoy telling you about it. Were the lambs tail-docked (a controversial procedure done to prevent an infestation called myiasis)? Were the sows put in farrowing crates, which prevent them from crushing the piglets but are considered inhumane by many? Let your farmer or butcher know you are interested; nothing could please them more.

BRAD FARMERIE

PUBLIC, NY

Brad is the kind of guy who invites you in for a quick bite, and three hours later, you've sipped cocktails at his speakeasy gin bar, Madam Geneva, and eaten an eight-course tasting menu that, had it ended with fireworks, would not have seemed inappropriate. He is the kind of guy that spends all day in the kitchen explaining boudin, even though he is running three restaurants and a bar, not to mention being a dad and carrying the mantle of a Michelin star.

There's a rumor that Edison did his AC/DC experiments on horses in this neighborhood, so my brother jokes that it happened in this back room. The horse head above the door is a monument to those horses that never came out.

I really learned to cook in London. I was there for seven years. In England, you start training when you're a teenager, so I felt like I had a lot of catching up to do, and I worked constantly.

I'd discussed opening a restaurant with my brother, so together with his partners at AvroKO, we created PUBLIC and the adjoining space, the Monday Room, which is a bar and has a separate menu. We like to keep that pretty experimental. Right now it has a very meat-centric menu. I use a lot of wild game. I almost got arrested for having kangaroo on the menu. I wasn't trying to hide it, I had no idea it was against the law.

I felt like I needed to have the experience of hunting. My writer buddy Manny Howard organized a trip. Basically, this guy Uncle Bubsy (gotta love Uncle Bubsy) owns the right to hunt boar on this island off the coast of South Carolina. So the deal is, when you find wild boar, the dogs go after them. The boars actually give up pretty quickly. I think they realize they'll do better in a fight than a race against the dogs. These feral hogs are just burly. Someone gets the job of coming up behind and picking up the boar's hind legs. Then someone else comes in with a knife and stabs it through the armpit to the heart. I was completely terrified, but the second time around, I did it. I think because of my experience with butchering, I had a pretty good instinct about where to put the knife. Then you drag the boars back to a cabin and just process everything. We made sausage with the intestines, and cooked and cured all the meat.

It's a perfect memory. In fact, I don't think I would do that trip again, just because it could never compete.

"I ALMOST GOT ARRESTED FOR HAVING KANGAROO ON THE MENU. I WASN'T TRYING TO HIDE IT, I HAD NO IDEA IT WAS AGAINST THE LAW."

PORK RILLETTES

Rillettes are a great savior of sorts. In the "good old days" they were a way to preserve the beauty of the pig's bounty and insure there would be some for later. The concept is that slowly steaming the meat in liquid draws out the fat; the chunks then slowly cook in the fat until they are tender. Traditionally, after hours of cooking, the chunks would be flaked with a fork and mixed with the remaining fat within the pot, hardening to slightly stringy meat surrounded with fat. I prefer to puree the whole thing, making a simple, spreadable goodness.

We throw a slight Asian bend to this recipe with the aromatic spices and soy sauce, but the real star of the show is the vinegar, which not only acts as a preserving agent but also balances the delicious porky richness with acidity.

2 pounds high-fat pork scrap or pork belly, cut into 1-inch cubes
1 cinnamon stick
2 cloves
3 star anise fruits
2 cardamom pods
4 cloves garlic
1 thumb ginger, peeled and sliced thinly
¼ cup soy sauce
½ cup rice vinegar
¼ cup Chinese black vinegar
2 tablespoons cold water
Duck fat (optional)

Put pork in a heavy-bottomed pot. Place cinnamon stick, cloves, star anise, and cardamom on a piece of muslin (cheesecloth) and tie it closed, adding it to pot. Put garlic, ginger, and soy sauce in a food processor or blender and process to a fine puree. Pour this into the pot, add the vinegars and water, and stir thoroughly.

Cover pot, place over low heat, and slowly bring to a boil. Reduce heat to a very low simmer and continue to cook, covered, for 10 minutes. This draws the fat and moisture out of the meat.

Uncover and cook for an additional 2 hours, stirring every 10 to 20 minutes to make sure the ingredients aren't sticking. At the end of the cooking time the pork should be falling apart and much of the liquid should be evaporated. Allow to cool slightly, and remove spice sachet from pot.

Working in batches, scoop meat, fat, and liquid out of pot and place in a food processor. Pulse to a coarse puree, place in sterilized jars or ramekins, and seal while still hot (the easiest way is to make sure containers are sterilized is to take them directly from the dishwasher after a cycle or boil briefly). Cool and let sit in fridge for a day to let flavors meld. Serve at room temperature within a week. If you wish to keep it longer, top chilled rillettes with a layer of duck fat. Sealed with the fat, rillettes will keep in the refrigerator for up to 2 months. Once the seal is broken, eat within a week.

Serves 6 to 8 as an appetizer

GRILLED RACK OF VENISON

WITH SALSA VERDE

One of my favorite dishes, this came to grace the menu at Public thanks to my good friend and chef de cuisine of Double Crown, Chris Rendell. His salsa verde is good on almost anything—even bread—but I'm particularly partial to the way it works with venison. New Zealand venison, or other lean farmed version, is well worth the effort in finding, as long as you don't overcook it and keep it toward rare/medium rare. This recipe uses the rack, but you can just as easily substitute the loin, tenderloin, or even a cut called leg loin, which is exceptional on the plate and easy on the wallet.

1 8-rib rack of venison (about 2 pounds), cleaned of all sinew, preferably New Zealand or farmed venison, 2 smallest ribs removed
Olive oil
Sea salt
Freshly ground pepper

Salsa Verde
1 tablespoon cabernet sauvignon vinegar
2 ounces (about ¼ cup) stale sourdough, crusts removed and diced
⅓ cup finely chopped parsley
½ cup picked finely chopped basil
2 boquerones (marinated white anchovy), do NOT substitute salted anchovy
1 clove garlic, minced
1 tablespoon drained capers
1 cup extra-virgin olive oil

For the salsa, pour the vinegar over the bread and allow it to soak for 15 minutes. Then combine all of the salsa ingredients except the olive oil with the soaked sourdough bread. Place the mixture in a food processor or high-speed blender with about one-third of the oil. Place the blender on high speed to puree the ingredients as quickly as possible. It is VERY important that the ingredients are mixed at high speed and just until they become a nice puree. Processing at a low speed will make the mix stringy and may turn the herbs brown. Add enough of the remaining olive oil to get a nice sauce consistency. Refrigerate until needed.

Lightly oil and season the meat with salt and pepper. Preheat the grill and cook the venison to rare to medium rare, 10 to 18 minutes, depending on meat and grill temperature. Internal temperature measured with a meat thermometer should be 130°F for medium rare. Test frequently to keep meat from overcooking. Remove the meat and place it on a warm tray or plate to rest for 5 minutes. Internal temperature will increase about 5°F.

Carve the rack of venison so that there are 6 equal portions, each with one rib attached. Top with a dollop of room-temperature salsa verde and serve.

Serves 6

Everyone got rabbit skulls with feathers and rhinestones for Christmas last year. I'll bring home skulls and my wife will clean them and paint them. Right now I'm looking at a pig skull and a goat skull and rabbit skulls that we have arranged on our table, and rabbit faces that she cured and stuffed. Home taxidermy. Definitely takes using the whole animal to the next level.

I first used whole animals from Bellwether Farms in Sonoma, when Cindy was only doing spring lambs. My angle was always more as a restaurant chef: How can I put this animal on the plate? Instead of buying a box of loins and doing consistent pork chops, I realized: I can smoke part of this and make a pork chop out of this, or I can do it whole and slice it so I can use every part of the pig.

When I realized how much better the meat was that has been thoughtfully farmed, I started driving out every Wednesday to

RYAN FARR

4505 MEATS, CA

Ryan Farr makes exquisite hot dogs. He is part of the rock star butcher phenomenon, according to the New York Times. *He has worked at some of the best restaurants in the world. Like his hot dogs, though, there's a limit to the grandeur. Ryan is just a super-nice guy. He answers his phone every time it rings, he hugs without ambivalence whenever you see him, and he seems totally lacking in irony.*

I first met him at a Meatpaper *magazine party, where he was slowly and almost wordlessly butchering a half hog from Devil's Gulch Ranch in a bottleneck of one hundred or so people. The performance felt more like art than food preparation and so spawned conversations more in the vein of mortality and morality than of roasts and chops.*

His company, 4505 Meats, buys whole animals, butchers them, and serves the meat, mainly in the form of hot dogs, hamburgers, and sausages. He also teaches butchering to home cooks interested in carnal knowledge.

Nicasio to pick up a couple dozen rabbits and a pig from Devil's Gulch Ranch. This was before Mark was really delivering to San Francisco. He was still just doing ranch kills, so they were these 250-pound pigs and they were just massive. That's a lot of meat to go through, especially for a fine- dining restaurant. So it became really important that I had a game plan and knew what I was doing, otherwise it would sour or spoil. I got into charcuterie and salumi. I had a huge wine cellar filled with salumi, hams, and everything hanging. I learned to cure meats through trial and error. Curing is very precise. Everything is about exacts. It definitely breaks your heart when you lose something you've made.

I started doing hot dogs because I needed to make rent. It was also curiosity because I didn't know how they made skinless hot dogs. I knew how to make forcemeat and mortadella and bologna and all that. So I figured that out and it turns out I like the dogs in casings much better. The concept of the dog I had growing up was the Ballpark frank that plumps when you cook it. Mine definitely do plump up. They'll burst on you if you don't watch. Flavor-wise, we put bacon in them, which melts at a lower temperature than regular pork fat so that lovely bacon grease pops all over the place. Really, though, with a dog, there's no reason to make something that's going to smack you around with flavor.

I think the main reason I began cooking was that when I was a kid I had to find a way to get more food for myself. I didn't think my mom was giving me enough so I had to plump up.

DAMN GOOD HOT DOGS

This is the original hot dog recipe that made it all happen . . . a variation of the dogs we currently make and sell nationwide. Using a mixture of meats and fat gives it the silky texture that I love.

8 pounds pork butt
4.8 pounds chicken
5 pounds beef
2.2 pounds beef fat
2 cups nonfat powdered milk
1/3 cup egg white
5 cups simple syrup
1/2 cup salt
2 teaspoons pink salt *
6 tablespoons paprika

1/3 cup white pepper
1/5 cup dried parsley
1/2 tablespoon dried thyme
2/3 cup chili powder
2 tablespoons cayenne powder
2 1/2 tablespoons garlic powder
1/2 tablespoon poultry powder
3 1/2 cups ice water
About 35 feet Grade-A sheep casings

Cut all meat and fat into 1-inch cubes, let rest in freezer until semi-frozen and temperature is below 40°F. Mix together all of the non-meat ingredients (not including water) and let sit in the fridge. Mixing ahead of time helps hydrate the milk powder.

Grind all the meat through a fine die. You can store in the refrigerator or the freezer, but it is important to keep the temperature below 40°F at all times.

Put all meat in a chilled mixing bowl and use paddle attachment or mix thoroughly and slowly. Mix in the other ingredients on low speed until everything is integrated and very sticky.

Turn mixer on high and let it whip for 4 minutes, adding the ice water slowly.

When it is pureed, stuff hot dog mix into grade-A sheep casings. Keep refrigerated until ready to cook.

Makes about 60 1/3-pound hot dogs

* Curing salt. Necessary to inhibit growth of bacteria. Use and store with caution. See page 288.

See also Sausage Basics, page 32.

BRESAOLA MADE WITH BEEF TRI-TIP

This recipe is spectacular and I'm crazy to share it. As far as cured meats, it is pretty straightforward. It is one of the most popular Italian dry-cured beef dishes. Please see safety tips on dry curing on page 144.

5 pounds beef tri–tip	2½ teaspoons garlic powder
2 cups fine sea salt	3 tablespoons berbere spice
2 tablespoons dextrose	1 tablespoon onion powder
2 teaspoons pink salt *	2 teaspoons ginger powder

Grind all spices, salt, and sugar together in a spice or coffee grinder. Deeply rub half of the dry mix all over the tri–tip and let cure in refrigerator for 7 days in an airtight container or bag.

Remove tri–tip from the container, discard liquid, and rub the remaining cure on the beef, letting it cure for 7 more days in the refrigerator.

Remove tri-tip from the bag, rubbing off any spice and salt clusters. Hang and air dry for 2 to 3 hours at room temperature. Once the outside surface is dry, hang beef at 60°F with 65 percent relative humidity for 31 days, or until the meat is dry and solid throughout.

Slice very thin against the grain.

Makes about 3 pounds dried meat

* Curing salt. Necessary to inhibit growth of bacteria. Use and store with caution. See page 288.

DRY CURING

CURING meat may seem an esoteric art. In reality it is derived from the PEASANT necessity to use every SCRAP of a freshly killed animal. Most *sacrificios*, or slaughtering TRADITIONS, meander similarly. There is infinite sense inherent in these. Spreading out the preparation of MEAT is economical and prudent. It allows you to have varying experiences from the same animal: first day—slaughter; then EAT the liver, kidney, and heart, which are the most perishable parts; make BLOOD sausage with the intestines as casings; second day—make FRESH sausages and prepare salami and hams for curing.

Dry curing is a temperamental process, dependent on air and humidity, and involves safety and sanitation issues that may deter novices. Safety is important: you can make yourself or someone else very sick from mold and rot with improperly cured meats. Your equipment must be sanitized. A little bacteria will multiply with abandon during the days of hanging. Dry curing is probably a bigger endeavor than most home cooks should try, but we wanted to introduce the concept with this salami recipe and Ryan Farr's Bresaola (page 143). I highly recommend Michael Ruhlman and Brian Polcyn's *Charcuterie* and Paul Bertolli's *Cooking By Hand* for more knowledge and how-to's before attempting dry curing. If you persevere, you will have a cook's satisfaction from continuing a tradition that's been practiced for centuries.

The recipe below is my family's, handed down from my great-grandfather, who emigrated from Italy. It strikes me as an excellent salami primer, tasting straightforwardly of meat and salt, time and patience.

SALAMI

5 pounds pork butt, frozen and then thawed in the fridge (this will kill trichinae, as well as keep the meat cold enough to prevent the fat from smearing)

2½ pounds beef (aged beef, if possible; the flavor is particularly good for salami)

1½ pounds pork fatback

About ⅔ cup salt, or approximately 3.5% of the total weight of the meats

1 teaspoon pink salt *

¼ teaspoon lactobacillus plantarum, a starter culture you can find at a beer, cheese, or winemaking store

3 tablespoons black pepper, cracked

1 cup red wine

2 cloves garlic, crushed

2½ tablespoons fennel seeds

10 feet beef middle casings

* *Curing salt. Necessary to inhibit growth of bacteria. Use and store with caution. See page 288.*

Keep meat and fat very cold, even partially frozen, throughout the process so your fat remains distinct from the meat in the finished sausage. Grind the fat while cold through the large die into a bowl set in ice. Grind pork and beef on the largest die when semi-frozen and then keep in the refrigerator/freezer at a temp of around 34°F. Most refrigerators keep food at 38°F or below, so you may have to adjust yours.

Mix all ingredients by hand, keeping the meat below 36°F at all times. Once everything is mixed thoroughly, stuff into beef middle casings (see Sausage Basics, page 32, for instructions).

Next is the incubation, which requires vigilance. Stuffed salami is incubated at 85°F to 90°F for 1 to 2 days. The relative humidity is kept at 75 to 85 percent. I use an old freezer cabinet that I modified; depending on your location and the season, you may need a humidifier or dehumidifier to maintain consistency.

During this period, you want "good" bacteria to flourish. The lactobacillus plantarum and nitrite insure that the bad bacteria do not flourish along with it.

Finally, the drying. Hang the sausage in a cool, dark, humid space until it is completely stiff throughout, about 21 days. During this phase the salami will lose between 35 and 45 percent of its water. The temperature should be 55°F to 65°F, with a relative humidity of 70 to 80 percent. The high humidity allows the salami to dry evenly and thoroughly. Mold will form on the outside of the salami. Fuzzy or greenish mold is bad. Throw out your salami if this develops. Dry white mold, which creates a protective layer, is desirable. If it smells off, if it is mushy or not dried through, do not eat it. At the conclusion of the drying phase, the salami can be held without refrigeration.

Makes about 6 pounds of salami

NATHAN FOOT

NORTHERN SPY FOOD CO., NY

I picture Nathan as an infant, swaddled in an apron, curled up in a roasting pan. He was born to do this. His career took shape in San Francisco, where he worked in very serious restaurants. Northern Spy Food Co. does not seem like a serious restaurant at first glance. It's in New York's East Village, a youthful neighborhood, and has very reasonable prices. Which makes it all the more romantic that back in the kitchen lives Nathan and his stock, which he adds to, but never throws out, letting it develop under his watch.

I don't ever want to hire someone like me. I put so much pressure on myself, I don't sleep well at night. Even if people are really stoked about the food, I don't totally believe it.

If a special comes back uneaten, I get a little bummed out. I'm just psyched about every dish I send out. And those specials are where I can sneak in my fine dining background. I'm not a chef who is just into ordering and sitting in the walk-in—I'm about cooking. I'll probably always do the butchering here. I'm not as fast as some dudes out there, but I know what I need to get from the pig.

I went to CCA, they're a for-profit cooking school. Pretty much if you can fill out the application, you're in. Afterwards, I tried working at the Four Seasons, I thought maybe I should make money and be responsible. But given who I am and my issues with authority, I quit after six months. They have this whole purchasing department, there were no market runs, no buying directly from farms, and I knew I could never change that. I needed some inspiration.

I learned to butcher at Elizabeth Daniels. I was putting my hands on proteins, I was given a position of responsibility and I was totally into it but I was still pretty green. I had bad habits from banquet cooking, like being wasteful. I wasn't very aware of the discipline needed to work in a kitchen. I didn't know how to work small. I didn't learn how to check my ego. But I got over myself.

At Massa's, I saw the lobster going out and I thought, *I want to work here.* Ron Siegel is unlike any chef you've met,

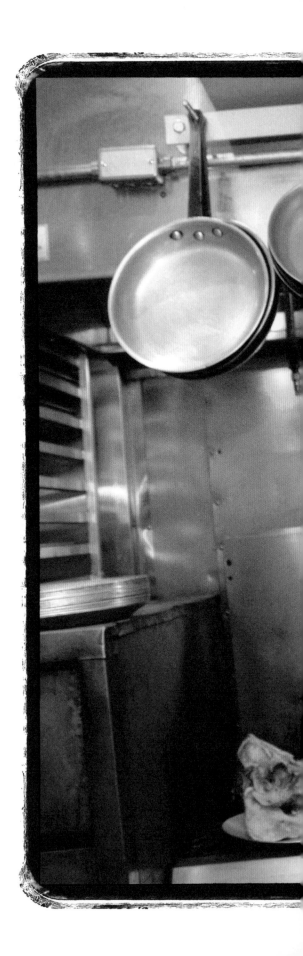

he's like a truck-driving, beer-drinking guy. He's got a really high food aptitude, in a very non-pretentious way. I left Massa's with a really good foundation. That became my new standard.

I decided to give Myth a shot. I got an opportunity to take over that kitchen for a while. I changed some stuff, like I only know how to do sauces my way. They had done everything Gary Danko style, finishing everything with butter. I don't use butter in sauces. After I left Myth, I came to New York.

I don't have a reputation in this town yet. I want to show that my kitchen has skill. It's not just some guy at the burners with a bunch of mercenary line cooks. In my heart, I can't allow any food to go out without me looking at it.

HEADCHEESE

First we called it headcheese on the menu and it didn't sell. When we put it on as pork terrine, it started going! It may seem even more intimidating to prepare it, but this recipe is straightforward, balanced, and transcendent.

Braising Liquid
2 stalks celery
2 carrots
1 onion
1 tablespoon olive oil
6 cups stock (pork or chicken)
1 bunch thyme
1 bunch rosemary
2 cloves
½ teaspoon star anise
½ teaspoon allspice
1 bay leaf
1 tablespoon peppercorns
1 teaspoon fennel seed
1 teaspoon coriander seed

1 pig head, about 15 to 25 pounds
1½ cups green pistachios
5 tablespoons white-wine vinegar
2 cups finely chopped parsley leaves
Salt and pepper

Preheat oven to 350°F. Chop coarsely the celery, carrots, and onion. Heat oil and sauté over medium heat until onion is translucent. In a pot large enough to roomily fit your pig head, combine the onion mixture and stock. Add the rest of the braising ingredients. Bring stock to a boil, reduce to a simmer, and cook about 2 hours, until flavorful. The amount of liquid needed should halfway cover the head and will depend on how large your pot is, so add water if you think it's necessary—but don't dilute too much, as a lot of the flavor from your terrine comes from this liquid.

Toast pistachios in oven until lightly golden; set aside. Decrease oven temperature to 300°F.

Strain the braising liquid. Lay the pig head, face up, in the pot, and pour liquid over head. As stated above, this should cover head at least halfway, and can completely submerge it if your pot is deep enough. Cover with foil and braise until you can easily remove the jaw from the skull, about 3½ to 4 hours. You want the meat to be soft but not completely melted; there should still be some structure. If your pig head is not completely submerged in liquid, occasionally baste it with the liquid during braising.

Remove braising liquid to a separate pot, strain, and remove the fat when it has cooled. Let the head cool slightly and remove meat and fat from it before the fat sets. Use an ice bath to cool your fingers while working. Tear bite-sized pieces and set meat and fat in separate piles. Use any skin that is soft enough to be palatable. Throw away any brain, glands, inner ear, and the roof of the mouth. I usually exclude the ears, eyeballs, and snout, but you can include. If you include the tongue, peel before adding. Watch out for and remove little bones.

Line terrine mold or loaf pan with plastic wrap. In a bowl, add meat and fat so you have a 90:10 ratio of meat to fat. Add enough strained braising liquid to cover meat. Add white-wine vinegar, a tablespoon at a time, to taste. Add pistachios. Mix gently, so as not break down the fat too much. Add parsley. Stir again gently, so each bite will have some parsley and pistachio. Salt and pepper to taste. Do not oversalt. The vinegar will taste stronger now than when terrine is set. Pour the meat gently into the lined terrine mold and cover with plastic wrap. Refrigerate overnight.

To serve, cover terrine completely with a flat dish and flip gently to remove. Slice with a very sharp knife. Serve with a sprinkling of salt, Dijon mustard, pickled vegetables, and bread.

Makes one terrine

ROBERT GRANT

THE BUTCHER SHOP, MA

Robert is the Chef de Cuisine at The Butcher Shop, part of Barbara Lynch Gruppo's, including No. 9 Park, B&G Oysters, Stir, Drink, Sportello, and Menton. The kitchen is like a galley. Nearly claustrophobic in scale, it is by necessity a model of efficiency and camaraderie. Upstairs is a restaurant with a butcher block plunked down in the midst of the dining room, strange and lovely. Barbara's success seems to have a lot to do with the sense of curiosity and ownership bubbling up everywhere. Or maybe Robert is just a special case.

I would say the majority of my butcher skills and knowledge have been self-taught here. When I started I didn't realize what a huge opportunity this was for me to just learn and make mistakes and grow. Now I take advantage of every second. It has been a career changing experience. I feel really good about what we've accomplished and the direction we're headed.

The space is broken down into the retail/butcher space and the restaurant space. But it feels integrated and holistic. When the sun goes down, we turn the music up a little and it gets completely packed, way over capacity. The butcher counter stays open until 8 pm every night, so we'll be cutting meat up and people will be around just watching and asking questions, having a drink. We've worked really hard to get to know the meat, so we can pass that on to the guests. We explain why a non-USDA graded rib eye from PT Farm is more expensive than a prime graded rib eye from Maryland.

I grew up in Denver and my first cooking job was at Cook's Fresh Market which was a little gourmet market, with a hundred-plus cheeses that I got to know. Big pastry shop, meats, fish, deli, retail, imported stuff. It was the best possible start a young cook could have. I worked every possible position in that market. I learned so much there.

I went to Bouchon for my externship from Johnson & Wales and I didn't even go back for graduation. I just stayed in Vegas. I worked through every station and every shift. It really shaped me as a cook. And those were the only other two places I ever worked.

We started a CSA because there wasn't one in the city. It has a monthly pick-up and we change animals every month. For April I bought three sixty-pound lambs from a Vermont family farm. You subscribe a month at a time and we stretch the pick-ups over three weeks. Being in a very urban environment, people have small kitchens and limited time to cook, so we've really made it user friendly.

The first week CSA members watch me break down the animals. This month they'll go home with a tied lamb leg roast and a double rack chop or two. The second week, they'll pick up a couple pounds of sausages and two to three pounds of lamb shoulder: whole, cut, ground, or marinated. The third week we'll do some dry aged lamb loin and confit shanks. I wanted to bring the full service butcher into the CSA, so you're getting a lot of value. My goal is to introduce people to the idea of a CSA and then show them how to utilize the meat and how important it is for American farmers.

For February I bought a rosé veal calf from Animal Farm in Orwell, Vermont. People were way into it. They have this tiny little herd of Jersey cows and she makes probably the best artisan butter in the country for French Laundry, Per Se, No. 9 Park. Barbara basically bought one cow, Hopi. Hopi lives at Animal Farm but all of her butter goes straight to No. 9.

CRISPY VEAL SWEETBREADS

These are fantastic. Crunchy on the outside and meltingly flavorful in the inside. You can use 1½ cups of all-purpose flour instead of the cornstarch and chestnut flour. The chestnut flour is worth trying though; it gives a nutty flavor and a lighter, crunchy crust, and accommodates our gluten-free diners.

1 pound veal sweetbreads
¼ cup kosher salt
2 tablespoons white wine or distilled vinegar
1 quart buttermilk
1 cup cornstarch
½ cup chestnut flour
Kosher salt and black pepper
Grapeseed or canola oil

Sauce
1 tablespoon butter
1 tablespoon minced onion
1 tablespoon minced carrot
2 tablespoons minced truffle shavings
½ ounce Madeira
½ cup beef demi-glace
Few drops truffle oil (optional)

The process of preparing sweetbreads has several important steps: poach, peel, and press. When you first get yours home, give them a good rinse/soak in cold water. While they are soaking, put on about a gallon of water to boil. When the water has reached a boil, add kosher salt and white wine. Set up a bowl of ice water to transfer the sweetbreads into when they are done poaching. Gently place the sweetbreads into the boiling water and give them a little stir. Cook about 2 to 3 minutes. They should be slightly firm on the outside, but still feel doughy on the inside. Transfer to the ice bath. Once cool, it is time to peel the outer membrane off, which should be relatively easy to do with your fingers. Once all the thin membrane is removed, spread sweet-breads out evenly on a sheet tray lined with a clean dish towel. Cover with another towel and place another sheet pan of the same dimensions on top. Leave the sweetbreads in the refrigerator with a couple of pounds of weight on top until you are ready to cook them.

Portion the sweetbreads into 1- to 2-ounce pieces and submerge in the buttermilk. Soak them for at least 30 minutes.

Prepare the sauce: heat the butter in a saucepan and sweat down the onion and carrot. Add the truffle and deglaze with the Madeira. Add the demi-glace and simmer for 10 to 20 minutes. Add a few drops of truffle oil, if desired, to intensify flavor. Set aside.

Prepare a dredge by mixing together the cornstarch and chestnut flour with a couple of pinches of kosher salt and a few grinds of black pepper. Heat a large skillet or frying pan and add ½ inch of oil. Working with a few pieces at a time, drain off excess buttermilk and thoroughly coat sweetbreads in the dredge. Gently add the pieces to the hot oil, leaving plenty of space in between them. If you overcrowd the pan, the temperature of the oil will drop and you will have greasy—not crisp—little nuggets. Cook about 3 minutes per side, or until they are deep golden brown and super crunchy. It may take a couple of rounds to fry all of the sweetbreads; hold cooked ones in a warm oven to retain heat and crispness.

Serve family style with sauce as accompaniment. We also usually add a carrot puree and pickled shallots.

Serves 4 to 6

SEARED DUCK BREASTS

WITH SPICED CHERRIES

This is one of Barbara Lynch's recipes. Duck is one of her favorite things to eat, especially when it's got some nice crispy skin on it. Though it can be made year round, the accompaniments in this dish celebrate early summer, specifically the arrival of fresh cherries in June and July. The sweet and tangy spiced cherries are a perfect foil for the rich, gamey meat.

Spiced Cherries
1 tablespoon black peppercorns
1 cinnamon stick
1 star anise
1 clove
1½ pounds sweet cherries, pitted
¼ cup sugar
½ cup dry red wine
¼ teaspoon red wine vinegar

4 boneless, skin-on Pekin duck breasts or
   2 Moulard duck breasts
Kosher salt
Freshly ground black pepper
Fleur de sel
2 tablespoons chopped fresh chives
1 tablespoon pulled-apart chive blossoms
   (optional)

To make the spice cherries: Tie the peppercorns, cinnamon stick, star anise, and clove in a cheesecloth sachet. In a medium saucepan, combine the cherries, sugar, red wine, and sachet and bring to a simmer over medium-low heat. Reduce the heat to low and cook, stirring occasionally, until the liquid is reduced to a syrup and the cherries are quite soft, 45 minutes to an hour. Remove and discard the spice sachet, stir in the red-wine vinegar, and remove the cherries from the heat. The spice cherries can be made ahead. They will keep for up to a week, covered and refrigerated. Serve the cherries warm or at room temperature.

    Season the duck breasts with salt and pepper. Heat a large skillet over medium heat. Add the duck breasts skin side down and cook for a few minutes to brown the skin. Reduce the heat to medium low and continue cooking to render more fat and further crisp and brown the skin, about 12 minutes more. Pour or spoon off some of the accumulated fat and turn the breasts over to finish cooking on the other side. (To check for doneness, use an instant-read thermometer; 135° to 140°F is right for medium rare, which is how I like it.) Transfer the cooked breasts to a plate or platter and let them rest for 6 to 8 minutes in a warm place.

    Slice the duck and divide it among four plates and top with the spiced cherries. Finish with a pinch of fleur de sel and a sprinkling of chopped chives and chive blossoms, if you have them.

Serves 4

BRAISED CHICKEN THIGHS

WITH ROSEMARY AND GARLIC

This is another great recipe from Barbara Lynch. It is surprising just how delicious braised chicken can be. When you make this, your kitchen fills with a wonderful fragrance. Serve with mashed potatoes and you have a truly satisfying meal.

2 tablespoons vegetable oil, plus more as needed
8 skin-on, bone-in chicken thighs, trimmed of
  excess fat and skin
Kosher salt
Freshly ground black pepper
3 garlic cloves, sliced

1½ tablespoons finely chopped fresh rosemary
1 cup dry white wine
1½ cups chicken broth
2 tablespoons chopped fresh parsley
Fresh lemon juice to taste
Fleur de sel

Heat the oil in a large skillet over medium-high heat. Season the thighs with salt and pepper and cook them skin side down without moving them until the skin is crisp and golden, 6 to 8 minutes. If your pan can't accommodate all 8 with space in between, sear the chicken in batches. Use a spatula to flip the chicken over carefully and sear the other side for 2 to 3 minutes. Remove the thighs from the pan and pour off all but about 1 tablespoon of the fat. Lower the heat to medium, add the garlic and cook, stirring, until fragrant and lightly colored (don't let it brown), about 2 minutes. Add the rosemary and cook for another minute. Add the wine, bring to a boil, and cook until the wine reduces by about three quarters. Add the broth.

Return the chicken to the pan, cover with the lid slightly ajar, and simmer, stirring occasionally, until the chicken is cooked through and fork-tender and the liquid in the pan has reduced by about two thirds, about 30 minutes. Transfer the chicken to plates or a serving platter and keep warm. If necessary, return the sauce to the heat to reduce further. Stir the parsley and lemon juice into the sauce in the pan and pour the sauce over the chicken. Sprinkle with a little fleur de sel and serve.

Make ahead: The chicken can be made 2 days ahead (without the parsley and lemon juice) and refrigerated, covered. Reheat it over low heat, partially covered, until heated through, about 10 to 15 minutes. Add the parsley and lemon juice just before serving.

Serves 4

RAISING YOUR OWN CHICKENS

I wouldn't claim any special expertise in **CHICKEN** farming, but I do have a contented **BROOD** of four in my backyard. The transition from not having chickens to having chickens is really pretty straightforward. You can buy **FERTILIZED** eggs, chicks, or poults (teenagers). Poults are usually available at feed stores and don't require **INCUBATION**. Chicks, however, come in the mail, which is a beyond-exciting package to receive. Also, if you order chicks, you can buy them from a **HATCHERY** that has heritage **BREEDS**, which are oftentimes ridiculous and wonderful.

Chickens need nooks to sleep in at night (and to be protected from predators, which is a varied and prolific crowd when you're a chicken) and to lay eggs, if they are hens. Around that nook you can build a yard with, yes, chicken wire, so they can scratch and bathe in the dirt and eat their chicken feed in a contained but open area. You can also let them out in the yard. They will eat all your snails. They will also probably eat all of your greens, sometimes seemingly just out of spite. If my garden is at a tender stage, or I just don't want chicken bacchanalia among the rows, I like to throw them lots of leafy vegetables, which makes the egg yolks nearly orange and viscous with nourishment.

Hens need protection from weather and

predators. In the summer, make sure they always have lots of water, and before winter arrives, you will need to weatherize the coop: heating lamps for freezing conditions and waterproofing for wet conditions. Predators will mostly be kept out by a yard-high fence of chicken wire, but you may also need to line it with chicken wire at ground level, so nothing can crawl from underneath. It is also important to have a completely enclosed coop you can lock up at night.

If you manage to evolve from pet owner and egg eater to small-time farmer, you may want to try a classic coq au vin recipe. This will be a feast and a memorial to a hen whose laying days have passed, either from age or broodiness. Open a good bottle of wine and remember her well.

JESSE GRIFFITHS

DAI DUE SUPPER CLUB & BUTCHER SHOP, TX

I didn't know about Jesse when I got to Austin but everyone I met told me I had to find him. It's an apt introduction to a chef without a restaurant and a butcher without a storefront. Jesse's businesses live by word of mouth. Dai Due Supper Club hosts farm dinners and the Butcher Shop pops up at farmers' markets. In the commissary kitchen where he makes his sausages, I also honed my theory that if you ever want to cause a little fracas in Texas, just ask a room full of people where to get the best barbecue.

I like the Salt Lick, but I mean, they do use sesame oil in their coleslaw.

I grew up in North Texas. I moved down here eleven years ago. In my mind, Austin was this super-cool town that just had to have super-cool restaurants. But, it turns out, Austin's less sophisticated than I thought.

I had my real food epiphanies in Europe. The first time I went I was served fish on a plate with just a slice of lemon. And I was like, *What the heck is this? You're too lazy to make a sauce? But then I ate it and it was like, Ohhhh. I get it, I get it.* The fish was fresh and delicious. The lemon was really good, too. I got a job working in a kitchen in Venice because it was off-season. It was just the chef and me, and we cooked for each other all day. It was awesome. Then my wife and I went back to Europe together and worked on a few different kinds of farms: cheese, goat, and vegetable. At night I read the *River Cottage Meat Cookbook* in its entirety. He said it all.

We came back and for a while I lived out in the country. I was shooting squirrels and making paella with it. Just trying to figure it out. I thought, I don't want to touch another stalk of celery that was picked by a slave in Mexico. I mean, if you're not part of the solution, you're part of the problem. And so we were like let's start cooking using only foods from around here. We'll see what happens. We did our first dinner for seventeen people and it just took off.

We also got serious about not eating dirty meat. For the most part I am a vegetarian unless I know I'm getting grass-fed, clean meat. And just because it's local doesn't mean it's good. All agribusiness is local somewhere.

SMOTHERED PORK CHOPS

These pork chops are tender and moist. If you've never brined your meats before, you will always brine after tasting this recipe.

1 cup salt	4 onions, sliced
1 cup brown sugar	Salt and pepper
3 star anise	2 tablespoons flour
4 bone-in pork chops	1 quart pork or chicken stock
2 tablespoons lard	1 bay leaf
Flour for dredging	

Make a brine by boiling a gallon of water with the salt, sugar, and anise. Cool completely. Brine the chops for 12 hours in a nonreactive container in the refrigerator.

Preheat the oven to 350°F. Heat the lard in a large ovenproof pan over medium heat. Dredge the chops in flour, shaking off excess. Brown them thoroughly in the lard and remove to a plate. Add the sliced onions to the pan and cook, stirring often, until softened. Season with salt and pepper, to taste. Add 2 tablespoons flour to the onions and stir well. Slowly add the stock, stirring and scraping the pan. Return the chops to the pan, add bay leaf, cover and bake for 1½ hours in the oven. Serve with rice and greens cooked with bacon.

Serves 4

Butchering takes focus, it is really calming for me to come in and just take care of the carcass in front of me. The environment needs to emulate the philosophy. Aesthetics couldn't be more important. I had been looking at this butcher shop for probably four years. My partners, Angela and Melanie, live in the neighborhood, and it finally just felt like the right move.

I thought the fact that we were women would be a novelty, something that people would find amusing. But we were more excited about the fact that we were cooks than that we were women. It used to be that butchers were able to give cooking suggestions and be educated about what they were selling. Now, if you go to Safeway or something, people don't know anything about the meat they are selling. We wanted to bring back that old-school feeling.

We totally had a romantic idea about what it would be like to run a butcher shop! We wanted to sell rabbits and house-made baby food and meat sauces and strange meat cuts. I was super inspired about all the obscurities that restaurant people have access to. We found out those

TIA HARRISON
AVEDANO'S, CA

Tia is the owner of Avedano's, a retro-fitted butcher shop in the Bernal Heights neighborhood of San Francisco. She is also executive chef at Sociale, an upscale Italian restaurant, and a mom. Her schedule is ferocious but she seems moored by the physicality of her work.

She takes me through the wood-paneled walk-in cooler, carcasses akimbo on hooks. It feels like it is one hundred years ago in this room. Each carcass is from a farm in the area. The customers here have demands about source ranging from curiosity to moral righteousness and part of the impetus of opening the shop was to follow the animals back to their origins.

There is an aesthetic decadence to the particularity of her butchering and to every inch of Avedano's. The butcher block is clean and dips down the center from use. Tia takes the rounded muscle of a top sirloin and considers it quietly before she makes her first cut. Later, as we eat tacos made from the scraps and thick steaks with a hearty strip of fat, I swear I can taste that consideration.

things didn't sell easily at all. What really sells are rib eyes, New York strips, chicken breasts—the familiar stuff. So we can put weird cuts out in the counter, but there's got to be a lot of education involved. Really working the product and sampling things. It costs more for the smaller producers to run a responsible business and so you have to charge more for their products, which becomes an educated purchase for the customer. We are lucky that we have a lot of people who trust us by now, and are willing to try new things, but in the beginning, no.

Motherhood has changed the way I cook. I love cooking Italian food because it fits my philosophy: there doesn't have to be much in the way of bells and whistles. I don't need to be confused by what I eat. I just need something that is made with really good ingredients, something simple. Braising is awesome because it's something you can prepare ahead and let cook. It's less stressful and you come out with an amazing meal using cuts of meat that are inexpensive. There are so many things you can do besides stews and lamb shanks—I don't know if people understand how many applications there are for braising.

My daughter doesn't get creeped out by the animals at the shop. She told someone that her mom cuts up rabbits and eats them. Sounds a little gruesome to someone who hears it out of context. But it's just normal to her.

OSSO BUCCO

This dish is traditionally done with veal shanks, but lamb is cheaper and works just as well. Be sure your butcher gives you meaty pieces; otherwise you will have long pieces of bone when the meat pulls away with cooking. Serve osso bucco with an herb or Parmesan polenta, and a citrus gremolata.

⅓ cup flour
Salt and pepper
4 pieces veal or lamb osso bucco,
   about 12 ounces each
3 tablespoons olive oil, plus extra for drizzling
3 tablespoons butter
1 onion, chopped
½ cup chopped celery
½ cup chopped carrots
4 cloves garlic, coarsely chopped
2 bay leaves
1 cup white wine
2 cups chicken stock
1 tablespoon fennel seed
4 sprigs marjoram, leaves picked
2 cups diced fire-roasted tomatoes
3 tablespoons finely chopped fresh Italian parsley

Gremolata
Grated rind of 1 lemon
Grated rind of 1 orange
1 to 2 tablespoons freshly grated horseradish
2 tablespoons chopped fresh Italian parsley

Season flour with salt and pepper, to taste. Coat the shanks in the mixture. In a large, heavy skillet on medium, heat oil and butter. Sear shanks on all sides, about 3 minutes each side. Remove the browned shanks and set aside.

Add onion, celery, carrots, garlic, and bay leaves to pan, and sauté. Season with salt and pepper. Raise heat to high, add the wine, and deglaze the pan. Return shanks to pan and add the stock, fennel seed, marjoram leaves, and tomatoes. Drizzle with olive oil. Reduce heat to low, cover, and cook for about 2 hours, or until meat is tender. Baste a few times during cooking. Sprinkle with chopped parsley and stir into the sauce. Remove the cover and continue to simmer for 10 minutes to reduce liquid.

Combine gremolata ingredients in a small bowl. Serve osso bucco with polenta, with gremolata as garnish.

Serves 4

BRAISED LAMB RISOTTO

WITH ROASTED BELL PEPPER

Lamb makes this an elegant and substantial risotto, perfect for late winter or early spring.

1½ pounds lamb shoulder, cut into 1-inch cubes
2 teaspoons salt
2 tablespoons extra-virgin olive oil
1 cup rosé wine
1 sprig rosemary
5 cloves garlic
2 bay leaves
3 cups water
2 cups arborio rice
About 6 cups vegetable stock
3 tablespoons balsamic vinegar, plus extra for drizzling
½ cup minced roasted red and yellow bell peppers
2 cups chopped arugula
1 cup grated pecorino (or Parmesan) cheese
2 tablespoons butter

Season lamb with 1 teaspoon salt. Heat 1 tablespoon oil in a large pot or a cast-iron skillet over medium-high flame. Sear the meat until brown on all sides. Add wine and deglaze, scraping all the brown bits from bottom of pan. Add remaining salt, rosemary, garlic, bay leaves, and water. Reduce heat and simmer 1½ hours, stirring occasionally. Add enough water to maintain stock toward the end if needed.

Heat a second large pot, add 1 tablespoon olive oil and rice, and cook for a few minutes to release some of the starches. Add 2 cups of stock and lamb, and bring to a simmer, adding stock 1 cup at a time until rice is al dente. This could take 30 minutes.

Put the first pot back on the heat, add vinegar, and deglaze. Simmer for a couple of minutes. Add remaining ingredients and stir to combine.

Drizzle risotto with vinegar and serve with a large salad.

Serves 4 to 6

SHORT RIBS
WITH POMEGRANATE BARBECUE SAUCE

This recipe yields extra sauce, which you can use on sandwiches or freeze for next time. You will have also have beef broth left over. Remove the fat and keep in the freezer for when you want to make some amazing gravy.

4 beef short ribs, cut thick and at least 2½ inches
    long (approximately 3½ pounds)
Salt and pepper
2 tablespoons olive oil
1 large carrot, diced
½ medium white onion, diced
3 celery stalks, diced
1 bay leaf
4 cups beef stock

Sauce
½ white onion
4 cloves garlic
¼ cup red wine vinegar
2 cups pomegranate juice
4 cups ketchup
1 tablespoon mustard powder
½ cup cola
¼ cup brown sugar
1 teaspoon liquid smoke
1 tablespoon chili flakes
2 teaspoons kosher salt
2 teaspoons cracked black pepper

Season short ribs with salt and pepper to taste. Heat olive oil in a sauté pan over high heat and sear ribs on both sides. Place ribs in a braising pan (or a cast-iron pot) along with the mirepoix (carrot, onion, and celery) and bay leaf, and pour in stock, adding water to cover as necessary. Bring mixture to a boil, lower to simmer, cover, and braise for 3 hours.

Meanwhile, puree the white onion and the garlic cloves in a blender with the red wine vinegar. Combine with remaining ingredients in a saucepan over low heat. Simmer for an hour or until the sauce is reduced by about half and flavors come together, stirring occasionally to keep it from sticking.

Transfer ribs to a clean, shallow baking dish, discarding the bones as they fall off and removing some of the fat (if you wish). Cover in barbeque sauce to taste and broil on middle rack, 4 to 5 minutes per side. Serve over noodles, mashed potatoes, crusty bread, or with your favorite side dish.

Serves 4

HOW TO CUT A CULOTTE STEAK

Culotte Steak is so **DELICIOUS**, simply grill it and serve with some really good olive oil and **FLAKED** sea salt. **[1]** Place the top sirloin cap with the fatty side down and remove the tough silver skin. Place the knife under the piece, blade up and slicing away from you. **[2]** Flip over. This entire piece is called the top sirloin cap and the fatty layer on the outside of any piece of meat is also called a fat cap. **[3]** Make an incision in the fat cap lengthwise and remove the fat on the smaller side. All of the fat is unnecessary but leaving some on enhances the flavor. **[4]** Remove the tip and set it aside. The portion used for steaks should be fairly uniform. **[5]** Steaks from this piece are more tender when they are cut thick. These are about an inch thick. **[6]** Besides your lovely culotte steaks, you will have the tip, which you can slice and use for stir fry or fajitas; the fat cap, which you can render or use for flavor when cooking a tougher piece of meat; and the silver scraps, which you can add to anything braised or stewed.

(1) (2) (3)

(4) (5) (6)

CHRIS HUGHES
BROKEN ARROW RANCH, TX

Broken Arrow Ranch was founded by Chris's father, Mike, who had previously traveled the world as a salvage diver. Between pulling up the remains of the Lusitania and the Challenger, it dawned on Mike that people in other parts of the world loved to eat the wild game, like deer, that were considered pests back home on Texas ranches. Broken Arrow culls the non-native species from ranches to save more grass and feed for livestock. A few nights a week, the mobile processing unit goes out to a ranch that has requested their service. The rancher guides the shooter as they stalk through the darkness.

We try to harvest year round. It's kind of feast or famine sometimes. If we get too much rain, it really prevents us from going out, because the ground is too muddy, and the ranchers don't want us tearing up the roads. When there's drought conditions, then we start getting a lot of calls, because there's not enough feed for both the cattle and the deer.

It's not about putting a bullet into an animal and killing an animal. It's about putting a bullet in that animal in the right spot so that its death is instantaneous and humane. We'll take up to 300-yard shots, but when you start getting out that far, the risk of not making a clean shot increases, so it kind of depends a little bit on the conditions. Heck, if you practice, you can train on the target pretty quickly. Whether or not the animals scatter depends on how recently they've been hunted. As the evening progresses, they get smarter, and they move out in pretty short order.

It's actually better to reuse your casings because the first time you fire a bullet, it's a little bit loose in the chamber. After you fire it, all that metal expands and basically molds itself to your chamber and it fits perfectly so you don't have as much variation in your bullet. We discard after about four uses because then it starts to wear down and it'll crack—that's bad.

This is the only way we've ever harvested. We bring in the deer, lay it on the cradle, and do some of the initial cuts and skinning. Then we hang it up and pull down the rest of the skin. We take out the guts and remove the head and put it outside. Once that's done, we weigh the animal and pay the rancher based on the weight. Then we start the cooling process. So typically within the hour, the animals are hanging. We can fit about forty at one time. This is a one-room show.

We actually have three MPUs (mobile processing units), the third one we leave in South Texas. We harvest down there using a helicopter, which is the only way, because you're on 800 square miles of ranch with only maybe three roads cutting through. Plus, these animals are very, very shy. If you get within 200 yards, they're going to know before you know.

We only have one skinner here, but we actually have five skinners there. We also use the hides. Once we pull out all the water and they're stiffened up, we'll send them out to a tannery in San Antonio. Mainly furniture manufacturers purchase them.

CARNE GUISADA

(VENISON STEW WITH CACTUS)

Mexican flavors are deeply integrated into Texas cooking. When I'm out of Texas for more than a few days, I start craving this carne guisada with warm, fresh tortillas. Like all stews and braised dishes, this one tastes even better after the flavors have been allowed to meld and set in overnight. If possible, prepare a day ahead.

2 dried ancho chiles	2 large tomatoes, diced
2 tablespoons corn oil	2 tablespoons tomato paste
2 pounds venison stew meat	2 to 3 tablespoons cumin powder
Salt and pepper	1 cup beef stock (optional)
1 medium onion, chopped	1 cup cooked nopalitos,* cubed or in strips
2 garlic cloves	

Add dried ancho chiles to a small pot of boiling water and cook until soft, about 10 minutes. Drain and set aside until cool enough to handle. Remove stems and rinse away seeds. Using a food processor, puree the chiles with a splash of water. Set aside to add to stew later.

Heat the oil in a large skillet or Dutch oven over medium-high heat. Season venison with salt and pepper. Working in small batches, brown meat on all sides and set aside in a bowl. Add onion and sauté until transparent, about 5 minutes. Add browned venison, chili puree, garlic, tomatoes, tomato paste, cumin powder, and 1 cup water or beef stock. Cover and simmer over low to medium-low heat until meat is fork tender, about 1 hour. After about 30 minutes, taste and adjust seasonings. You can simmer up to 3 hours depending on how finger-pulling tender you want the meat, but be careful that the sauce doesn't overly reduce and become bitter. Add water as needed to prevent drying out—you should have a thickened gravy when it's done cooking.

When the venison is tender, stir in the nopalitos and cook 5 minutes more to heat them through. Serve with flour or corn tortillas, refried beans, and Mexican rice.

Serves 4 to 6

* Nopalitos are the small pads of prickly pear cactus—thorns removed—that have been cut and boiled until tender. Their taste and texture is similar to green beans. Depending on your location, you may be able to find fresh nopalitos at the market. Precooked, jarred varieties work well and are found in ethnic aisles and stores. Give the cooked nopalitos a quick rinse before adding to stew. If you can't find nopalitos, you can still enjoy this dish without them.

WILD-GAME CHILI

Everyone here has their own chili recipe, and as the weather turns cold the pots start simmering. Here's how I make my pot of "Texas Red." No beans allowed. The key is cooking it slowly for several hours.

2 pounds coarsely ground venison
1 pound coarsely ground wild boar
2 tablespoons cooking oil
2 (12-ounce) cans/bottles ale, or beer if preferred
1 large onion, chopped
3 cloves garlic, finely chopped
1 jalapeño pepper, finely chopped
2 chipotle peppers canned in adobo sauce, chopped, sauce reserved

1 tablespoon adobo sauce
1 tablespoon tomato paste
4 to 5 tablespoons chili powder (you can mix favorites, like ancho and cayenne)
4 tablespoons ground cumin seed
1 tablespoon paprika
1 teaspoon salt
¼ teaspoon black pepper
2 tablespoons cornstarch (optional)

Combine the venison and boar meat. In a heavy pot with tight-fitting lid, heat cooking oil and brown meat in small batches, setting aside each batch as it is browned. Return browned meat to pot, add ½ can of ale and cook covered over low heat for about 1 hour. Stir occasionally to prevent sticking, and add ale if the liquid evaporates. While meat is cooking, chop the onion, garlic, jalapeño, and chipotle. To make a mild version, split jalapeño in half and remove seeds and internal membrane (responsible for most of a pepper's "heat") with a spoon before chopping. Leaving more of these makes the chili spicier.

Drain the pot's juices into a skillet and sauté the onion, jalapeño, and garlic in the juices until onion is softened. Pour this mixture back into the pot with the meat and add adobo sauce and tomato paste. Cook covered over low heat for 2½ to 3 hours, stirring occasionally and adding more ale if needed. The chili should cook at a low simmer, not a boil.

Add chili powder, cumin seed, paprika, salt, and pepper, and adjust. (If you desire a thicker chili, make a slurry with 2 tablespoons cornstarch and a little water. Stir in the cornstarch mixture just before chili has finished cooking.)

Serve over tamales or corn chips with cheese and sour cream.

Serves 8 to 10

ROB LEVITT
MADO RESTAURANT, IL

Allie and Rob Levitt named their restaurant after a story about Fernand Point, chef of France's famed La Pyramide. It is rumored that every dish first had to win over his wife, nicknamed Mado, before it could be served in the restaurant. Allie and Rob's collaboration is more modern and overt but the charm is en pareil. Two haute cuisine hotshots (both have worked at some of the finest restaurants in New York and Chicago), cozily sharing their talents with you—and with each other.

Rob: Once a month, we'll do our family dinners.

Allie: We push all the tables together and it's just one menu. We did a mutton dinner recently. We made mutton empanadas, mutton chorizo, roasted leg of mutton, mutton chops, and a mutton ragù.

Rob: I started cooking when I went to the University of Illinois. I was a music major, playing saxophone in wedding bands. A friend of mine was leaving town for the summer, so I got his dish-washer job. Very quickly I took to being in a professional kitchen. I was never going to be the musician that I wanted to be. It takes a lot to admit that, but I think when I did, I was ultimately much happier. On the other hand, the more I got into cooking, the more I enjoyed it.

Allie: We met at the CIA, and then we both cooked in New York. Rob did his externship at Park Avenue and I was at Gramercy Tavern, doing pastry.

Rob: When I was in school, I entered a recipe contest. I won a trip to Barcelona. I show up with my suitcase full of black clothing. Fortunately I wasn't so New York hardened. I realized—this is nice. People are nice. I was looking for a change.

Allie: 9/11 helped us leave, but we already wanted to go. There's just so much pressure there. We started in New York with really fancy food and we appreciated the training, technique, and discipline, but just we just thought—let's peel it back a little bit.

Rob: We decided we needed to do our own thing. The people that own this space who are now our partners asked if we were interested in doing something. And I said, *Yes, but I'm not interested in being your chef. My wife and I have an idea for a restaurant.* Over the years working in Chicago, we became familiar with farmers around the area. We realized using whole animals is the sensible way to go. If we had to get in cut pork chops it would be five dollars a pound, whereas whole pigs come in at $1.45 a pound. There's not a part we don't use anymore. We make cracklings. We use the pig's head for stew. The bones and the trotters go into stock.

Allie: It's like Rob always says, farmers don't raise a pork chop, they raise a pig. And where we can't get whole animals, we ask what they need to get rid of. There's different cliques and we run in the old-school-revival clique—buy local, butcher your own, preserve your own.

Rob: We get a little annoyed when people are say it's so much work to go to the green market. We do it with hardly any staff. Or they complain about how you can't get by on local in the winter. Really? 'Cause we did. If you find people with greenhouses, there's carrots and beets and kale and beautiful salad greens.

Allie: Potatoes, onions, turnips.

Rob: We put a list up in the restaurant of our farmers. It's not just product to us, it's a family. When I worked at 312, we were really busy and I was working a ton. My reward was a 280-pound hog. The chef called me down to the basement. He and three dish-washers have this giant hog on a rolling cart. All he asked is that I cook the ribs for the staff. That was the first time I butchered a whole pig. Then it was all I wanted to do. When *Cooking By Hand* came out, I read it cover to cover, three times in a row.

Allie: A farmer who had borrowed it brought it back the other day. And we're like, *Oh, good, he can put it back under his pillow now.*

"IT'S LIKE ROB ALWAYS SAYS, FARMERS DON'T RAISE A PORK CHOP. THEY RAISE A PIG ... WE RUN IN THE OLD-SCHOOL-REVIVAL CLIQUE— BUY LOCAL, BUTCHER YOUR OWN, PRESERVE YOUR OWN."

PIG HEAD STEW

Guests often ask us, "What are the delicious little white noodles in this fabulous stew?" They look at us funny when they hear "pig ears." Everyone should make this at least once.

Pig-Head Meat

1 pig head (preferably with tongue, ears, and jowls intact; butchers tend to leave the jowl on the shoulder), all hair removed
1 head garlic, cut in half
1 onion, quartered
10 sprigs thyme
10 sprigs marjoram

Sauce

3 tablespoons olive oil or lard
1 onion, medium dice
3 carrots, cut into ¼-inch rounds
1 bulb fennel, medium dice
1 teaspoon red chili flakes
Pinch of salt
2 cups crushed canned tomatoes
Reserved pig-head cooking liquid

Polpettini (little pork meatballs)

1 pound pork shoulder, cut into 1-inch chunks
¾ pound country bread, cut into 1-inch chunks
3 tablespoons salt
2 teaspoons cinnamon
2 teaspoons smoked paprika
1 teaspoon ground ginger
1 teaspoon red chili flakes
1 tablespoon finely chopped rosemary leaves

Stew

3 cups chickpeas
¼ teaspoon salt, plus a pinch
3 bunches black kale
3 cloves garlic, thinly sliced
Dash olive oil
¼ cup marjoram leaves
Red chili flakes

Cooking the pig head, sauce, and polpettini can all be done up to 2 days prior to serving. Place the head, the garlic, onion, thyme, and marjoram in a heavy-bottomed pot. You could also use a roasting pan over two burners and cover with foil. Add water to cover. Bring to a boil, reduce to a gentle simmer, and cook the head for about 4 hours, or until the meat is just starting to fall off the bone. Carefully remove head from pot. Strain the liquid and reduce by half. When the head is cool enough to handle, pull off all the edible parts. Besides the obvious cheeks and other exposed meaty bits from the back of the head, there are big chunks of meat under the eye sockets and along the snout. The snout, too, is quite delicious in a lip-smacking, gelatinous way, and should be coarsely chopped and added to the mix. The tongue needs to be peeled and then coarsely chopped, along with the ears. Left-over skin, fatty bits, and the skull can be discarded. Refrigerate.

To make the sauce, place the oil, onion, carrot, fennel, and chili flakes in a heavy-bottomed pot. Add a generous pinch of salt and cook over medium heat until the vegetables are tender but not brown. Add ½ cup of the crushed tomatoes and cook until all the liquid has cooked out and the tomato begins to caramelize. Add the remaining tomato and pig-head liquid, and simmer for 20 minutes. Cool, cover, and refrigerate.

For the polpettini, preheat oven to 350°F. Make sure the temperature of the meat is 36°F or lower so that it mixes well. Combine meat with all other ingredients and grind through the coarse plate of a meat grinder or a food processor. Mix well. Form mixture into 1-inch meatballs and place on a baking sheet lined with parchment paper. Bake for about 20 minutes, to about 137°F internal temperature. Cool and refrigerate.

The day of: preheat oven to 250°F. Place chickpeas and a pinch of salt in a pot; cover with water to 1½ inches above the beans. Bring to a boil, then transfer to oven, checking once after 45 minutes to make sure they remain covered in liquid. Add boiling water if they are dry. Cook about 1 hour and 15 minutes.

Remove the ribs from the kale and coarsely chop. In a pot sweat the garlic with olive oil and ¼ teaspoon salt. Add kale and set the heat to medium low. Cook slowly for about 25 minutes, or until just tender.

To assemble the stew, bring the sauce up to a boil and add the head meat. Add the chickpeas, meatballs, and kale, and season with salt, to taste. Add the marjoram leaves and red chili flakes to taste. The stew should be a bit brothy. If it seems too dry, add a splash of hot water. Divide among 8 warm bowls and drizzle with a little extra-virgin olive oil.

Serves 8

CRISPY LAMB BELLY

This dish is both a touch exotic and universally applauded. Much is done the night before; you just need to focus on the breading and frying before serving.

1 boneless lamb belly and breast, 8 to 10 pounds, trimmed of excess fat	4 cups chicken stock	Pork fat (preferred) or canola oil for panfrying
3 sprigs rosemary	Salt	1 pound baby arugula
1 onion, coarsely chopped	3 cups all-purpose flour	1 cup toasted almonds
1 head garlic, split in half crosswise	5 eggs, beaten with ¼ cup water	(Marconas are particularly delicious)
	6 cups panko	
	3 tablespoons lemon juice	
	6 tablespoons olive oil	

Preheat oven to 325°F. Place the lamb, rosemary, onion, garlic, and chicken stock in a baking dish just large enough to hold everything. Cover and braise for 2 hours or until very tender. Remove meat and strain liquid into a pot. Reduce liquid by three fourths. It should be thick and syrupy. While the liquid is reducing, shred the meat, discarding most of the fat and tissues (a little lamb fat is okay). Mix shredded meat and reduced liquid, and add salt to taste. Press into loaf pans lined with plastic wrap. Cover and refrigerate overnight. Unmold lamb from pans. Cut 16 equal (about ½-inch-thick) slices and refrigerate.

Set up a breading station: 3 bowls, the first with flour, the second with beaten egg, and the last with panko. Place a baking sheet next to the last bowl. Remove lamb slices from fridge. Coat lightly with flour, then egg, then panko, then back to the egg, back into the panko, and onto the baking sheet. If necessary, work in small batches: the lamb slices should stay cold until you are ready to bread them.

Preheat the oven to 350°F. Mix together the lemon juice, olive oil, and a pinch of salt. Set vinaigrette aside. Heat ½ inch pork fat or oil in a large, heavy skillet over medium flame until it shimmers. Add a few slices of lamb and fry until each side is crisp and golden brown. Remove to a baking sheet, sprinkle with a little salt, and repeat with all the slices. Allow a minute or two between batches for the oil to get hot again. Place lamb in the oven until hot all the way through. Check this by inserting the tip of a paring knife into the middle of one for 10 seconds and touch it to your bottom lip. If hot, it's ready. Place 2 slices on each warmed dinner plate. Mix the arugula and almonds and dress with vinaigrette. Taste for salt and place a little salad next to the lamb. We usually serve this with a dollop of aioli or some really good hot sauce.

Serves 8

SCOTT LEYSATH

THE SPORTING CHEF, CA

Scott is the guy you want to take hunting with you. He has been chasing down coveys since he was a kid. Plus, his wit is dry enough to start a fire. He is the Sporting Chef, taking his love of cooking game to the airwaves on HuntFishCook. He has sponsorships, a TV show, cookbooks, and a life full of masculine bonding and competitiveness. Not too far from the life of a professional athlete, it occurred to me, sitting in his well-appointed home, with his well-trained hunting dogs at slack attention. And a hunter that can turn a venison leg into a perfectly prepared filet is probably about as rare as pitching a perfect game.

What you really need when you go out hunting is a sharp boning knife, a nylon bag and a giant cooler with ice. Most guys will just leave the possibly gut-shot carcasses in the back of their truck while they bang around on a warm, fall day. I wouldn't want to eat that. Spend the fifty bucks to have it butchered by a professional, it's worth it. I also think a Jaccard meat tenderizer is a great investment, breaks down some of the tougher meat.

Hunting isn't catch and release, you have to cook it. Hunters bring home a ton of this stuff and their wives don't know what to do with it. If your game tastes gamey, don't blame the meat. If it's waterfowl, brine it with water, salt, and brown sugar to replace the blood with brine. With venison, don't overcook it. Well done does not mean less gamey, it is the opposite, in fact. Overcooked meat elicits that Clint Eastwood lip curl—not good. You don't need to hang a young doe, but if it's older, let it hang for a while.

Doing the TV show is the perfect gig for me. I've been serving this meat and catering for years. I can only watch a bass being caught so many times. I think the cooking part of it adds an interesting element to the show.

I grew up hunting. We weren't shirtless yokels out shooting squirrels, we had licenses. I'm a bird man, mostly. You head out to the blind in the morning and you can tell right away if it's going to be a good day. If you don't hear any ducks, that's a bad sign. It's not uncommon to spend up to a million to get into a club. They'll have a beautiful lodge, blinds with whole kitchens set-up inside, and access to a lot of good hunting. I take my son, Jake, with me. I give him a "buck a duck" to pluck them. It's a spiritual experience to be out there, so it may seem inconsistent to some people to shoot at them. You really have to respect the animals, not use them for target practice.

"I GREW UP HUNTING. WE WEREN'T SHIRTLESS YOKELS OUT SHOOTING SQUIRRELS, WE HAD LICENSES. I'M A BIRD MAN, MOSTLY."

DUCK BREAST AND BEER SANDWICH

How's that for an attention grabber? Well-seasoned duck breasts simmered in beer with sweet onions and garlic—oh, my! I recommend enjoying this recipe with a full chilled tankard of your favorite foaming ambrosia. The sandwiches are handy for the outdoors, but you can also serve the duck with wild rice.

1 pound boneless duck breasts, skin removed
Salt and pepper
3 tablespoons olive oil
2 medium yellow onions, sliced into thick rings
2 tablespoons light brown sugar
4 cloves garlic, chopped
2 tablespoons grainy mustard
1 red bell pepper, sliced into thin strips
Pinch chili flakes
1 cup flat dark beer
4 tablespoons mayonnaise
4 sandwich rolls
4 lettuce leaves
4 tomato slices
4 slices provolone cheese (or your favorite)

Season the duck breasts liberally with salt and pepper. Heat 2 tablespoons of the oil over high heat in a large skillet and sear breasts quickly on both sides, but not past rare. Remove and set aside. Add remaining oil and onions. Reduce heat to low and cook onions 4 to 5 minutes. Add brown sugar and stir. Cook until sugar has melted and coated the onions, about 3 to 4 minutes more. Add garlic and next four ingredients and simmer until liquid is reduced to about ¼ cup. Return breasts to pan, cover, and cook to medium rare, checking at 5 minutes. Remove duck and slice thinly on the diagonal.

Spread mayonnaise on rolls and add lettuce, tomato, and cheese. Divide duck, peppers, and onions among sandwiches.

Serves 4

VENISON JERKY

A great way to use up a whole bunch of deer, this jerky recipe is particularly good with older, tough animals. If you don't have any deer meat or antlered game, try it with trimmed, skinless duck or goose breasts, but increase the oven temperature to 165°F. Make sure that you remove any fat, gristle, silver skin, etc. before marinating the meat. This jerky is not brined or cured, so it should be refrigerated or frozen if you plan on keeping it around for over 1 week.

2 to 3 pounds trimmed deer meat, slightly frozen
1 teaspoon hoisin sauce
1 cup soy sauce
1 cup pineapple juice
1 tablespoon brown sugar
¼ cup rice vinegar
1 teaspoon minced ginger
2 cloves garlic, minced
1 tablespoon (or more) Tabasco or Asian chili-garlic sauce

The barely frozen meat will be easier to slice. Slice meat with the grain, as thinly as possible, into strips. Combine the rest of the ingredients in a large bowl. Add meat and toss to coat evenly. Cover and refrigerate 12 to 24 hours.

Place two baking sheets on lower rack of oven to catch drippings. Preheat oven to 160°F. Remove marinated meat from fridge. Place on paper towels and squeeze to remove as much moisture as possible. Place meat strips in a single layer, not overlapping, directly on oven rack above the baking sheets. Make sure oven door is cracked open about ½ inch so that moisture will escape. Turn meat over every two hours. Meat is done when it is still slightly pliable, not so dry as to be crisp and breakable. This will take 4 to 5 hours. If storing, let meat cool before putting into sealed container in refrigerator. The jerky will keep for 1 to 2 months.

Makes about 1 to 1½ pounds jerky

PRIMAL CUTS: VENISON

The **DEER** is an animal apart. This is a sprinter and a vaulter, full of **MUSCLE** and **FOREST** and **FIELD**. The primals are primal. There is farmed deer, more domesticated and **FATTY**, but it still begs treatment apart from farmyard creatures. While many hunters use barbecue **SAUCE** and shoe-leather doneness to try and ward off **GAMINESS**, my field research suggests that rarer is better for a clean, **GRASSY** succulence. A young doe may not beckon **AGING** but it will benefit most deer.

SHOULDER

The workhorse shoulder is full of fat and gristle and relaxes once it has had a good, long braise. Ask your butcher to pull out the mock tender before it becomes stew meat or a roast. The mock tender is a little muscle worthy of the grill. Bone-in shoulders can also be seasoned and braised for several hours until the bone pulls away cleanly.

Cuts: mock tender, blade chops, stew meat, boneless shoulder roast, bone-in shoulder roast

FLANK, PLATE, AND RIBS

These generally get boned and then tossed into the grinding bucket, but if you are weary of venison chili, venison spaghetti, and venison burgers, lightly pounded flanks are great on the grill, and ribs can be slow-cooked and slathered with an earthy, spicy barbecue sauce.

Cuts: ground venison, stew meat, ribs, and flank steak

BACKSTRAP, OR LOIN

Located on either side of the inside of the spinal cavity, the backstrap or loin is often mistakenly referred to as the tenderloin. The loin is what many hunters use for steaks, grinding or drying the rest. It is a tender piece and is best served rare or medium-rare as noisettes or chops.

Tenderloin is the most delicate and tender cut of the backstrap. These flat pieces should be cooked quickly at very high heat to insure a nice sear and a pink center. Overcooking a tenderloin would be a real shame.

Cuts: chops, boneless country-style ribs, boneless loin, boneless loin noisettes, tenderloin

LEG

Like all legs, the venison leg is made up of muscles that will cook better if they are separated at the seams. Cooking muscles separately means more consistency and tenderness, as all the grains are of one mind. Steaks should be cut thick so there will be a variation in temperature

from the outside to the center.

Cut the top sirloin into nice steaks and do not cook past medium rare or you will get a tough, gamey piece of penance. Like the top sirloin, you can use the sirloin tip for steaks, or a sweet little roast. The whole round can be cut into fajita meat and cooked high and fast. It also makes a good roast, especially when seamed out and butterflied, so it cooks evenly and moderately fast. It contains the top round, bottom round, and eye of round, so you can also divvy it into those muscles for three elegant roasts. These muscles can also be totally denuded and grilled, pan-seared or broiled until medium rare. Before serving, slice across the grain.

Cuts: top round (roast or steaks), bottom round (roast or steaks), eye of round (roast or steaks), top sirloin (roast or steaks), sirloin tip (roast or steaks)

SHANK

Venison osso bucco, of course. Also perfectly good for adding to your ground or stew-meat stash, though most hunters have a healthy inventory of that already.

Cuts: shank, osso bucco, ground meat, stew meat

OFFAL

Venison offal is a perfect celebration of a successful hunt. Flour-dusted liver and kidney fried over a campfire in a bit of venison fat, or grilled heart, sliced thin and served rare, are respectable trophies.

ground venison
stew meat
ribs
flank steak

top round
bottom round
eye of round
top sirloin
sirloin tip

BACK

LEG

FLANK,
PLATE,
RIBS

SHANK

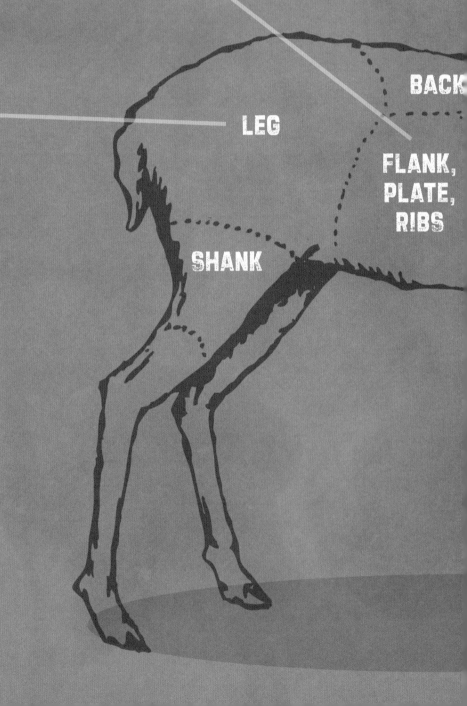

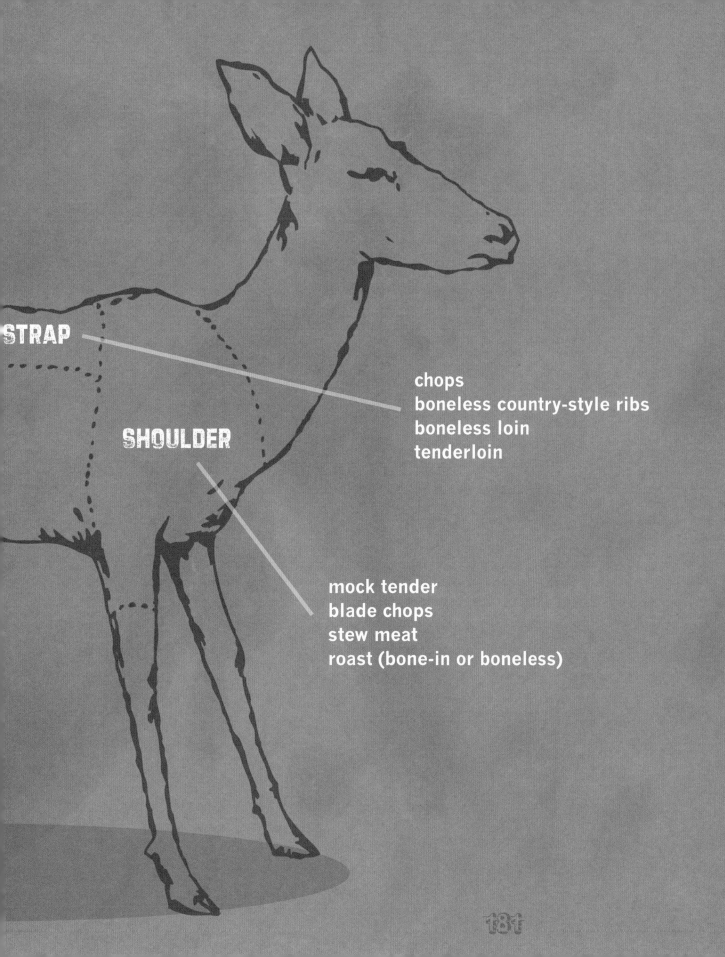

STRAP

SHOULDER

chops
boneless country-style ribs
boneless loin
tenderloin

mock tender
blade chops
stew meat
roast (bone-in or boneless)

DONALD LINK

COCHON BUTCHER, LA

I had to rib Donald Link a little about his stature in New Orleans and so I nicknamed him "the Mayor." On my flight into Louisiana I overheard three conversations about his restaurants and his butcher shop. While I sat in Cochon Butcher, the fawning created a discernible uptick in the humidity. Clearly a prodigal son, he has a majestic air. Relaxed and tensile in the same breath, like a napping lion. He has a whole New Orleans storyline wrapped up in his relationship to food. Born of a rice empire that held fast to fecund country traditions, he headed off to culinary school. At forty years old, he owns three restaurants—Herbsaint, Cochon, Cochon Butcher, as well as Calcasieu, an event space. The butcher shop has a counter of take-home, house-cured, fresh meats and also serves a daily rotating menu of sandwiches. An empire with a long memory.

Can I get a box of cigars back here? There are restaurants that basically just heat stuff up and send it out, and then there's real cooking. Our muffaletta is the perfect example. Instead of just buying generic meats from around town, all the salumi is homemade. Our bread, on the other hand, is from a local baker. I thought about making our own bread but that would take a huge piece of business away from this guy. Why am I going to hire someone when there's a great breadmaker just down the road? In France, they do the same thing—the boulangerie is right next to the butcher. If someone else can make it better, you shouldn't do it yourself, and vice versa. That's the philosophy I've built my businesses on.

Maybe the salumeria is not a southern tradtion, but the tasso and the boudin are. That's stuff my family has been making for years. I grew up with pig butchery. Still to this day, I go and make sausage with them. Usually it's after deer-hunting season. Everyone makes the sausage together and then they split it up. Very communal. I've got deep roots here in Louisiana. My family came over from Germany in 1880 and started the rice business. They developed a system of irrigation and managed to get it on the trains going into New Orleans and get the marketing going. They still do farm most of the rice here.

I personally much prefer to buy whole animals. I would do it even if it weren't more economical, but it is. I also think it's good for my sous chefs to have to really look at what they're doing and make decisions. *Here's a whole lamb. This is how much it cost, this is how much we need to make. Tell me what your plan for this lamb is, from head to toe. Whatever you want to do, it's your choice.* It's nice to be able to let the animal decide that, instead of just looking at a piece of paper that says: make this many chops, this many ribs. Now that's a great education, because you have to make money or you won't stay in business, and you need to create something interesting. People are always trying to pin me down about what I'll be putting on the menu six months from now. I don't know what's going to be around then. When I get there, I'll figure it out.

I want to buy local, but to a point. I'm not going to buy junk. There's a chicken farmer up in north Louisiana—I met him at a market in Covington about a month ago—and pretty soon we'll have our first chickens from him. We've talked about this four to six months ago and now they're ready. I've had better-flavored chicken—you ever had a chicken in France? Man, that's like, perfect. It has fat. But the texture of this guy's birds is perfect, so we're having conversations about feed. That's what's so exciting about this process: together we can collaborate to make a better product.

There's a lot more opportunity to buy local than there was nine years ago. I think Hurricane Katrina had a huge effect. Since then, people are more motivated and interested in doing things in an old-school way and connecting more to their community. There are more young farmers growing better products and getting interested in local restaurants. Before Katrina, farmers never really thought of restaurants as a revenue source. They didn't trust that they would actually buy their stuff. We can't buy blood here, though. You got to go over the bridge for that.

"IF SOMEONE ELSE CAN MAKE IT BETTER, YOU SHOULDN'T DO IT YOURSELF, AND VICE VERSA. THAT'S THE PHILOSOPHY I'VE BUILT MY BUSINESSES ON."

MY BOUDIN

Boudin can mean many things: blood sausage, pork offal sausage, even a crawfish sausage. But in New Orleans it means a pork liver and rice sausage. Spicy, rich, and complex. I grew up making this recipe, and so we had to have them at Cochon Butcher.

2 pounds pork shoulder, cut into 1-inch cubes
½ pound pork liver, cut into 1-inch cubes
1 small onion, chopped
2 celery stalks, chopped
1 medium poblano, stemmed, seeded, chopped
3 medium jalapeños, stemmed, seeded, chopped
6 cloves garlic, coarsely chopped
4 tablespoons kosher salt
1 tablespoon black pepper
1 tablespoon ground white pepper

½ teaspoon pink salt *
2 teaspoons cayenne pepper
1 teaspoon chili powder
7 cups cooked white rice
1 cup chopped fresh parsley
1 cup chopped scallions
4 to 6 feet hog middles casings (optional), thoroughly rinsed

Combine the pork, liver, vegetables, and the seasonings, and marinate for 1 hour or overnight, covered, in the refrigerator. Place the marinated mixture in a large pot and cover meat with water (by 1 to 2 inches). Bring mixture to a boil, reduce heat, and simmer until the meat is tender about 1 hour and 45 minutes.

Remove the pot from the heat and strain, reserving the liquid. Allow the mixture to cool slightly, then put all ingredients through a meat grinder set on coarse grind. (You can also chop with a knife if you don't have a meat grinder, which is what I usually do anyway).

Place the ground meat in a large bowl. Using a wooden spoon or rubber spatula, mix in the cooked rice, parsley, scallions, and the reserved cooking liquid. Stir vigorously for 5 minutes. When the boudin-rice mixture is first combined, it looks very wet and it's pretty spicy. Don't worry; after poaching, the rice absorbs the excess moisture and much of the spice. The wet texture and extra spice ensure your final boudin will be moist and full of flavor.

At this point you can feed the sausage into the casings (if desired). To do this, slide about 2 to 3 yards of casing onto the nozzle. Tie a knot on the end of the casing before the meat starts to come out. Guide the sausage on to a sheet pan that has a little water on it, to keep the casings from drying out and cracking. Twist the sausage into 6- to 8-inch links, as you like.

Poach the links gently in hot (not bubbling) water for about 10 minutes, then serve. Alternately, you can use the mixture as a stuffing for chicken, or roll it into "boudin balls," dredge in breadcrumbs and fry in hot oil until golden brown.

Makes 4 pounds of sausage

* Curing salt. Necessary to inhibit growth of bacteria. Use and store with caution. See page 288.

BUTCHER SPECIALS

- FRIED DRUM POBOY, DRESSED 9-
- MARINATED CRAB CLAWS W/ REMOULADE
- HOT SAUSAGE & PEPPERS ON FRENCH BAGUETTE 9.
- WHITE PIZZETTA W/ HOUSEMADE PICANTE SALAMI, ARUGULA & BANANA PEPPERS 6-
- GRILLED MANCHEGO CHEESE, BUTCHER BACON & TOMATO 10-

HOT BOO-UDIN!
BOILED PEANUTS!

BRAISED RABBIT

WITH BACON-SAGE DUMPLINGS

These noodle-like dumplings, made with bacon fat, are a true taste of Southern cooking. They're easy to prepare and delicious, so it's easy to understand why they were a staple (plus they make good use of that can of bacon fat under the sink that everyone used to have). But the best thing about these tender dumplings is that they really soak up the flavorful braising juices and take on the flavor of the rabbit.

I find that it's easiest to braise the rabbits whole, but if you buy them pre-sectioned, that's fine, they'll cook in the same manner. When you are picking the tender meat off the rabbit, avoid shredding it too finely (larger pieces of meat make a nicer presentation), and be extra careful to pick out small bones. I always pick the meat twice to make sure that I've gotten every last one.

Braise
2 rabbits, 2½- to 3-pounds each
Salt and black pepper
Flour
3 tablespoons vegetable shortening
4 slices thick-sliced bacon, sliced into lardoons
1 small onion, coarsely chopped
2 stalks celery, coarsely chopped
1 small carrot, sliced into 1-inch rounds
2 cloves garlic, smashed
1 cup dry white wine
½ bunch fresh sage
½ bunch fresh thyme
6 cups chicken stock

Dumplings
2 cups flour
½ teaspoon baking powder
¼ cup chopped fresh sage
¼ teaspoon salt
¼ teaspoon black pepper
5 tablespoons chilled rendered bacon fat

Stew
2 tablespoons vegetable oil
1 medium onion, finely chopped
2 parsnips, medium dice
1 poblano, finely chopped *
2 carrots, medium dice
2 stalks celery, finely chopped
5 cloves of garlic, minced
1 tablespoon dried oregano
5 bay leaves
2 teaspoons salt
½ teaspoon black pepper
⅓ cup vegetable oil
3 tablespoons whole-grain mustard
½ cup dry white wine

Season rabbits generously with salt and pepper. Just before cooking, dust the rabbits with flour and shake to remove excess.

Heat a large cast-iron skillet over medium heat. Add the shortening and bacon and cook, stirring, until shortening has melted and bacon has cooked halfway and rendered much of its fat. Drain the bacon fat from skillet (strain if necessary) and refrigerate until needed (the chilled fat will be used to make the dumplings). You should have about 5 tablespoons of fat. (If you don't quite have 5 tablespoons, you can add lard or vegetable shortening.)

Meanwhile, heat vegetable oil over medium-high heat in a large cast-iron Dutch oven. When the oil is very hot, add the rabbit pieces and cook until evenly browned, using tongs to turn rabbit as necessary. When the rabbit is browned, add the onion, celery, carrot, and garlic and cook, stirring, until the vegetables are coated with fat, then add wine. Bring the mixture to a boil, reduce heat and simmer until reduced by half. Add the sage, thyme, and chicken stock, return to a boil, reduce heat, cover, and simmer (turning the rabbit once or twice for even cooking) until the meat pulls very easily away from the bone, 1½ to 2 hours.

While the rabbit braises, prepare the dumplings. Stir together the dry ingredients in a mound on the counter or in a large mixing bowl, then add the chilled bacon fat. Use your fingers to combine dry ingredients with the fat until mixture resembles coarse pebbles. Make a well in the center of the mixture and add the water to the well. Use your fingers to work in the liquid and form dough. Knead briefly, just to combine, then shape the mixture into a ball. On a lightly floured surface, use a rolling pin to roll dough out very thin (a thin pie dough, a little thicker than fettucine) into a rough square shape. Turn dough over once if it starts to stick. Use a knife to slice the dough into 1 by 4-inch pieces, then set aside.

Bring a large pot of generously salted water to a boil. Add the dumplings and boil 3 to 5 minutes, until tender, and drain. Toss the dumplings with a small amount of oil to keep them from sticking together, then set aside.

When the rabbit is done cooking, use tongs to transfer it to a baking dish. Strain out braising vegetables and discard, reserving broth. Skim fat from broth and set aside. Using your fingers, separate rabbit meat from bone, feeling carefully for any small bones, and set aside.

Heat the reserved vegetable fat and vegetable oil in the Dutch oven over medium-high heat. Add the onion, parsnips, poblano, carrots, celery, garlic, oregano, bay leaves, salt, and pepper, and cook, stirring, until softened, about 5 to 7 minutes. Add the mustard and wine and cook, stirring, until pan is deglazed and most of the wine has evaporated. Add the reserved stock, scraping up any browned bits. Simmer for about 10 minutes, then add the reserved rabbit meat and simmer an additional 20 minutes.

To finish the dish, add the cooked dumplings, stir together just until warmed through, and serve. If you are not going to serve the entire dish at once, serve dumplings in a bowl and ladle the hot stew over the top, so the dumplings don't overcook and become mushy.

* When chopping poblanos and other chiles, slice them from the inside (rib side) of the pepper for a cleaner cut. If you have to cut through the thicker skin side it's easier for the knife to slip.

Serves 6 to 8

MIKE LORENTZ
LORENTZ MEATS, MN

Lorentz Meats doesn't sell anything except service. But they have done an extraordinary thing. Not only do they know how to do their business very well, they have studied how their customers should do their business very well. You can't be a successful butcher without successful farmers. It's a rare thing for a middleman to impart dignity on their role but Mike has done it by adding real value to his work, instead of just another fifty cents on the pound.

We built this processing plant in 2000 to help farmers bring their products direct to consumers. That was the big emphasis. Before that we were a little locker plant. We developed a slaughtering, cutting, processing facility all in one.

I'm second generation. Mom and Dad bought an existing locker plant back in '68. The amount of sanitation work that we do today, compared to thirty years ago, I mean, it's laughable. We would wash the saw once a week. We weren't the worst plant in the area, that was just kind of what people did. Now we have a third-party cleaning company come in every day. And we have a full-time quality control person who verifies their work.

My brother Rob and I wanted to do something that would actually drive the value of the business. We felt the best way to do that was to build a bigger facility and partner with local farmers to expand beyond just the two of us. We work with about 300 farmers who are doing direct marketing.

Now we're much more focused with what we encourage farmers to do, making sure they get a large enough transaction so that it's worth their while. We've worked with farmers since '68. In '90, when I came back from college and we were talking about our future, Rob was pretty adamant that he wanted to stay in the processing business, so as I looked at the customer list and noticed our top few customers got the majority of the processing done. And that's the "ah-ha!" moment. We don't need more farmers, we just need our farmers to do better in order to grow our business. So we came out with the Market Maker program. We got a grant from the USDA Rural Development to create a full-fledged curriculum, where we taught farmers how to do direct marketing.

It was calling Branding Your Beliefs. The average small farmer, they don't want to sell meat. They want to sell a connection to a farmer, because that's what they can most sincerely, consistently deliver. The meat is the by-product of the connection. It's almost like it's your coffee cup for being a public radio member.

I'm anti-farmers' market. It gets farmers trapped in this idea that they're selling meat. And they have all these inventory issues. At the end of the day I don't believe that they make any more money, they just work harder. I talked to a guy who was at the San Francisco Ferry Market, and he did $5,000 in three hours. We were having a heated discussion about whether or not that was worthwhile. He said something to the effect of, *You can't tell me I'm not making money.* And I said, *Yes, I can, because you can't tell me you are. You just know you've got a wad of cash and less meat on hand.* To do it well requires a sophisticated interaction between the processor and the farmer. And it has to be viewed as a very real business. Most people who are selling at the farmers' markets don't have good enough information on a daily or weekly basis. For all they know, their profits are completely wiped out because their pricing was based on incorrect numbers.

If you want to be in the meat business, twenty beef a week is about where your baseline needs to be. Anybody could get a .22 and shoot at a cow and say they're in the killing business. But it takes a little bit more than that to actually run a USDA plant.

FLANK STEAK FAJITAS

I love simple cooking techniques for grass-fed beef. The marinade and accompaniments bring complexity to a beautifully simple dish.

½ cup tamari
½ cup amontillado sherry, other medium-dry sherry, or cooking sherry
½ cup canned jalapeño chili peppers (approximately a third of an 11-ounce can)
¼ cup juice from the canned peppers
3 tablespoons gold tequila
1 tablespoon freshly squeezed lime juice
2 grass-fed beef flank steaks, trimmed, about 2 pounds total

2 or 3 large sweet onions, sliced thinly and lengthwise
3 large green bell peppers, seeded and sliced thinly
16 corn or 8 flour tortillas, or a combination of both
1 16-ounce container sour cream
2 avocados, diced and tossed in lemon or lime juice to preserve color
1 pound shredded Mexican 4-cheese mix
Salsas of your choice

Combine first 6 ingredients in a nonreactive bowl or large plastic food storage bag. Add flank steak, cover with plastic wrap if using a bowl, and marinate in the refrigerator overnight, turning occasionally.

One hour before grilling, remove steak from marinade and allow it to warm up to room temperature.

Preheat grill to medium high. Place pan on grill 4 to 5 inches above flame and cook onions and peppers until slightly blackened, about 10 to 15 minutes, turning often. (You can sauté these on top of the stove in a little olive oil instead, but you won't get the blackened quality.) Remove from flame and set aside.

Grill flank steak until medium rare to medium, 4 to 7 minutes per side, depending on the thickness of the steak (do not overcook, as flank steak will toughen). While the steak is grilling, wrap tortillas in foil and warm in a 325°F oven. Remove steak from heat and allow to rest, covered with foil, for 5 minutes. Slice thinly at an angle across the grain.

To serve, set out platters of meat, tortillas, grilled onions and peppers, sour cream, diced avocados (or guacamole), shredded cheese, and various salsas, and let your guests build their own fajitas. For quacamole, mash avocados just before serving, and add a tablespoon or two of minced onions, a tablespoon of minced jalapeños, and a pinch of salt.

Serves 6 to 8

MARINATED GRASS-FED BEEF

One of my customers, Gloria Goodwin Raheja, created this simple preparation for the Thousand Hills Grass-Fed Beef we carry. This is a preparation to turn to on nights when you have big expectations and low energy for dinner.

1 pound grass-fed round tip steak, cut into
⅛-inch-thick slices

Marinade
⅔ cup red wine vinegar
4 tablespoon olive oil
2 tablespoons Dijon mustard
3 cloves garlic, smashed
2 sprigs rosemary
1 teaspoon salt
½ teaspoon freshly ground black pepper

Dressing
⅔ cup olive oil
4 cloves garlic, smashed
4 sprigs rosemary
2 large shallots, sliced thin
4 tablespoons balsamic vinegar
3 tablespoons red wine vinegar
Salt and pepper

2 cups baby arugula
½ cup crumbled Roquefort, gorgonzola,
  or high-quality blue cheese

Whisk together vinegar, oil, and mustard, and then add all other marinade ingredients. Stir and add beef. Marinate for 2 hours or overnight in refrigerator.

Heat oil with garlic and rosemary in a heavy skillet over medium-high heat for about 4 minutes or until garlic begins to brown. Discard garlic and rosemary. Add the meat and cook for about 1 minute for medium rare. Remove the meat and set aside. Add shallots and vinegars to skillet, salt and pepper to taste, and cook for about 2 minutes over medium-low heat. Lightly dress the arugula and divide among four plates. Divide meat among plates, drizzle with more dressing, and crumble cheese on top. Serve immediately with extra dressing on the side.

Serves 4

MORGAN MAKI

BI-RITE MARKET, CA

Morgan Maki is the tuning fork of Bi-Rite Market's meat department, simultaneously grounding it and radiating energy outward. In the pulsating heart of the good-food movement, Bi-Rite stands out as one of the most innovative and profitable centers of sourcing integrity. Its mission statement, "Creating Community through Food," rings through Morgan like a mystic chord. After an early career striving in highly competitive, top-tier kitchens, Morgan is finding fulfillment in connecting not just with his kitchen comrades, but with consumers and growers, too.

There's no soigné shit going down over here but I think what we're doing is important to people. Shopping here might be the first step you take to: A. think more about what you're putting inside of your body; B. think more about how your personal choices affect everyone around you.

I teach a class here where I show everybody how to break down a chicken and make stock, because people will come in and they'll buy two chicken breasts instead of a whole bird, which costs less. One customer wanted to know if he could cure a ham at home, so he shows up with a scooter and rolls out with a twenty-five-pound hog leg and, like, six boxes of salt to pack it in. He brought in a little piece for me to taste the other day. It'd been about three months. It had mold all over it and it was beautiful. He was so proud and it's like you see this little spark inside of somebody. That's worth more to me than anything I ever did or made when I was working in fine-dining kitchens.

At a certain point I just had to leave perfection-obsessed kitchens. I didn't want to work six days a week, fourteen hours a day, because I was getting sick, physically and mentally. I needed to enjoy my life a little more and exercise and see some sunshine. There's a lot of guys that go to culinary school and it's like they've got stars in their eyes and they don't understand that it's about suffering and cutting yourself and burning yourself and working too much and drinking too much and collapsing at the end of the week.

When I got the job at Bi-Rite, I pitched the whole idea of sourcing farm-specific meat. The produce department already had amazing vegetables—like Full Belly and Dirty Girl. The owner, Sam Mogannam, was like, *Bring me a game plan. If you can make it work, then you can do it.* In two years we went from sixty grand in average monthly sales to a hundred grand.

We bring the farmers in here sometimes and they sit out in front and shake everybody's hand. It's a lot of networking to bring in good stuff and so everyone has to understand that sometimes, if it's really hot in August, the lambs don't eat. So being able to keep multiple options open and be flexible with farmers and explain to the customers so you teach them that it doesn't come from the lamb factory—it comes from a field sixty miles that way and its been sweltering out there.

During the summertime we'll all work on the Bi-Rite family farms in Sonoma, which grow a lot of the vegetables we use in the kitchen. I'll take my bicycle up there, put on an old pair of overalls, and help out on my days off.

The people that come into the market, they're my friends now; they come over to my house for dinner. It's become such a huge element of my life, being part of a neighborhood. All the other places I lived, working kitchens, I didn't know my neighbors. We'll have a party in the backyard of Bi-Rite and it'll be sixty people and everybody will contribute something to share.

LAMB SPEZZATINO

Do not let the multiday process of this recipe intimidate you! The steps are easy and there is very little to do on the day you serve, so you can relax with your dinner guests. Be sure to have a great salad and a fabulous crusty bread to mop up the sauce.

5 pounds lamb shoulder, cut into 1-inch cubes
2 tablespoons brown sugar
Pinch of chili flakes
Pinch of ground fennel seed
Kosher salt and black pepper
1 leek, sliced thinly
1 yellow onion, chopped into ¼-inch pieces
2 carrots, sliced thinly
2 stalks celery, diced into ¼-inch cubes
3 cloves garlic, chopped
1 bulb fennel, trimmed, cored, and diced into ¼-inch cubes

4 or 5 sage leaves, finely chopped
1 sprig rosemary, finely chopped
½ bunch thyme, finely chopped
2 tablespoons grapeseed oil
1 tablespoon tomato paste
2 cups dry red wine
2 quarts chicken stock
3 pounds garganelli or penne pasta
½ pound butter, sliced
½ pound grated Parmesan cheese, plus additional for the table

Two days before you plan to serve it, toss lamb with sugar, chili flakes, fennel seed, and salt and pepper to taste. Allow to cure overnight in the fridge.

The day before serving, prepare the leek, onion, carrots, celery, garlic, fennel, sage, rosemary, and thyme. Put one tablespoon of grapeseed oil in large cast-iron pot (or other large flat-bottomed pot with shallow sides) over high heat. Add half the lamb in small batches to pan and allow to brown on all sides (lowering the heat as it browns). Be patient and don't disturb the meat until it has browned, and then turn it. Once the first half is seared and brown on all sides, remove from pot, add the remaining tablespoon of grapeseed oil, and sear the rest. When the second half is seared, add back the first half, along with the vegetables and herbs. Cook over medium heat for a few minutes; then increase heat and add tomato paste. Cook on high for another 2 minutes, until you can smell the tomato paste getting sweet and bitter. Remove the lamb from the pot.

Add wine, scrape any bits of meat off the bottom of the pan, and cook until wine has reduced by three quarters. Return meat to pot, along with chicken stock, and transfer it, covered, to a 275°F oven, where it should slowly cook until lamb is very tender, about 2 hours. Remove from oven, allow to cool, and refrigerate overnight.

A few hours before serving, pull the braise out of the fridge and warm it up a bit on the stove. Strain out liquid and put the meat and vegetables aside. Return liquid to pot and simmer, reducing liquid by about one third over the course of an hour, until it reaches a thick sauce consistency. Combine everything again and hold until ready to serve.

Cook pasta according to package instructions. Heat up the braise and divide between two pots. Add half the pasta to each pot and fold in half the butter and cheese to each over low heat. When everything is evenly incorporated and the sauce is shiny and sticking to the pasta, serve immediately, with more grated cheese.

Serves 12

BOURBON-BRAISED PULLED-PORK SANDWICHES

This is a bit of a crash course in braising, a technique that cooks spend their lives constantly trying to perfect. If it doesn't turn out great the first time, remember that practice—lots of practice—makes perfect. And you'll be happy to spend time on it, as the final result is robust and sweet, and makes plenty of delicious sandwiches.

3½ pounds pork shoulder
Kosher salt
3½ tablespoons black pepper
5 tablespoons fennel seed
6 tablespoons chili flakes
3 tablespoons olive oil
1½ pounds yellow onion, coarsely chopped
½ pound celery, coarsely chopped
½ pound leeks, coarsely chopped
½ pound fennel, coarsely chopped
½ pound carrots, coarsely chopped

8 cloves garlic
375 ml (about 1½ cups) bourbon
   (Makers Mark works fine)
¼ bunch rosemary
¼ bunch thyme
¼ bunch sage
1½ bay leaves
¼ cup honey
4 cups chicken stock
1 cup dried cherries

Two days before serving: Remove the skin and cut the shoulder into manageable pieces. Season with salt to taste, pepper, fennel seed, and chili flakes, and cure in refrigerator overnight.

One day before serving: In a large vessel, heat oil and brown shoulder pieces in small batches at medium-high heat. It's important to regulate the heat of the pan by not crowding the meat. Take time to brown the shoulder well on all sides and build a good fond (the browned, caramelized bits of meat) on the bottom of the pan. Put meat aside and drain excess oil and fat from pan. Add onions, celery, leeks, fennel, carrots, and garlic. Cook until soft and beginning to caramelize.

Add bourbon and use the liquid to scrape all of the fond off the bottom of the pan. Turn heat up to high and reduce the booze until it is almost gone. Be careful while doing this, because it can ignite; if this happens, cover the pan—to put out the flames—and reduce heat. Return meat to pan when the reduction is done, add the herbs, honey, and chicken stock, and bring the braise up to a slow simmer (160° to 170°F).

Cover top of pot with parchment paper, put the whole thing in an oven at 275°F, and cook for 4 to 5 hours. Check the braise periodically to make sure that it is not cooking too hot: you should see only occasional bubbles rising to the surface of the fluid. The braise will be finished when you can put a fork into the meat and turn it without using much force. Allow the braise to cool to room temperature and refrigerate overnight.

On the day of the meal: Pull the pot out of the fridge, warm it up on the stove, and strain the liquid. Put the liquid back in the pot and reduce it by half. Chop your dried cherries and add to the liquid. Discard the vegetables and pick the meat apart into small pieces. Return the meat to the pot and incorporate it into the sauce. You're ready to make sandwiches.

Serves 6 to 8

FAVORITE SAUCES

Sauce separates an **OH, LA** from an **OH, LA LA**! When I asked **CHEFS** how they suggest improving the reputation of a home **COOK**, they offered up these favorites. I love them all for their versatility. Likely you'll find the **INGREDIENTS** for at least one in your pantry:

VINAIGRETTE

"If people knew how much a simple sauce like a vinaigrette can improve their cooking, they would be amazed." —Tia Harrison, Avedano's

This is perfect for a salad, but it is also a classic baste for meats and poultry. The most important thing is the balance of oil and acid to create an emulsion. There are myriad variations, once you get the technique.

4 tablespoons vinegar (white wine, red wine, rice, balsamic, herb or chili infused, etc.) or lemon juice
4 teaspoons Dijon mustard
salt and pepper to taste
12 tablespoons olive oil (or sunflower oil, walnut oil, hazelnut oil, or a mixture of these, etc.)

All ingredients should be at room temperature. In a bowl, whisk together the acid (vinegar or lemon juice), Dijon mustard, and salt and pepper (you can also add garlic, spring onion, and/or herbs at this point). Slowly drizzle the olive oil into the mixture while constantly whisking, to emulsify into a dressing.

SALSA VERDE

"I am a huge fan of this on meats of all kinds."
—Jason Barwikowski, Olympic Provisions

This is a rustic salsa, and you can play with the elements: heat (green chilis, horseradish, black pepper, chives or spring onion, garlic); herbs (parsley, tarragon, cilantro, basil); acid (vinegar, capers, cornichons, Dijon, lemon juice)

8 spring onions, trimmed
2 cloves garlic, halved
3 cornichons, halved
2 sprigs fresh tarragon, stems removed
1 bunch fresh parsley, stems removed
1 anchovy
juice of ½ lemon
1 tablespoon vinegar (white or rice)
6 tablespoons olive oil
black pepper

Pulse everything except the last four ingredients in a food processor, retaining some variation in texture. Put this chunky mixture in a bowl and add the lemon juice, vinegar, and olive oil, stirring gently. Pepper to taste.

Serves 4

GLACE DE VIANDE

"This is a great all-purpose sauce for finishing lamb, beef, pork, or poultry."

—Morgan Maki, Bi-Rite Market

3 pounds mixed bones (beef, lamb, pork, poultry, etc.)
2 pounds yellow onions
1 pound celery
1 pound carrots
1 tablespoon grapeseed oil (or olive oil)
1 pound mixed trim (sinew, connective tissue, skin, etc.)
1 tablespoon tomato paste
1½ cups dry white wine
3 bay leaves
1 teaspoon black peppercorns
2 sprigs rosemary
2 sprigs thyme
About 20 cups stock (page 73)

Roast bones at 450°F for about 30 minutes, for even browning and liquefaction of excess fat. While bones are in the oven, wash, peel, and coarsely dice mirepoix (onion, celery, and carrots). Remove bones from oven, and carefully drain fat from roasting tray.

In a stockpot with a little grapeseed oil in the bottom, caramelize all of the trim over a medium-high flame. Next, add mirepoix and continue to cook over the same flame until the vegetables also begin to caramelize. Then add tomato paste and cook until it begins to caramelize as well. Last, add 1 cup of the wine, deglaze, and reduce by 90 percent. This is a very important step in the sauce-making process.

Building up a fond and caramelizing all of these ingredients in this order creates lots of bitter, sweet, and savory tastes that will lend balance and complexity to the finished product.

Place bones, herbs, and peppercorns in a stockpot and cover with stock. Begin heating the stock over a medium-high flame. Meanwhile use the remaining half cup of wine to deglaze the fond left on the hot roasting tray. When the wine has reduced by half and all of the little bits of caramelized protein are scraped from the bottom of the tray, pour into stock and give it a swirl.

Leave the stock alone until you notice a bit of foam and scum accumulating on its surface. Then reduce heat to low and carefully skim stock at 1-hour intervals. This stock should run about 170°F for 3 to 4 hours.

Scoop and discard spent bones and vegetables and strain stock through a fine sieve or cheesecloth. Return stock to the stove over medium heat with the stockpot slightly off center on the burner; while reducing, oils and scum will accumulate on one side of the pot, making skimming easier and more effective. Check reduction about every 45 minutes and skim. This could take 4 to 5 hours.

When the sauce has reduced to the desired consistency and/or will tightly coat the back of a spoon, check the seasoning. If necessary, add a bit of salt and balsamic vinegar to adjust and balance the flavors. Cool to 50°F, then refrigerate overnight. The sauce is ready for use.

Makes about 5 cups

MARSHA McBRIDE
CAFÉ ROUGE, CA

As a female meat maven, I hate to focus on gender, but Marsha has this palpable woman-ness. Unlike many women who are successful in the upper echelons of fine dining or the meat world, she doesn't seem to be in conflict with masculinity. There's no ironic nod to her butchering prowess being unusual for a woman. I just adore that, I could curl up in it. Having a butcher shop in her restaurant is a phenomenon being replicated all over the country but Marsha has been holding it down for 14 years, not to mention creating a stable of talented charcutiers that have come through Rouge before most of us had ever heard of sopprassata. Scott Brennan is running the meat counter now and has even begun teaching butchery classes in the restaurant. I spoke with Marsha about her life in meat.

I studied criminology. I was director of a group home for runaway children in Hayward for seven years. Then I enrolled at the California Culinary Academy, where I learned my first butchery skills.

It was considered unusual when I began expressing a passion for meat. At the Culinary Academy, a German instructor would not allow female students the rugged task of breaking down a hindquarter of beef. Another male instructor would not allow women on their period to work with charcuterie because he thought the meat would be tainted.

Quang Nguyen was a terrific butcher and subsequently taught me several tricks of the trade during my tenure at Zuni Cafe. The importance of a lot of trial and error cannot be minimized. We do a lot of experimentation at Café Rouge.

I intended to open a butcher shop but quickly realized that the odds of profitability were limited. So I decided on a compromise of a restaurant and a meat market under the same roof.

The meat market has paid my bills some months, particularly with the financial downturn that hit us hard in

2008. I currently need four full-time butchers to make the shop work, so we're definitely keeping busy.

On my father's side of the family, there are several farmers who immigrated from Scotland in the 1860s. They raised citrus, avocado, and grapes in the central valley and Southern California. My cousin, Jeanne McCormack currently supplies Cafe Rouge with lamb and goats and is a third generation rancher in Northern California.

GOAT GRATIN

This casserole is based loosely on the French home-cooking standard, le miroton. *If you fear goatiness, please turn the page. This dish celebrates the sweet carnality of the goat with abandon.*

3 pounds boneless goat shoulder, cubed
½ quart goat's milk
1 pound gold potatoes, sliced ½ inch thick
Salt and pepper
¼ tablespoon extra-virgin olive oil
2½ pounds yellow onions, sliced thin
1 tablespoon chopped garlic

1 small bunch parsley, chopped
1 small bunch thyme, chopped
¼ cup white wine
3 cups bread crumbs or 2 cups panko
Capricious cheese or any dry goat cheese
   you like, grated

Soak goat meat in goat's milk overnight in fridge. Slice meat thin, reserving milk. Soak potatoes in goat's milk, aside from the goat, for 1 hour. Pat goat dry, season with salt and pepper to taste, and then brown meat in a large sauté pan in the olive oil. Remove meat. Sauté onions in same pan until slightly golden; add garlic, parsley, and thyme. Cook for 10 minutes and set aside. Deglaze the pan with wine.

Layer the bottom of a casserole dish with half the onion mixture. On top, place the goat and then the potatoes in a layer; finish with remaining onions. Almost fully cover top layer with goat's milk and deglazing liquid from pan. Mix bread crumbs with goat cheese and sprinkle over gratin.

Cover and cook in 350°F oven for 1½ hours; uncover and cook for another 20 minutes, until cheese and bread crumbs are toasted and liquids are bubbling.

Serves 6 to 8

MEXICAN RED POZOLE

This soup can be as spicy or as mild as you choose to make it. The pork hocks add a terrific flavor and the chiles are incomparable—your search for them might lead you to a great Mexican grocer. This recipe came to me from my sous chef, Julian Martinez, who has been making pozole for years.

Pork Hocks
4 to 6 pork hocks, to yield about 1 cup cooked meat
½ onion stuck with 4 cloves
4 cloves garlic
½ teaspoon peppercorns
1 tablespoon dried oregano
1 tablespoon kosher salt

Hominy
1 pound ready-to-cook pozole hominy
2 cups chicken stock
1 onion, cut in half (both halves are for the mirepoix)
3 celery stalks
2 carrots

3 dried New Mexican chiles
3 dried ancho chiles
2 dried guajillo chiles
½ onion, diced
3 cloves garlic, diced
½ teaspoon peppercorns
1 tablespoon dried oregano
1 teaspoon ground cumin
1 to 2 tablespoons olive or grapeseed oil
1 cup chicken stock

Garnishes (optional): tortilla chips, shredded cabbage, finely diced onion, thinly sliced radishes, wedges of lime, diced avocado, dried oregano, chopped cilantro, sour cream or yogurt

In a large pot, combine pork hocks, onion with cloves, garlic cloves, peppercorns, oregano, salt, and enough water to cover the ingredients. Bring to a boil, reduce heat to low, and simmer for 2 hours, or until meat is very tender. Strain off foam and fat every once in a while, and add water to cover if necessary. Remove meat and reserve 2 cups of the pork broth.

Meanwhile, in another pot, add the hominy, stock, onion halves, celery, and carrots. Bring to a boil, reduce heat to low, and simmer for at least 1 hour.

While the pork hocks and hominy are cooking, take the dried chiles, remove the stems, and soak them in some of the liquid from the pork hocks.

Sauté the diced onion, diced garlic, peppercorns, oregano, and cumin in oil until the onions are translucent and golden.

When the dried chiles are soft, put chiles and the sautéed onion mixture in a blender with enough pork liquid to cover. Blend until thin, and then strain the liquid. Reserve the strained solids for use as a garnish with the pozole. Reserve the strained chili liquid to add to the pozole.

Remove the meat from the bones and cut into small pieces: you should have about a cup of meat. Remove the vegetables from the hominy. Add meat to the pot of hominy, along with 3 to 4 cups of liquid: the reserved chili liquid (about a cup), 2 cups of pork broth, and the remaining cup of chicken broth. Bring to a boil over medium heat, reduce heat to low, cover, and simmer for 30 minutes, or until meat and hominy are very tender. Serve with your choice of garnishes.

Serves 6

TOM MYLAN
THE MEAT HOOK, NY

The canon of Tom Mylan mostly begins in his years at Marlow & Sons, where he helped open a shop, edit their food journal, Diner, and finally, create Marlow & Daughters, the first butcher shop in contemporary New York environs to buy only whole animals sourced locally. When we spoke, his new shop, The Meat Hook, was still partly conceptual and under construction. I met one of Marlow's owners, Mark Firth, at a party and expected him to bristle a bit at the mention of Tom, who had just left. Mark leaned in and shared the story of when Tom became a butcher. He was pushed downstream in a basket, only to land at the reedy shores of Fleisher's Grass Fed & Organic Meats to sleep upon a couch and learn upon a block. Mark knew there is no owning Tom, because the story of his becoming is the story of transcendence. A skill becomes a zeitgeist and a butcher becomes a prophet.

The first time I met Josh Applestone from Fleisher's, I thought, *I wish I was man enough to do this.* Lifting and throwing around heavy carcasses and cutting stuff with super-sharp and dangerous knives. There's a swagger and bravado and aura of cool that comes off of that. Women have always been hot for the butcher. If you talk to any old-school butcher, they all have stories about women giving them their number or whispering stuff in their ear.

I started training as a butcher at Fleisher's three years later. After six weeks, I had the bare minimum of knowledge and almost no skills whatsoever. That began the home-school era of my learning, I watched a lot of YouTube videos, bought a lot of DVDs shot on camcorders by weird guys in the Midwest that ran butchering lockers, that sort of thing. After six months I was a passable butcher.

Josh was really evangelical about restaurants buying whole animals. He ultimately convinced the Marlow group to be the guinea pigs. We were the first restaurant group to just jump into the deep end. A year ago there was no whole animal butcher shop in the city and now there's three. Granted, I opened two of them. There's Marlow & Daughters, the Meat Hook, and Dickson's. It definitely started in restaurants. Honestly, I'm kind of not that interested in the "who did what first" kind of game. Anybody with any sort of intelligence and vision could see it coming. We are teaching ourselves to do shit the way they did it eighty years ago. Our meat basically goes from the farm to the slaughterhouse, onto a truck, and to us.

Obviously one-hundred percent of our customers are coming in because we have really good meat and it's local and they are willing to pay more for better quality. But fifty percent of those people really want the whole story and when they buy a big steak they want to be able to share the farm it came from and how many months old it was when it got killed and what the breed is and how long it hung for. That's the draw. All meat has a story, it's just that our story is really awesome, and industrial meat's story is gross and freaky—it makes animals do things they're not designed to do, eat things they shouldn't eat, grow faster than they should grow. The end result is seldom positive.

Some shops are almost poisonously alpha and testosterone. As far as our shop, we are definitely dudes but we're not creepy. Quite honestly, half the people we've trained or have apprenticed with us are women. It takes a very particular person to be a good butcher. You definitely have to have a really well-developed sense of humor. Your heart has to be in the right place and it's rare to find those people anyway. It's so fashionable right now to become a butcher that we are bombarded with a lot of flighty idiots. You have to be smart, in a very particular way. Not like Asperger's smart, you have to be "intelligently" intelligent.

SHEPHERD'S PIE

Shepherd's Pie is one of the best things you can make to get the most out of your meat dollar, as well as being one of the most satisfying of all comfort foods. This recipe livens up the typical preparation by using lamb as well as beef, and adding a dense curry to the mix.

3 red potatoes, peeled and quartered
1 small yellow onion, diced
1 large carrot, peeled and chopped
5 cloves garlic, finely minced
½ pound ground lamb
½ pound ground beef
1 cup fresh or frozen peas
1/4 cup very good quality curry powder
1 beaten egg
½ bunch of chives, finely chopped
½ cup sour cream
Salt and pepper to taste

Preheat the oven to 375°F. In a pot, cover the potatoes in salted water, bring to a boil, and then simmer until very soft.

While potatoes are boiling, sauté onions, carrot, and garlic until soft; set aside. Using the same pan, season meats with salt and pepper to taste, and cook until brown. Return onions, carrot, and garlic, and add peas and curry powder. Mix well and cook for 5 minutes on low heat to let the curry flavor the meat.

Drain liquid from cooked potatoes and add egg, chives, and sour cream to the pot. Mash potatoes until smooth.

Spread meat and vegetables evenly in the bottom of a casserole dish. Spread potatoes on top of the meat, making sure the mix is even and looks like something you ate in elementary school.

Bake in oven for 20 to 30 minutes or until the top turns a light, crispy brown.

Serves 4

PRIME RIB

Prime rib impresses. It's big and expensive, so if you're going to do it, do it right! Make sure that your roast is properly seasoned: this recipe uses a brine injection to get salt into the heart of the loin. A meat thermometer takes the guesswork out. Leftovers are delicious in sandwiches the next day.

¾ cup salt for brine
2 cups warm water
1 extra-large brine-injecting needle
5-bone rib loin, chine bone off
¼ cup kosher salt
¼ cup coarsely ground black pepper

Start this process at least two days before you intend to roast the meat: mix the salt with the water and whisk until it is completely dissolved. Load the brine into an injector with a 6-inch spray needle. Stick the needle right into the middle of the meat from one end and gently press down on the plunger of the needle. Be patient and allow time for the beef to take the brine in as you very slowly remove the needle, allowing the brine to penetrate the whole length of this side of the loin. Repeat on the other side of the loin. Rub the exterior down completely with kosher salt and allow the loin to rest for two days so that the salt can equalize.

Remove loin from refrigerator a few hours before roasting to allow it to come to room temperature for the sake of even cooking. Put into a clean roasting pan and season with pepper.

Preheat oven to 450°F and roast for 25 minutes. Lower the temperature to 225°F and roast until the center reads 110°F with meat thermometer, about three hours. Remove from oven and let rest for 20 minutes before slicing. You can serve with Yorkshire pudding, roasted carrots, and a salad.

Serves 10 to 12

BUFFALO WINGS

Buffalo wings must be really hard to do well, because there are so many mediocre ones out there. The key is Frank's RedHot. It is essential: substitute other hot sauces at your peril.

Dipping Sauce
1 cup mayonnaise
1 cup plain yogurt
1 cup crumbled blue cheese
1 cup finely chopped fresh herbs (thyme, parsley, and rosemary)
5 cloves garlic, pressed
1 tablespoon black pepper
Juice of ½ lemon
Salt

1½ cups flour
½ cup cornstarch
2 tablespoons salt
1 tablespoon finely ground black pepper
½ gallon vegetable oil
4 pounds chicken wings
2 cups Frank's RedHot cayenne pepper sauce
2 cups clarified butter

Combine all of the ingredients for the dipping sauce, adding salt to taste, and mix them well so their flavors start to marry. Set aside.

Combine flour, cornstarch, salt and pepper. Heat oil in a heavy Dutch oven or home fryer. Use a clip-on thermometer to monitor your oil temperature. You can start frying when oil is 370°F.

Coat the wings in the flour mixture. Deep-fry wings in small batches and remove to paper towels to drain.

In a large metal bowl, combine the clarified butter and hot sauce. Add wings and toss, and serve with the dipping sauce. Go Raiders!

Serves 4

DEBONING A CHICKEN

Deboning a chicken is the very first **BUTCHERY** lesson. And it is one that every home cook should have under his or her belt. **MASTERING** this skill can be the difference between someone who is just **WINGING** it in the kitchen and someone whose culinary creations are worth preening over. Practically, **BONELESS** chicken on the grill or cooked under a brick has less chance of drying out, since the thickness is more consistent. Besides, there is no finer sight than a home cook dispatching a poultry **CARCASS** with grace.

How to debone a chicken. **[1]** Cut along both sides of the backbone from the "Pope's nose" to the neck. Cut out the backbone at the base. **[2]** Open up the bird, applying some pressure to the sides to flatten the bones. **[3]** Find the bottom of the rib cage on one side and cut behind it to release it from the flesh. Pull back from the bottom of the rib cage to remove it from the breast meat. **[4]** Make an incision along the leg bones. **[5]** Begin pulling the end of the leg bone out and clean meat off it with your boning knife. **[6]** After removal of the leg bones and rib cage, you have one piece that looks like this. **[7]** Make a cut at the base of the wing, removing the bone at the joint. Clean meat off the bone to the first joint and then remove the rest of the wing entirely. **[8]** Repeat on the other side.

(1)

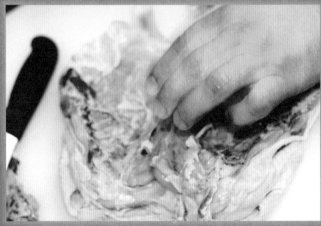

(2)

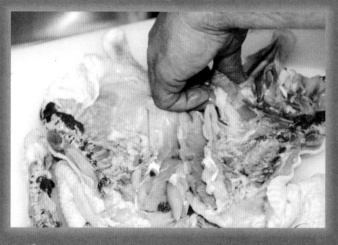

(3)

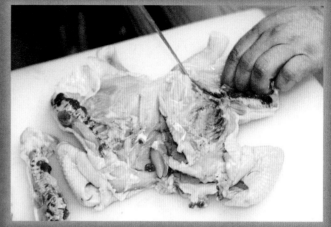

(4)

(5)

(6)

(7)

(8)

ERIKA NAKAMURA
AMELIA POSADA
LINDY AND GRUNDY'S, CA

Amelia and Erika just got married and gave birth to a bouncing baby butcher shop, just as full of their primal aspirations as any firstborn. They apprenticed under Josh Applestone and their shop is a sister store to Fleisher's in Los Angeles, a food culture more associated with starlets pushing food around a plate than with farm-specific chuck roast. Collectively, they have worked in sculpture, event planning, education, fine dining, and media. Every ounce of that history colors their counter.

Amelia: You need to try her sausage!

Erika: It's cool, it's a kimchi pork sausage. It's spicy.

Amelia: *Muy* spicy.

Erika: I was born and raised in Japan, so I have these kinds of Asian tastes, I can't help it.

Amelia: And I'm like, can't we just make a taco sausage and call it a day?

Erika: It started out with me just wanting to pursue butchering as a career, and opening a shop seemed like the logical next step.

Amelia: I was a vegetarian for basically my entire life. I never had a hamburger until a couple of months ago. And now I'm living it, breaking down lambs, taking their tongues out. Before this, I was doing the flowers for the St. Regis. I'd say out of all the things I've done in my life, this is what I'm most proud of. And I think everyone was kind of like . . . *You? With the red lipstick?* But I love it.

Erika: I just get this exhilarating feeling from it. As a sculptor, I always had an intimate connection with the materials I was using, wood or metal or plastic. Meat has that same quality for me, whether it's the fleshier, moist quality, or the fat. I just think I have some sort of romantic relationship to it.

Amelia: She was having an affair.

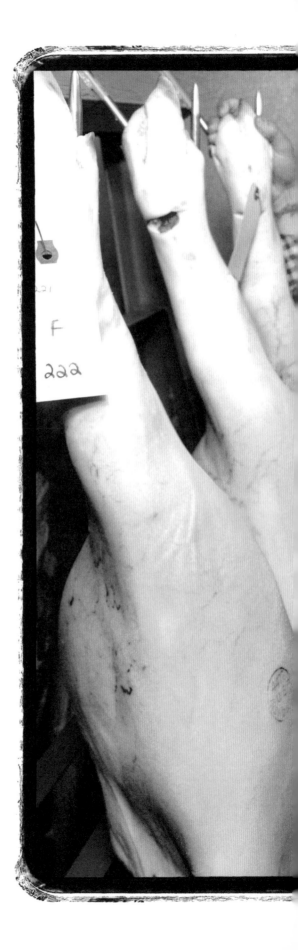

Amelia: We want to change the way people buy and think about meat in L.A. It's so important. People can choose to be blind or they can choose to treat the earth and animals the way they should be treated. It's a responsibility we all have as a society to the environment and to our community.

Erika: It's like my mother, who has been my harshest critic in the whole process and also my biggest supporter, and she's totally that stereotype of a middle-aged woman who shops at Costco for all of her stuff. But as I talk to her about this stuff, she shops at Fleisher's now. If I can get my mom to do that, then the possibilities are endless.

Amelia: When we graduated from our Fleisher's apprenticeship, we got to go to the Butcher Blackout. Basically, we got hazed. By a bunch of butchers! Josh Applestone and Tom Mylan started it after Tom did his apprenticeship. It's all this rowdy eating and drinking, which leads up to arm wrestling. We barely made it out alive.

Erika: It's true. I puked once and kept going.

Amelia: It began at Fleisher's and then we took a van to the Meat Hook in Brooklyn.

Erika: It's like a frat house inside of a fifteen-person van, I'm not kidding.

Amelia: We really want to bring it out to California. Maybe we'll start our own thing! It'll be like, the Ladies' Butcher Blackout. We'll have a mani-pedi sess . . .

Erika: No, no!

Amelia: . . . and pillow fights!

GINGER GARLIC GLAZED PORK

This pork is like candy. It is adapted from Chinese char sui *pork, which literally means "fork burn," referring to the traditional way of cooking pork on a fork over a fire. You will not be able to stop eating it!*

½ cup coarse sea salt
2½ cups light brown sugar
2 pounds boneless pork shoulder (butt)

1 tablespooon minced garlic
1 tablespoon minced ginger

Combine salt and sugar in a bowl and mix well. Place the roast in a suitable-size container and dry rub with the garlic and ginger. Next, thoroughly rub in the sugar/salt mixture. Transfer the roast to a large sealable plastic bag. Allow the rubbed meat to cure for 48 hours in the refrigerator. Turn the bag every 12 hours or so to insure that all of the meat's surface area is well coated.

Preheat your oven to 365°F. Place the roast in the center of a roasting pan and cover it with a tent of foil. Roast for approximately one hour, until internal temperature reaches 150°F. The exterior should be crisp; the interior should be pink and supple. Pull the roast out of the oven and allow it to rest for 20 minutes before cutting. This allows all of its interior juices to be redistributed, so the roast will not lose any of its moisture and tenderness. Serve hot or cold, thinly sliced on a platter, as a ramen garnish, or as accompaniment.

Serves 6

DIRTY DUCK RICE

You will make this rice dish over and over again. You will play with it, tweak it, and perfect it to your taste!

1½ cups short-grain white rice
1 tablespoon grapeseed oil (or vegetable or olive oil)
5 black peppercorns
¼ medium onion, sliced thin
1 duck breast, 1 to 2 pounds, cut into ¾-inch cubes
Salt and pepper
1 cup enoki, oyster, or shiitake mushrooms
½ can julienned bamboo shoots
2 cloves garlic, minced
¼ cup mirin (sweetened Japanese cooking wine)
¼ cup sake
½ cup chicken stock
1½ tablespoons low-sodium soy sauce
Thinly sliced green onions or shredded nori (dried seaweed) as garnish (optional)

In a clean pot (with tight-fitting lid),* gently wash rice with cold water. Drain.

Heat oil and peppercorns in a deep pan over medium flame. Add onions and let sweat. Lightly dust cubed pieces of duck with salt and pepper to taste. Add duck to pan and sear until there is a change in color. Lower heat and add mushrooms, bamboo shoots, and garlic. Toss to combine, deglaze with mirin and sake, bring to a quick boil, and turn off the heat.

In the rice pot, combine chicken stock, soy sauce, ½ cup water, and duck-mushroom mixture; stir. There should be just 1¾ cup liquid: not enough, and the rice will turn out hard; too much, and the rice will be soft and bloated.

Cover and turn heat up high. Bring mixture to boil and immediately turn down to low/simmer. DO NOT lift the lid at any point of this cooking process! Cook for 15 minutes, then turn heat off. Remove lid and allow to rest for 5 to 10 minutes. This insures that the grains of rice will hold their shape. (If your rice seems too wet, add 3 layers of paper towels to top of pot and cover quickly. This will help absorb excess moisture while rice sits.) Using a wooden spoon/spatula, gently mix the rice in a folding motion, working your way from the outside in. Serve with a garnish of thinly sliced green onions or shredded pieces of nori (dried seaweed).

Serves 4

* If you have a rice cooker (preferred method), simply wash rice until it turns clear, and drain the rice of any extra moisture. Combine ingredients in rice cooker, secure the lid, and follow regular cooking instructions.

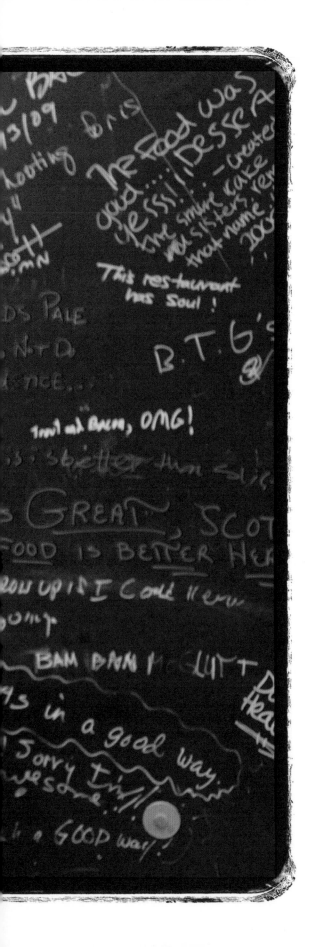

SCOTT PAMPUCH
CORNER TABLE RESTAURANT, MN

Scott is a serious wisenheimer, as my mom would say. Cooks are generally funny and vulgar but Corner Table's kitchen is like a Benny Hill episode on fast-forward. The corner table is actually in the kitchen, and for $125, you will be fed until you beg for mercy, and sign the chalkboard, pictured here, with your impressions. I can only imagine this would be a very silly night. The ribaldry isn't the only thing at a fever pitch. Scott is working on creating his own food system, with all the intensity, playfulness and vision of a kid building a fort. There are farm dinners, voracious sourcing, and classes. Some of his customers have even formed relationships with his farmers for their home cooking. Raise the flag high!

I don't feel like we're a chef-driven restaurant anymore. We're a farm-driven restaurant. I write menus based upon what the farmers give me. There are probably seventy farms we've used over the last five years. I grew up where a lot of these farms are, southern Minnesota. It was a given that I was going to buy from them. I know people that claim to be a local restaurant, and they don't buy their eggs locally, because they think it's too expensive. Well, then you're not really a local restaurant; you're just another restaurant who uses that as a marketing concept.

I didn't start cooking until I was twenty-seven. I sold hotel and convention space. The banquet stuff at the hotel was pretty cool and they let me play in the kitchen. At a certain point, I was spending more time in the kitchen than anyplace else. I got fired.

At Minneapolis Community and Technical School I ended up getting a really good cooking instructor and I was like, *I'm starting the game late. Can you give me any more than the textbook?* He turned me into his sous chef for the program.

I came out of school and worked for Modern Café, here in town. I heard that the chef hated culinary students. I got a little ballsy in the interview and dared him into giving me a start. *If you like me, you don't have to interview anymore.*

If I'm terrible, you can still say that culinary students suck.

The first day, he stood over my shoulder and eyeballed me the whole time. I did breakfast, lunch, and dinner for him for a year. One day, I told the owner he should fire his chef. He was like, *Well, do you know anyone better?* We were in the middle of service, so it's not like he could kick me out on the spot. He promoted me.

I got to the point where I wanted to start my own thing. This building used to be a little mom and pop Italian place. I joke it was a mob deal. The owner and I had breakfast. We didn't talk business at all. The bill came, and he wrote a number on the back of it—I'm assuming it's rent. He slid it to me, and then I slid it back to him with a different number, and then he slid it back to me, and that was it. We shook hands and he gave me the keys.

The point of the Tour de Farm dinners is to really educate people. I think everybody talks about knowing where their food comes from, and people are in CSAs, which they're all proud of, but a lot of people are still missing the boat. They don't understand how much work went into it. When they talk about farms they think of production, a staff of forty-five people. But the guy I sit and shoot the shit with every Thursday is the guy who is out there feeding the hogs, doing everything.

You're not asking someone to eat differently; you're asking somebody to change their views. And that's the most difficult thing to ask anybody to do.

RUSTIC HAM

I love a country ham for Sunday supper. The curing requires a little forethought, which makes it all the more rewarding. The sweetness in the brine makes this succulently satisfying, and perfect fodder for a little red-eye gravy, if you add some coffee.

12- to 18-pound ham, bone in, skin on

Brine
1½ cups kosher salt
1 cup brown sugar, tightly packed
1 cup maple syrup

6 teaspoons pink salt *
8 cloves garlic, crushed and skin removed
1 tablespoon black peppercorns
5 whole dried bay leaves
8 to 10 sprigs fresh thyme

Stir all brine ingredients together until dissolved. This brine can be multiplied or reduced, depending on ham size. Add the ham to the cold brine, and lay a heavy plate on top of the floating meat to keep it submerged. Cure the ham at the rate of 2 pounds per day (If you make a smaller roast and it cures less than 3 days, you can omit the pink salt).

Rinse off the ham and pat dry with a towel. Refrigerate the ham for one day to dry the skin and get it ready for roasting or smoking. Slow-roast for approximately 4 to 6 hours at 275°F, to internal temperature of about 155°F.

Serves 10

* Curing salt. Necessary to inhibit growth of bacteria. Use and store with caution. See page 288.

BARBECUE BRISKET

This is a crowd pleaser: double it or triple it and feed your neighborhood.

4 tablespoons extra-virgin olive oil
4 to 5 pounds beef brisket, boneless
1½ teaspoons salt
1 teaspoon black pepper
2 tablespoons smoked paprika
1 medium onion, finely chopped
1 medium carrot, finely chopped
½ celery rib, finely chopped
2 cups red wine
3 apples, cored and cut into bite-size pieces
2 cinnamon sticks
Thyme sprigs
1 fresh bay leaf (or 2 dried)
2 cups beef stock, plus additional if needed

Sauce
Braising vegetables and liquid
6 ounces whole tomato
½ cup brown sugar
1 teaspoon smoked paprika

Heat 2 tablespoons oil in a heavy, wide, ovenproof 6-quart pot over moderately high heat until hot but not smoking. While oil is heating, pat brisket dry and season with salt, pepper, and smoked paprika. Brown beef on all sides, about 20 minutes total, and transfer with tongs to a bowl. Pour off fat from pot, then add remaining oil and cook onion, carrot, and celery over moderately low heat, stirring occasionally, until softened, about 10 minutes.

Preheat oven to 300°F. Stir vegetables, then add wine and apples; scrape up any brown bits. Increase heat to high and boil until liquid is reduced by half, about 10 minutes. Return beef (with any juices) to pot, and add cinnamon sticks, fresh thyme to taste, bay, and stock. Bring to a simmer, then braise, covered, in middle of oven until very tender, about 4 to 5 hours. Once beef has cooled off, take two forks and shred all meat.

For the sauce, remove vegetables, apples, and juices, and place in a blender. Add rest of sauce ingredients and process to a thick puree. Add sauce back to the shredded meat. Bring to a simmer for an additional 30 minutes. Use additional beef stock to adjust consistency to taste.

Serves 8 to 10

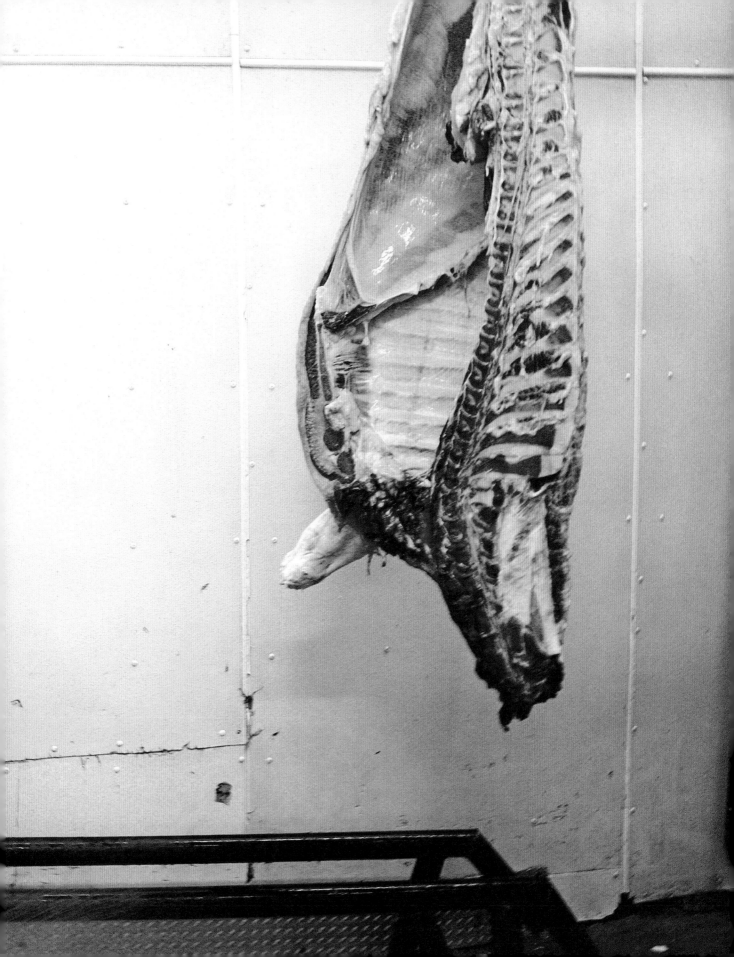

MIKE PHILLIPS

CRAFTSMAN RESTAURANT, MN

Mike doesn't own Craftsman, which makes his work all the more extraordinary. As the chef he has helped establish Tour de Farm dinners with Scott Pampuch aided in developing the city's local food initiatives and created a farm-direct buying program to rival any I have seen. It doesn't seem to be about bravado or profit, at all. Upstairs at Craftsman is the kitchen, but downstairs is Mike's haven, his cured meat workshop where he experiments and teaches others. His Midwestern humility threatened to belie his talents, but the truth is in the salumi. When he started slicing, I thought, "So he does know how to brag."

I dice the fat for salumi in the walk-in cooler because I don't have any refrigeration out here and if I take too much time it will smear and then I've got trouble. So when I'm prepping I have to run back and forth from the walk-in. I've only had one or two bad batches in all my years of doing this.

Nitrates have a horrible rap. One study out there was conclusive and it was about eating burnt bacon every day. Celery powder? Come on! You find more traces in a stick of celery than you do in a cured product. It's such a farce, especially from the natural foods world. There's no difference in flavor.

I started curing hams ten years ago when I saw a picture of Paul Bertolli surrounded with all of his meat. Then I started reading and the pigs were from Iowa and Minnesota. I thought, *Wait a minute, those are my pigs! Why don't we keep them here?*

One of the places I get pigs from is Hidden Streams Farm, which has formed a little cooperative of five or six other farms that have different kinds of produce like milk cheese, vegetables. It gives people more choices and it saves costs. On the menu right now we have venison, lamb, pork, duck, rabbit, and trout—all raised within a hundred and fifty miles. We bought eleven lambs and we knocked them all down in one day. Everything gets butchered and then if we need to freeze it, we can. That works best for the farmer and it's efficient for us.

The meat industry in the US just sells water. It's interesting to visit bigger plants because you really see how the business works. If you buy a tumbler to marinate, for instance, it speeds up the process, and then you can sell that ham before the bill on the meat is due. Not like in my kitchen, where everything is done by hand.

I have so many people asking me to buy salami but I can't resell from the restaurant. I want some regional identity for this area and I think cured meats would help. Minneapolis hasn't had the best food reputation.

I have a notebook with every recipe I've ever done. You can check it out. There's just so much mistrust in the food world. Everybody's so secretive; I couldn't get anyone to teach me how to cure meats. People spend so much money figuring out how to make stuff, they get greedy about their market. It would be nice if we could all learn from each other.

> **"I STARTED CURING HAMS TEN YEARS AGO WHEN I SAW A PICTURE OF PAUL BERTOLLI SURROUNDED WITH ALL OF HIS MEAT."**

MIXED GRILL OF LAMB

WITH CHICKPEA STEW

This dish is in the spirit of a feast. A resplendent, King Henry VIII-style feast with grog wine and candlelit, table-bending, ribald abundance. In the spirit of butchering a whole animal, the dish makes a place for almost every part of the lamb. While Henry may have thrown a royal tantrum if tongue or kidney was missing, you are king of your own castle, so cook what you can source and what your guests can eat. Each element has its own yield (in parentheses), if served alone; but when you grill all the elements and assemble the stew, you will serve 10 to 15 people, depending on how many King Henry-size appetites are at the table.

1 rack of lamb, cut into rib chops
  (yields 4 or 5 servings)
1 lamb heart (yields 2 servings)
1 lamb liver (yields 2 servings)
2 lamb kidneys (yields 2 servings)

Marinade
12 cups olive oil
2 teaspoons salt
2 teaspoons pepper
2 sprigs rosemary
2 sprigs thyme
2 sprigs oregano
4 fresh bay leaves

Lamb Tongues (yields 6 servings)
1 carrot, chopped
1 onion, peeled and chopped
1 stalk celery, chopped
Sachet of herbs and spices: rosemary, thyme,
  allspice, nutmeg, black pepper, parsley, etc.
7 cups chicken stock
1 cup white wine
6 lamb tongues

Lamb Sausage (yields 8 servings)
3 pounds lamb trim (50:50 fat-to-lean ratio)
2 tablespoons harissa
⅔ cup chopped parsley
⅓ cup chopped onion
2 cloves garlic, minced
1 tablespoon ground coriander seed
1 teaspoon allspice
Salt
About 6 feet hog casings, 32 to 35 mm
  in diameter

Chickpea Stew (yields 4 servings)
1 carrot, ⅛-inch dice
1 onion, ⅛-inch dice
1 stalk celery, ⅛-inch dice
½ pound guanciale, diced
3 fresh bay leaves
2 cloves garlic, minced
2 cups canned whole tomatoes, chopped
2 quarts chickpeas, soaked overnight
1 gallon chicken stock
2 cups salumi ends from dry cured ham,
  salamis, pancetta, or coppa
Salt

In a bowl, combine the marinade ingredients. Marinate the rib chops in about half the marinade. Refrigerate until ready to grill. Cut away and discard the top of the heart, where the connective tissue, ventricles, and auricles are. Slice in 1-inch-thick pieces. Cut the liver into 1-inch-thick slices, discarding any connective tissue. Slice the kidneys in half lengthwise. Cut out and discard the middle connective tissue. Place the heart, liver, and kidney pieces in the remaining marinade. Refrigerate until ready to grill.

    Place all the tongue ingredients, except the tongues, in a large pot and bring to a boil. Add the tongues and reduce heat; simmer for 1½ to 2 hours, until the skin will peel off the tongues. Occasionally skim off any foam. Remove the tongues, cool, and peel. Refrigerate until ready to grill.

For the sausage, grind all the trim or use a food processor, keeping meat at 36°F or colder. Add rest of sausage ingredients and salt to taste. Stuff into hog casings. (See Sausage Basics, page 32.) Refrigerate until ready to grill.

For the chickpea stew, sweat the vegetables, guanciale, bay leaves, and garlic in a covered heavy-bottomed nonreactive pan on low heat. When the onions and the guanciale fat are translucent, add the rest of the ingredients and simmer until the chickpeas are done to your liking, about 1½ to 2 hours. After one hour, check every 15 minutes. Add a little salt early on and adjust to taste later as you cook. Add a little stock if your stew starts to dry out before the chickpeas are done.

The Mixed Grill: This is the combination of all of the marinated elements plus the sausage, grilled and served on the chickpea stew. Get the grill very hot, because you want to cook everything so it gets a nice sear but doesn't overcook, which will increase gaminess and toughness. Grill the chops to 140°F internal temperature. Grill the lamb tongues, kidneys, heart, and liver to medium rare. Cook the sausage all the way through. Let the meat rest for five minutes. Warm the chickpea stew and arrange mixed grill on top of it. Garnish with chopped flat-leaf parsley. This makes a beautiful family-style arrangement or sophisticated individual platings.

Serves 10 to 15

Lambs and goats have a long **HISTORY** of domestication and are straightforward in construction. Their flavor is **PRIMEVAL**, like **GRASS** and cliff faces and **SALTY** air.

SHOULDER

The rough-hewn shoulder is fatty and flavorful. It makes a lovely roast, netted up with neat heft. It has the perfect meat-fat ratio for stew. Shoulder chops are a grocery store perennial: round bone chops on the arm side and blade chops on the dorsal side. The foreshank is cut off the shoulder and is gorgeous whole or sliced into osso buco for a wet, braised comfort food. Add the neck to stock or soup, to leach out the meat and flavor from the bones. I have also had it boned and skewered. Cooked quickly on high heat, the neck meat is silky and sweet.

Cuts: square-cut shoulder (whole without arms or neck); bone-in or boneless roast, which can be divided into inside (rib roast) or outside (arms and outside the ribs); blade steaks or round bone steaks; foreshanks; neck, and stew meat

RACK

The ribs of the goat and the lamb become the rack. This is a restaurant favorite. I have met many a farmer who has lamented he could not breed a lamb with three racks and one leg. They are lovely frenched to expose the bone. A waitress friend of mine called these "meat circles with bone handles." Of all the meat on these heady beasts, I find it the least flavorful, though that may be part of why they are so popular. The rack can be roasted after a searing, but should be served with a good deal of pink.

Cuts: rack (hotel or split rack, chined or chine on, cap on or cap off, frenched or not), rib eye roll, and rib chops (frenched or not)

LOIN

The loin is a foppish muscle, elegant and hardly used. I favor loin chops over rib chops because they have more bone. The loin can be served as a roast, as can the tenderloin, which nestles into a T-bone or porterhouse (not usually distinguished in a lamb or goat, but a good butcher will separate them for you).

Loin chops should not be cooked through; they will be dry and livery-tasting. They should always have the titillation of a seared outer crust and a nearly raw pearl in the center. Cook them hot and fast, and interfere as little as possible with seasoning.

Cuts: Loin roast (saddle or split, bone-in or boneless), loin chops, tenderloin

LEG

Leg of lamb is a personal favorite. It is gamey and brutish, with its big bone, so clearly identified as a leg. I love the ceremony of it. It is a dish for only a crowded table; it must be seasoned and roasted and carved in convocation. It is religious in its metaphors, all sacrifice and spring, the whole mess of life. For a smaller set, you can roast or grill the muscles separately to medium rare, crusted with salt, pepper, olive oil, and fresh herbs.

The hindshank can be cooked on the leg, if you are serving it whole. If you are cutting leg steaks (grillable) or boning the leg, you can save the hindshank to braise along with the foreshank, as whole pieces or sliced into osso buco.

Cuts:: hindshank; leg roast (bone-in, boneless or semi-boneless); leg steak roasts, whole or divided into separate muscles (inside round, outside round, knuckle, sirloin, and eye of the round); kebab meat

BREAST

The breast, or belly, usually stays on the loin, but a good butcher will separate it for you. It is lovely roasted or cured into bacon. Remove the riblets, marinate in a spicy herbal marinade, and grill.

OFFAL

The head has cheeks and a tongue and brain. These articulated tidbits are all very small and you would probably want more than one animal's worth to make anything. Yet, coupled with the kidneys, heart, and liver, you have the makings of a rich pâté, which will imbue your spirit with the sweet fortitude of the lamb. The term "lamb's fries" is often used for the liver and other offal, including, in many countries, the testicles.

rack (hotel or split rack, chined or chine
    on, cap on or cap off, frenched or not)
rib eye roll
rib chops (frenched or not)

loin roast (saddle or split,
    bone-in or boneless)
loin chops
tenderloin

LOIN

LEG

hindshank
leg roasts (bone-in,
    boneless or semi-
    boneless)
leg steak roasts (whole
    or divided into
    separate muscles:
    inside round, outside
    round, knuckle,
    sirloin, and eye of
    round)
kebab meat

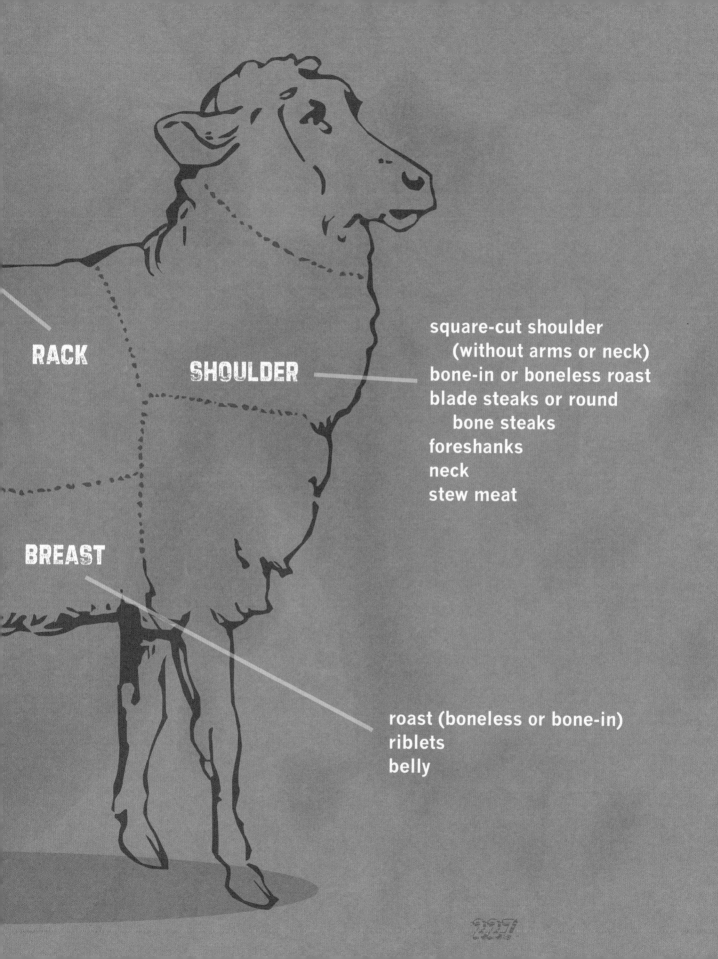

RACK

SHOULDER

BREAST

square-cut shoulder
   (without arms or neck)
bone-in or boneless roast
blade steaks or round
   bone steaks
foreshanks
neck
stew meat

roast (boneless or bone-in)
riblets
belly

It all started as a blog. I was butchering at the Greene Grape in Brooklyn and writing about meat, as a former vegetarian. When I moved to Portland, I made a business out of it. You have to figure out something to do for yourself or you're never going to get anywhere. The blog was a way to start talking about things I was learning. Nothing against vegetarians and I hate people who think I'm saying anything against them. Be a vegan, be vegetarian, but know that you're not actually changing any industry. You're just opting out, not actually supporting small farmers who treat their animals well.

When I got here, I developed BCN PDX, the next installment of my Bacon Gospel. BCN PDX is a party and tasting—five flights of bacon that I've made. Sometimes I just cover my costs, sometimes I make a tiny bit of money. I definitely know which flavors make people go crazy, like coffee and cocoa. People also really like the lighter flavors, like tea, five spice, and fruit. I have about sixty varieties and I'm constantly adding more.

I also do the Heritage Breed Supper Club, which are whole-animal dinners. When I first set up a relationship with the farmer, I visit and and have dinner and we talk. I meet the animals and I walk around and hear stories about their kids. I usually take friends. The farmers who are the most open are the ones I respond to. That's how I found Heritage Farms Northwest. They were my first farm. I got a couple red wattles from them. Apparently, it's been really good for them as well. They've been getting a lot of press. They're so good, and they graze on all these hazelnut orchards. It's such a rare thing because there's only 800-something in the world.

I became a vegetarian when I was twelve. It was my one piece of control. I had a pretty shitty life and it was the one thing I could do to be different. It totally pissed my parents off, but I had to cook for myself, so I learned.

When I lived in New York, there were so many queers in performance art, musicians, spoken-word artists. They have these big personalities, talking about their experience with sexuality. Sometimes you feel left out. You feel like you're not doing anything. But I am. I'm just very different, I'm working with food instead of my sexuality.

BERLIN REED
THE ETHICAL BUTCHER, OR

Berlin is just coming out of that magical phase of life where you begin to understand yourself but you are still malleable. He still has a million dreams and projects all dangling in front of him, like equally ripe pieces of juicy possibility. Potential— lush, heady potential.

It was a perfect day that we spent with the Deck family, in the model of the Ethical Butcher, whose post-vegetarian values mean he only sells meat that he buys direct from good farms. Berlin killed, eviscerated and plucked chickens that had spent their life on just such a farm. And in our post chicken-dinner promenade through the acreage, we came upon two calves, just hours old—and all full of blinky-eyed potential.

"BE A VEGAN, BE VEGETARIAN, BUT KNOW THAT YOU'RE NOT ACTUALLY CHANGING ANY INDUSTRY. YOU'RE JUST OPTING OUT, NOT ACTUALLY SUPPORTING SMALL FARMERS WHO TREAT THEIR ANIMALS WELL."

TEA AND PLUM ROASTED RACK OF LAMB

This recipe works with pork ribs or other favorite chutneys, like fig or raisin. The marinade and glaze is subtle and elegant, not overwhelming.

2 racks of lamb, 8 ribs per rack, trimmed and frenched
1 or 2 tablespoons kosher salt, or to taste
2 tablespoons Earl Grey tea leaves
1½ tablespoons five-spice powder *
⅓ cup plus 2 tablespoons plum chutney or jam
1 cup strongly brewed Earl Grey tea

Place lamb in a shallow container. Sprinkle salt, tea leaves, and five-spice powder onto lamb and rub in. For the best flavor, let this marinate for 4 to 12 hours, covered, in refrigerator.

Remove lamb from refrigerator and let come to room temperature. Preheat oven to 500°F. Pour ⅓ cup chutney on lamb and spread all over racks. Set racks bone side down on a baking sheet. In a small dish, mix brewed tea and remaining chutney, and set aside. Cook lamb in 500°F oven for 15 minutes. If rib bones begin to brown, cover with foil. Then immediately turn oven down to 325°F. Brush about a third of the tea-and-chutney glaze on racks. Return to oven and allow racks to roast for another 15 minutes. Check for desired temperature and continue roasting if needed.

rare—135°F
medium rare—140 to 150°F
medium—160°F
well done—165°F

Glaze again immediately after removing from oven. Allow racks to rest a few minutes before cutting. Cut between every second rib bone for 8 double chops.

Serves 6 to 8

* You can make your own five-spice powder by grinding 1 teaspoon sichuan/szechuan peppers, 1 teaspoon star anise, ½ teaspoon cinnamon or cassia bark, ½ teaspoon cloves, 1¼ teaspoon fennel seed, and ¼ teaspoon white pepper.

THAI COCONUT FRIED CHICKEN

Okay, wipe the vision of soggy coconut-covered fried something from your mind. This chicken is blessed with just a teasing of coconut and lime flavor.

1½ cans coconut milk
Juice and zest of 4 limes
1 tablespoons sriracha, or chili garlic paste
3 cloves garlic, sliced
Fresh kaffir
Fresh basil
Kosher salt and freshly ground black pepper
1 chicken, cut up, or 3 to 4 pounds chicken pieces
3 cups panko bread crumbs
Zest of 1 lime
¼ to ½ cup shredded coconut
2 cups shortening

Whisk coconut milk, lime juice, zest, and chili paste together, taste, and adjust acid and spice as needed. Add garlic, kaffir, basil, salt and pepper to taste, and mix well. Place chicken in large nonmetallic bowl or container. Pour in marinade, making sure each piece is completely covered. Cover and refrigerate for 12 to 24 hours.

Mix panko, zest, coconut, and salt and pepper to taste in shallow dish. Dredge chicken in mixture and let sit for at least 5 minutes. In two cast-iron or heavy pots with high sides to reduce splatter, heat shortening to 360°F over medium-high heat. Place chicken pieces, skin side down, into the two pots. Pieces should not crowd one another. Fry chicken until deep golden brown and turn. Lower heat to medium low and cook until done, 25 to 30 minutes. Remove pieces as they are done and drain on paper towels. Keep warm in the oven while the rest of the chicken finishes. Serve immediately.

Serves 4

BACON CURING THE ETHICAL BUTCHER WAY

The Ethical Butcher is a nonsmoker! I make my bacon by roasting a seasoned, cured pork belly. Here are 3 flavors from my catalog of nearly 60 flavors of local, heritage-breed bacon goodness.

2½ pounds heritage-breed pork belly, skinless and boneless, edges trimmed until uniform
Kosher salt
2 tablespoons ground cornmeal, for Jalisco version only

Backyard Memories Rub
1½ tablespoons kosher salt
½ cup crushed fresh raspberries or 2 tablespoons preserves
1 teaspoon french lavender
4 or 5 fresh sage leaves, chopped
¼ cup gin

Jalisco Rub
1½ tablespoons kosher salt
3 serrano chiles, sliced
1 jalepeño, sliced
1 dried guajillo, sliced
zest of 1 lime
1 teaspoon cumin
1 tablespoon chopped fresh cilantro
1 clove garlic, minced
¼ cup tequila

Python Rub
1½ tablespoons kosher salt
2 teaspoons crystallized ginger, sliced
½ teaspoon freshly grated ginger root
½ teaspoon ground ginger
2 tablespoons ground cacao
6 to 10 scotch bonnet peppers, stemmed and finely chopped (substitute habeñeros)
1 teaspoon shredded coconut

Rub entire pork belly with salt. In a bowl, mix rub ingredients of choice, except alcohol (for Backyard Memories and Jalisco). Rub belly with mixture until saturated. Place belly in a gallon-size sealable bag and add alcohol. Seal bag, squeezing out as much air as possible. Place on bottom shelf of fridge for 7 days. Turn slab over on day 3 or 4.

After one week, remove slab from bag. Preheat oven to 225°F. Place slab skin side up on baking sheet. For the Jalisco version, coat fat side of pork with 2 tablespoons ground cornmeal before roasting. Roast until internal temperature reaches 145°F. Remove from oven. Cool and drain slab on wire rack for 15 minutes. Place slab on plate and cover lightly with plastic wrap and place in fridge until completely cool; overnight is best. Bacon will keep for up to about 1 week.

Slice and cook bacon as desired. Can be used to make lardoons, strips, bacon bits, etc.

Serves 6 to 8

MAKIN' BACON

BACON is a pleasure so uncomplicated that there is no real rationale for resisting it. Bacon exists outside of shame, outside of consequence. **SMOKING** bacon at home is simple enough to be done with some regularity and yields dividends. If they should ever happen to meet up, the liquid smoke-flavored by-product from the grocery store will cower next to your **HOMEMADE** creation.

Ask your butcher to bone out a pork belly and leave the skin on. When you ask for one belly, you will be getting one side of a pig's belly, which can be up to ten pounds of meat. You can also ask for less. Three pounds is a nice chunk, enough to share some.

For the curing process, I prefer a dry rub, after which I let the belly sit for five to seven days in refrigeration. Below is a simple dry rub. Remember, this is called a rub, so be vigorous in its application. I encourage wild experimentation: add spice, heat, sweet, or tang. After curing in the dry rub, give the belly a good rinsing and let it dry in the fridge overnight before you smoke it. If you prefer pancetta, at this point, after rinsing you would skin it, roll it, tie it, and hang it out to dry. (See page 144.)

You can purchase a smoker for the next stage, or rig a homebrew contraption yourself pretty easily. If you create your own smoking device, use a roasting pan that you are no longer attached to. It should be large enough for your pork belly to lie stretched out, like Cleopatra. It should have a shelf in it that will separate the meat from the wood chips, like a roasting tray, a strainer, or chicken wire. The lid should fit tightly.

The wood shavings you use can be pre-bagged from a store or from any tree that grows something you find delicious or aromatic: almond, cherry, grapefruit, lilac, walnut. Look for hard wood and avoid sap. Soak the shavings in water for half an hour. Fill the bottom of your contraption with the shavings and turn the heat up high on the stove until the wood begins to smoke. Have a meat thermometer at the ready. I use the kind with a wire and remote reader, so I can keep the lid closed until it beeps. There is less chance of your kitchen smelling like bacon for days. Lay the belly on the shelf and close the lid. The temperature in this contraption should hover around 200°F. There will be smoke. Open a window, turn on a fan, and offer a generous waft to your neighbors. The bacon will be done when the internal temperature reaches 140°F. Let it cool in a civil manner, sitting on the stove. Or maybe in a turned-off oven, if you have a dog.

For one belly: ½ pound brown sugar; ⅓ pound salt; 2 teaspoons pink curing salt (see page 288); 1 teaspoon black pepper

JIM REICHARDT
LIBERTY DUCKS, CA

Jim discovered California cuisine as it was discovering itself, and came of culinary age with the luminaries of the food world. He has been the "duck man" ever since. His Liberty Duck is found on menus from Spago to French Laundry to Daniel. He was also on the vanguard of Slow Food as it planted roots in the US. Jim heads the Heritage Turkey Project, which encourages 4H kids to raise endangered breeds to promote biodiversity and learn niche marketing. These are things Jim knows a thing or two about.

I poach my eggs in duck fat. My kids thought it was normal to always have a couple gallons of duck fat in the fridge. I'm a fourth-generation duck farmer. I grew up with ducks. There were only two duck farms west of the Mississippi at that point. If our farm went under, we couldn't go down the road to work at another duck farm, so Dad wanted us to have something else. I was an architectural photographer for a while.

My family's duck was on the first menu at Chez Panisse; it was the only duck around. I started to hang out with some chefs and they wanted bigger, meatier birds, like they have in France. That wasn't available in the US. So I struck out on my own with birds bred to mature slower so they put on more weight in the breast.

My farm is a very simple operation. Food, water, and a little bit of warmth is all they need. I get day-old birds in the mail. They live for nine-and-a-half weeks. The normal commercial bird lives six weeks. At six weeks they stop gaining weight but we keep feeding because they get a more complete flavor. Regular birds are almost like veal. These guys have nice rich, red flavor.

The nice thing about ducks is that the old buildings work great. Current conventional chicken farming is down to like a quarter cent profit per pound. Those buildings have to be just the right temperature or they're losing money. Ducks aren't really in that world.

Slow Food USA decided to take on heritage turkeys to save breeds that were being eliminated because the commercial industry only uses the broad-breasted white. About seven years ago, Randi Seidner, one of our Slow Food co-leaders, got the idea to combine the heritage program with 4H and Future Farmers of America families. Slow Food bought the poults and the feed and the 4H kids raised them. The hope is that someone will take it on as a viable business. After two years we decided to start turning it over to the kids. We're letting them buy the feed, which leads to better farming.

We've been able to market all of the turkeys successfully before Thanksgiving. We do a community slaughter. There's the kill station and as soon as they've bled, you put them in a scalder, 140 degrees for ninety seconds. Then you put them in a picker, which pulls the feathers out with little rubber fingers. Then evisceration and chilling. We get first timers killing. There's not a big line to learn but people are willing. It's better than cleaning gizzards. For most everyone, the turkey slaughter is a good experience. Some people consider it part of their Thanksgiving tradition now.

DUCK LEG CONFIT

Duck confit is more french than smoking at the airport, more french than a pencil skirt at the grocery store. You should know how to make this because you never know when you might have to pass as un vrais francais.

4 duck legs
1 tablespoon sea salt
½ teaspoon ground black pepper
6 cloves garlic, crushed
1 shallot, peeled and sliced
6 sprigs fresh thyme
2 bay leaves, broken into halves
4 cups duck fat (olive oil may be substituted)

In a shallow dish, sprinkle-season the sides of the duck pieces with salt and pepper. Sprinkle the garlic, shallots, thyme, and bay leaves evenly over both sides of the duck. Arrange the duck, skin-side up, and cover and refrigerate for 1 to 2 days.

Preheat the oven to 225°F. Melt the duck fat gently in a saucepan. Brush or rinse the salt and seasonings off the duck and pat dry with paper towels. Arrange the duck in a single layer in a deep baking dish. Pour the melted fat over the duck legs so that they are completely covered. Place the duck in the oven and cook very slowly at a very low simmer—just an occasional bubble—2 to 3 hours. The duck is done when it is very tender, pulls away from the bone on the drumstick, and shrinks toward the thigh. Check the duck periodically so meat does not overcook and fall off the bone. The confit can be served immediately or cooled and stored covered in fat. It will hold up to 14 days in this condition, gaining flavor.

To serve later, bring to room temperature to soften the fat. Gently lift the legs out, scraping off excess fat. (The fat can be stored in the refrigerator and reused up to 3 times for making confit.) Heat a heavy-bottomed skillet over medium-high heat. Cook duck, skin side down, until skin is crisp, about 5 minutes. Turn heat down and cook the other side until heated through, about 5 minutes.

Serves 4

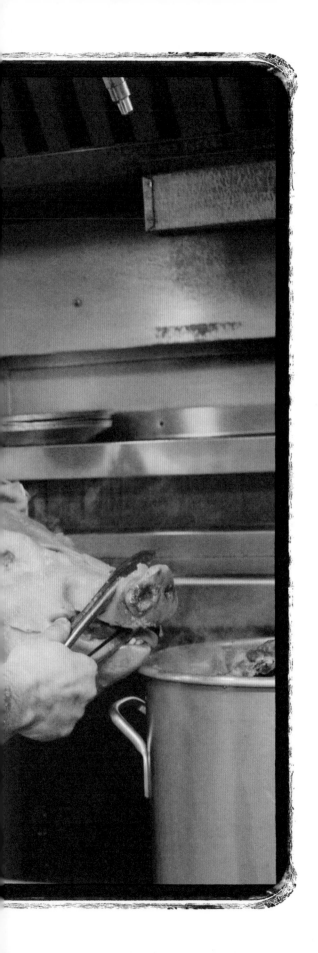

ARI ROSEN
SCOPA, CA

For my birthday this year, there was no question about where to eat. It was Scopa. On a hot Healdsburg evening, my friends and I grabbed the only outside table, and shared nearly everything on the menu. We shut it down, ending the meal with a visit from Ari, and the dainty digestifs and almond birthday cake he brought with him. I want nothing else from a restaurant. It is so familiar and yet it sparkles. Ari is like that, too. Maybe it's the unvarnished comfort of being terribly good-looking. Whatever it is, it's all over Scopa and his menu—genuine and generous. Like the very last bite of a birthday dinner, with your favorite people and a full belly.

I always dreamed about restaurants but I was on the psychology track in college, running a sleep laboratory on campus. I went to see my sister in Italy. She said, *Change your ticket and work here for a year.*

So I went to my favorite restaurant in Florence and said I would work for free. I got in the kitchen with Lorenzo Torini, who was insanely talented and intense. He was obsessed with El Bulli, geometric plating, intense technique but classic Italian influence. Italians don't like it when you go too far out of the box.

I got real good at Italian after Lorenzo got so frustrated with me, he went around the kitchen and wrote the Italian name for everything on notes and said, *You will know all of this by tomorrow.* I didn't have formal training so I had to learn culinary terms in Italian without knowing them in English. Then, even harder, I had to come back to America and try to be a credible cook.

One time I sent out a dish without sauce and he caught it. He pushed me up against a metal cabinet, took a frying pan and slammed it right next to my head and said, *I send out dishes, don't you ever send out a dish again.* My friend told me he did something like that here and he had to go to anger management courses.

Then I met Lucca Pecorini who is 100-percent Tuscanaccio, born and bred in the hills of Italy. That's where I first started dealing with whole animals, hogs from Franco Lecche, this short Sardinian with a barrel chest. Not too many restaurants in Italy buy whole animals, but people see pigs butchered, it's more a part of their culture. We were bootlegging it up with hooks hanging from the hood.

From Lorenzo, I got technique. From Lucca, I learned the poetry. Like, *In the war between Pisa and Florence, they cut off the salt so that's why there's no salt in Florentine bread.* Lucca must have thought I had way more experience than I did. He asked if I wanted to open a restaurant with him and two other chefs. I was twenty-four. The only people in the kitchen were the four of us. No one had specific dishes. It was like, *What dish are you doing tonight?* We spent sixteen hours a day on thirty covers. We only had a small number of plates, so we'd be waiting for people to finish their food and then we would run to the sink and wash them. It was a creative project. We weren't efficient at all and we worked from 7 am to 1 am, six days a week. We fought like dogs and we loved each other.

Family is super important to me, so that pushed me to go home. I was an ADD kid and my mom made me roll out pasta instead of giving me Ritalin. So we had pasta drying on the backs of chairs and chin-up bars. My parents were hippies, like *Little House on the Prairie* with floral shirts. At school we milked goats, cleaned the chicken coop, and once a year we slaughtered chickens. I went to horse camp at Mac Magruder's ranch and now I buy his hogs.

When I got back from Italy, I worked at Charlie Palmer's Dry Creek Kitchen for awhile. I was pining for Italy one night at a local bar and I met Dino. He was at a new restaurant called Santi and it sounded just right for me. He and I fed off of each other, whole animals galore, Bellwether Farms lambs, we had parties all the time. There's some tribal shit that goes on when you bring out a whole animal. It all comes down to that, for me, the celebration. There used to be feasts across the land! People are tradition hungry here.

I worked at Santi for three years. Dino and I would sit up all night, drinking grappa and playing *scopa* and talking about one day opening a restaurant together. Probably the day I signed the lease here, Dino called me and said, *I'm going to do a pizzeria in Geyserville, come join me.* At the time, I was really sad that we weren't doing it together but I think it's probably been better for our friendship.

No matter what, we stay open until 10 pm. You don't have to order a big entrée, it's like Sunday dining. We get a pig from Mac Magruder and then we've got four pork dishes on the menu. In Italy, we changed the menu every single day. It's getting harder to get the offal and the necks. Pretty soon it will be cheaper to get pork chops. Like, *Hey buddy, you only get two kidneys per animal. I've got to get top dollar.*

PORCHETTA

Porchetta is my favorite pork dish and this recipe adapts it for the home cook. Like most perfect dishes, there aren't more than 5 ingredients: pork, salt, garlic, rosemary, and sage. Though the ingredients are simple, it is labor intensive. Nevertheless, there is something incredibly festive about roasting a whole pig, especially when the final product has an irresistibly crispy exterior and a center that bursts with flavor and slow-roasted juiciness.

Ideally, porchetta should be roasted in a wood-burning oven to obtain its subtle smokiness, but it is equally delicious when cooked in an oven at home. Instead of using a whole pig, I use the center cut of half a pig to insure that it will fit. Even then, you need to cut the porchetta in half to get it in the oven.

15 to 20 cloves garlic
1 middle primal cut of pork, skin on (ask for a skin-on pork belly
  with the loin still attached to the belly) *
Kosher salt
1 cup finely chopped sage
½ cup finely chopped rosemary
Fennel seed, optional
Salt
Olive oil
Butcher twine or strong natural cooking string, free of plastics

The porchetta will work in a nonconvection oven, but a convection oven is recommended. Preheat to 500°F and turn on the convection fan. Finely chop the garlic in a food processor to yield about ½ cup of garlic paste.

Starting with the pork skin side down, roll it into a "Tootsie Roll," and check to make sure that the skin is not overlapping on the bottom. The two edges of pork skin should meet, creating a tunnel of pork without the bottom skin overlapping. You may need to cut away 1 to 2 inches of meat from one edge of the rectangle to make your perfect roll. Cut from the side opposite the loin so you don't lose any precious loin meat.

Be careful not to put any garlic, sage, or rosemary on the skin side of the pork, because it will burn during the skin-crisping phase. Sprinkle a thin layer of salt, about 3 tablespoons, evenly across the top of the pork. Massage the garlic paste into the meat also, spreading it evenly across the top. Then add the sage and rosemary, sprinkling throughout. Season with fennel seed to taste, if desired. There should be enough herbs covering the pork so that it looks herb-encrusted and no raw meat is visible from the top.

Tying the pork: Cut 15 to 20 two-feet-long strands of butcher twine or string. Taking one strand at a time, loop the string around the skin side of the pork and tie a knot securing the two sides together. You will need help to hold the pork roll closed while you tie. Work in tandem, moving from the top of the roll and working your way down, tying one loop every 2 inches.

When you are finished tying the pork, carefully roll it skin side up. Depending on your oven size, you may need to cut the roll in half. Place each roll on a flat roasting rack resting in its own roasting pan. Finally, rub the outside of the rolls with olive oil and give them a heavy sprinkling of salt to insure a delicious crunchy pork skin.

Crisping the skin: The key to a great porchetta is getting the pork skin nice and crisp. The idea is to blast it with high heat for close to 45 minutes, causing the skin to blister, harden, and turn golden in color. However, not every oven is made equal, so during the skin-crisping phase you will need to stay close at hand to check progress often. You will probably also need to flip the porchetta around once or twice to insure that the skin cooks evenly. (During the skin-crisping phase, a lot of fat is rendered and collected in the bottom of your roasting pan. It will cause smoke because of the high oven heat. Having a turkey baster on hand to remove the excess grease can help reduce the smoke. The smoke will subside after you turn down the oven.) You will recognize doneness by a caramelized golden color, blistering bubbles that form on top, and by tapping the skin to check that it is hard and crisp. As soon as the porchetta skin has achieved these 3 characteristics, turn heat down to 300°F and turn off the convection fan. If you don't have a convection oven, the skin-crisping phase will take longer, but it will still happen.

The porchetta will continue to cook for about another 1½ to 2½ hours, or until a meat thermometer reaches 140°F. Make sure to check the meat's temperature in a few different spots, because the ends of the roll will cook faster. After pulling the porchetta from the oven, let it rest for at least 20 to 30 minutes. The crisp skin will act as a natural insulator, holding some of its internal heat for up to a few hours before coming down to room temperature. Slice thin and serve. Porchetta is often served with salsa verde.

Serves 10 to 20

* Talk to your local butcher and preorder a skin-on pork belly with the loin still attached. Often this primal meat cut will come with the ribs still attached; remove or have the butcher remove the ribs from the loin/belly without separating the loin from the belly. You should end up with a flat rectangle of pork that has a raised cylinder of pork loin attached to one side of it.

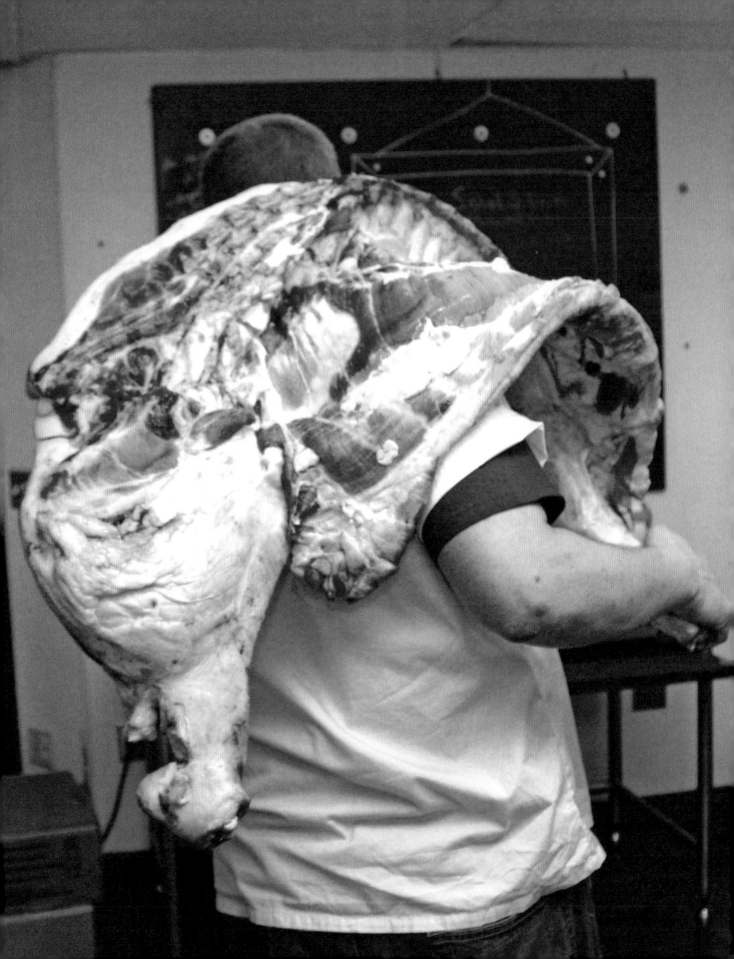

JOEL SALATIN

POLYFACE FARMS, VA

Joel has become the farmer-hero archetype in the real world drama to change the food system toward, as he puts it, "mob stocking herbivorous solar conversion lignified carbon sequestration fertilization" or "herbivores, perennials and movement." He also advocates freedom from regulation that hampers small producers. The depth of his commitment is not about revolution so much as stewardship. A covenant between God, Man, and Earth. It couldn't be more timely or timeless.

We believe we're just pilgrims and we're supposed to leave the earth better than we found it. It's just as inconsistent for a pro-lifer to stop off for a Happy Meal as it is for a tree-hugger to be for abortion. And both sides look at each other and say, *How can you reconcile those two?* They're equally inconsistent.

About half of our church community is into what we are doing. They're the home-schooling, grind-their-own-flour, raw-milk half. And then you have the Tyson chicken growers. This is big Tyson country.

People think our neighbors must lean on the fence and just fawn over what we're doing. But we're considered bio-terrorists around here. We don't vaccinate, so we're bringing in disease. We let our chickens run around here and commingle with redwing blackbirds, which are going to take diseases to their chicken houses. Oh, it's very serious. That same mentality permeates the USDA FDA, the food police in this country. And they consider me a Luddite and a threat to the greater system.

In the fifties and sixties people were enamored with white sugar and white bread and nobody was breast-feeding. That World War II generation, wonderful as it was, turned its back on everything that was noble about the agrarian economy and completely embraced the industrial economy.

My grandfather was a charter subscriber to Rodale's *Organic Gardening and Farming* magazine. Dad had a real conservation environmental ethic from his father. All the advice back then was to plant corn, build silos, graze the woods, and use chemical fertilizer, which was against dad's understanding of ecology and economics.

We had lost a farm in Venezuela. We essentially fled through the front doors as guerrillas came in the back in a junta in 1959. Dad saw the developing world as the new frontier, growing up in the age of exploration. It was his dream to farm there. We started over here when I was four years old. It was the most eroded, worn out, gullied, cheapest farm anywhere.

I always wanted to farm. I don't ever remember wanting to do anything else. But early on I wasn't sure I could just do farming, and I definitely had a flair for writing. I assumed I'd be a Woodward or Bernstein and uncover muck, write my bestseller and retire to the farm.

I got a part-time job at the local daily newspaper, did obituaries, police reports. I ate it up. When I got out of college they said, *We want you back as soon as you can*. I naturally got all the farm stories. A company that bought black walnuts came to Virginia and set up a buying station, so I went down to cover this new agricultural enterprise. You could pick up black walnuts and get paid for them, pretty amazing. It was a bumper year and they were inundated with hulls. The meat is one-third of the volume. They had to tow away the other two thirds. I asked if we could bring some home. They made the grass grow like magic. We said that we'd like to run an operation that did this. I gave my notice at the newspaper. Everybody in the world thought I was crazy. *You can't make money farming*.

The second year the nut company didn't come back and we were desperate for cash. We bought broiler chickens from a Mennonite family, pulled the old layer shelters out from the rafters and pastured poultry.

Direct sales is the only way to make any money as a small producer. A natural addition to the chickens was eggs, so we started with a little prototype egg mobile that I made on bicycle wheels. Then we had the idea of *piggerating* so we got a couple pigs to do the composting instead of having to turn it twice. People loved the pork. One thing led to another. You diversify to turn a hundred-dollar customer into a two-hundred-dollar customer.

Now my bride, Teresa, and I co-own T&E, a slaughterhouse in Harrisonburg. Some of the things that make good food pricier are the non-scalable government regulations that discriminate prejudicially against small producers. At our plant, we get the same stack of directives as a plant that does 40,000 beefs a week. We're paying eight times industry price just to get it into a package. Fifteen years ago, we got over fifty bucks a hide. Today it's five.

I wonder what it'll take for liberals, who have always trusted the government to take care of things, to realize that more regulations are not the answer. I speak to a lot of very liberal groups, environmentalists, foodies, and they just can't wrap their head around the FSIS actually doing something to harm local food.

The eternal optimist in me says, let it get bad. Maybe we'll reach the tipping point where everybody takes up their pitchforks and marches down to the capital. The problem is, for all of our growth, we're still only two-percent of the food system. Monsanto, Archer Daniels Midland, and Taco Bell are still way bigger. Five tractor-trailer loads a day, seven days a week, go into DC just carrying french fries.

We've got an incredibly food-illiterate culture. The religious right should be awestruck at biology and life and not looking at an arrogant manipulative paradigm of life. The creation has become worshipped much more than the Creator. And that's a shame.

OVEN-FRIED CHICKEN

This easy recipe is one of our all-time favorites. We serve it with mashed potatoes, gravy, and sweet corn for a great summer meal.

¼ cup butter	2 teaspoons salt
¼ cup lard	2 teaspoons paprika
1 egg, beaten	2 teaspoons pepper
3 tablespoons milk	1 chicken, around 4½ pounds, cut up
½ cup all-purpose flour	

Preheat oven to 425°F. Melt butter and lard in a 9 by 13-inch pan in hot oven. Mix egg and milk together in a bowl. Mix dry ingredients in a plastic bag. Dip chicken in milk/egg mixture, then shake in bag until coated. Place skin side down in melted butter/lard and bake for 25 minutes. Turn chicken and bake another 25 minutes, until crisp fried.

Serves 4

SHENANDOAH PON HAUS

American families, like communities around the world, have long gathered to harvest animals and share both labor and a feast. Scrapple, pon haus, and white pudding are variations on the theme of a hearty and nourishing home for the little bits left over in the butchering process. Traditionally made with scraps and offal, this recipe utilizes the pork butt.

4 pounds pork butt	Salt and pepper	2 cups cornmeal
1 tablespoon peppercorns	2 cups buckwheat flour	Butter
2 bay leaves	Fresh sage	Maple syrup

In a large pot, combine pork, 3½ quarts water, peppercorns, bay leaves, and salt and pepper to taste. Bring to a boil and lower heat. Baise until the pork falls apart, about 3 hours. Let the pork cool in the liquid. Remove the pork and grind.

Remove peppercorns and bay leaves from the braising liquid and reduce by half. Return the ground meat to the liquid.

Add buckwheat and sage to taste. Slowly stir in cornmeal, keeping a smooth consistency. Simmer until batterlike, stirring frequently.

Pour into loaf pans, let cool, and then refrigerate overnight.

Serve with breakfast by slicing and panfrying in butter. Great with a little fried sage and maple syrup.

Serves 10

FACTORY VS SUSTAINABLE

The economics of **FEEDING** people are complicated. Neither the **INDUSTRIAL** meat-packing industry nor **SMALL** farms that market directly to consumers were born fully grown; it has taken

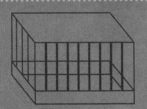

FACTORY FARM PIG

FERTILIZATION

Sows are artificially impregnated
PRO: Quick and cheap
CON: Lack of biodiversity

PREGNANCY

Pigs are held in metal crates with concrete floors
PRO: More pigs in less space
CON: Limited mobility can lead to trauma and distress

Piglets can be crushed by sows in tight quarters

NURSING & WEANING

Piglets nurse for 2 to 3 weeks; then weaned by week 4
PRO: Speeds production
CON: Piglets taken too early can exhibit anxious behavior, including biting at other pigs' tails.

Sow is immediately re-impregnated

Piglets' tails are "docked" (cut off) to prevent other pigs from biting them off

FATTENING

Pigs fatten on bonemeal, corn, soy, and other cheap feed
PRO: Pigs fatten faster
CON: Natural foraging tendencies and nutritional needs are ignored

Pigs are also fed antibiotics to avoid illness stemming from sub-par living conditions. But antibiotics can lead to the rise of resistant "superbugs"

SLAUGHTER

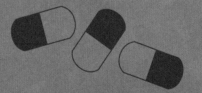

Pigs are slaughtered on-site at 6 months
PRO: Full vertical integration
CON: Huge numbers of pigs; little consumer oversight

Pigs are stunned, then hung up by their feet, and finally, cut and bled to death

SHIPMENT

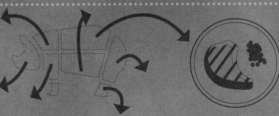

Pig is processed and shipped to various locations
PRO: Differing needs can be met simultaneously
CON: Fossil fuel consumption; spread of contamination

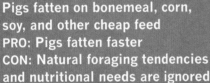

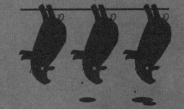

time for them to evolve to their present status.

I like this chart from my friends at **MEATPAPER** magazine because it shows the pig's **LIFE** in terms of a series of decisions made by farmers and butchers. A silent partner in both of these models is the **EATER**.

CHART DESIGN BY CHRIS YING & BRIAN McMULLEN

SUSTAINABLE PIG

FERTILIZATION

Sows are left with boars in the field

Sows are naturally impregnated
PRO: Genetic diversity
CON: Non-uniform animals; lack of control

PREGNANCY

Some producers hold their pregnant sows indoors in horse pens with "rub rails" that prevent piglets from being crushed.

Pregnant sow is often left in field to farrow (deliver).
PRO: Less stress on pregnant sow
CON: Piglets can sometimes be crushed

NURSING & WEANING

Piglets nurse indoors for 3 weeks, then go to the field; weaned at 2 months
PRO: Humane treatment
CON: More expensive

FATTENING

Antibiotics are not standard course

Pigs fatten on acorns, milk, and bread
PRO: Easier feed on pigs; environmentally friendly non–corn or soy feed
CON: More expensive

SLAUGHTER

Pigs are slaughtered from 6 months to two years at off-site slaughterhouses
PRO: Smaller number of pigs
CON: Pigs have to be transported to off-site locations

SHIPMENT

Pigs are often sold whole
PRO: Meat can be traced; less waste
CON: Fewer customers interested in buying whole hog

OLIVIA SARGEANT
FARM 255, GA

Farm 255 can be experienced as a restaurant, but that might be missing the point completely. There is a whole universe, a food cosmos orbiting around the dreamy downtown spot that is both unkempt and exquisitely art-directed. Jason Mann created a farm and a CSA and five of his friends opened a restaurant that bought the vegetables. They began a ranch that has meat enough for a CSA, Farm 255, and the newest addition, Farm Burger, which is a home for the vast quantities of ground meat that come from every beef carcass. Moonshine Meats is a new attempt by the Farm 255 crew at aggregating and distributing good meat, moving the community ever outward. There is also Farm cart, a sweet to-go caboose and a twinkly-lit stage for playing music until it is almost too late to ride your bicycle home. It is every bit as sweet as it sounds and after a day on their farm and a dinner full of its harvest, I felt like anything can be done. As long as you have six friends, lots of dirt, and twinkly lights.

No one had restaurant experience in a traditional sense when we started. It was definitely an adventurous step. It's all *chutzpah*, all *cojones*, all the time.

Self-teaching is incredibly valuable. My whole world was food. So, even though I had zero training, I was the opening head chef of our 140-seat restaurant. It was a ridiculous decision but I don't regret it, because it taught me how to be fearless.

We're going into our eighth season of Full Moon Farms. The CSA started with the farm and was the backbone of the restaurant—125 guaranteed customers right there. We started the meat CSA last year. We started the livestock program three years ago.

The first year and half was like a purchasing melee. It was pig's feet sticking out of people's cars, and driving to the Atlanta farmers' market every Saturday morning before service, a Volkswagen Golf full of vegetables, because none of the farmers would come to me.

We still have this element of compromise and decision

making that is the most fascinating part of our model. In a perfect biodynamic system of interdependencies, it only made sense to have animals that were harvested for the restaurant. All in the name of research and experimentation, which is our underlying ethic.

The livestock program is about to grow a good bit for Farm Burger. The beef are 100 percent grass fed. Jason, who runs the farms, feels strongly that a tenet of his practices is adaptability and flexibility. It's the same with the "locavore" argument and the whole-food movement: flexibility has to be a tenet, because it's a tenet of agriculture. At the basis of agriculture is the weather, so stability is not rampant. That's the same way we make decisions in the restaurant.

Learning compromises was the exciting part and the difficult part of the first two years. A restaurant has to have an exorbitant number of onions to operate. So, that's one area where we make an exception. We had to make a decision as to what came first, organic or local. Those are two philosophies that we believe in. And local food—we wanted that to be the decision that we made first.

We really want to communicate that local food is not expensive, elitist food. It's not a fancy restaurant. And Farm Burger's based on the concept of volume. It's a six-dollar local grass-fed burger. It can't have a 50 percent food cost and be a solvent business. The basic idea is that it's accessible, it's economic, it's ethical, it's affordable. The conceit behind our restaurant is that when you are buying local food, you're taking out a lot of the middlemen in the process. So, in many ways, local foods end up being a lot cheaper.

Farmers have to be entrepreneurial. They have to be smart at business and marketing. They have to be articulate at educating the consumer. That can't fall to a different sector of people. It can't be the nonprofits, it can't be the schools. It has to start with the farmers.

It's not that we have this radically successful, profitable business model, but we have a really interesting one. It's a very collaborate venture, between a farm and a restaurant.

PIG TROTTERS

Our recipes are designed to utilize the entire animal. Raising our own pigs, slaughtering one at a time, and paying on hanging weight means we must maximize our investment and use all parts. Luckily for us, pig is great. Ears, feet, skin, bellies, and trim all transform into luxurious moments of meaty, fatty goodness perfect for Old World preparations. This recipe, from Head Chef Matt Palmerlee, calls for pork shanks. The resulting disks make crispy, delicious appetizers.

2 whole pork shanks, at least 6 inches each, hoof on	1 tablespoon butter
2 carrots, large dice	2 tablespoons Dijon mustard
1 white onion, large dice	Salt and pepper
3 stalks celery, large dice	1 teaspoon fresh thyme
A few bay leaves	1 tablespoon fresh chopped parsley
A few juniper berries	Flour
A few cloves	2 whole eggs, beaten
2 shallots	Panko
	Extra-virgin olive oil

Prepare your pig feet by washing them well and cutting them if necessary. Boil in water for 5 minutes and discard the water. Place them in cold water along with carrots, onion, celery, bay leaves, juniper berries, and cloves. Simmer for 3 hours. Strain the broth and reserve.

Remove skin, meat, gelatin, and tendons from bones. Roughly chop meat, gelatin, and tendons together. Add chopped skin to make a ratio of 1 part skin to 2 parts meat mixture. Put it all in a bowl and add enough cooking liquid to just moisten it.

Quick-sauté shallots in butter, and add to meat mixture with mustard, salt and pepper to taste, thyme, and parsley. Place mixture in center of a 2-foot-long piece of foil and tightly wrap, creating a roll. Let sit in refrigerator for 24 hours for gelatin to set. Next day, cut into 1-inch discs with foil still on, then unwrap each individually. Dredge with flour, then egg, then coat with panko. Heat ½ inch of olive oil in a sauté pan, and fry on each side until golden brown. Serve with grilled bread and condiment of choice, such as fruit mostarda or onion jam.

Serves 4 to 5

PORK BELLY CONFIT

This recipe by Chef Matt Palmerlee is as decadent as you can imagine. You will taste a bit of this, feel a little guilty, and stick it in the fridge. Then it will call to you in the middle of the night . . . Should I get up to fry just a tiny piece up? You are safer if you invite a bunch of people over to eat it all at once!

5 pounds pork belly, skin off (heritage-breed, pasture-raised)	4 tablespoons salt
	4 cloves garlic, chopped
½ tablespoon ground cinnamon	Bouquet garni of thyme, bay leaf, and rosemary
½ tablespoon ground cloves	White wine, enough to cover belly
¼ tablespoon ground allspice	2 to 3 quarts rendered pork or duck fat
3 tablespoons ground black pepper	Canola oil, if needed

Rinse belly and pat dry. Rub all sides with cinnamon, cloves, allspice, black pepper, salt, and garlic. Lay flat in deep baking dish, skin side up. Add bouquet garni and enough wine to just cover entire belly. Refrigerate for 24 hours.

Next day, remove belly from wine and pat dry. Liquefy fat in a pan over low heat. Place belly in clean deep baking dish and cover entirely with the melted fat. If you do not have enough to cover, you can supplement with canola oil. Bake at 250°F for 2 to 3 hours, or until both fatty and meaty parts are fork tender. Let cool completely, resting in fat. Refrigerate in the fat for a day before eating, for more flavor, if you can resist. Store the confit in separate containers in portions you will use. To serve, wipe off lard, cut into squares and reheat until crispy brown by pan frying or deep frying. Serve with mustards and green salad. The pork confit will keep in the refrigerator, in the fat, for up to a month.

Serves 12 to 16 as an appetizer or 8 to 10 as a main dish

To me it's all about passion. That passion is what I saw in my dad, Jack, and I had to take a stab at it myself. I'm selling the best stuff money can buy and people just love you for it. What's better than that?

What's better than being liked? I learned all the fine skills from my dad. He was very charismatic, and he was a worker bee, like me. If I left some meat on the bones, my dad would throw it on the scale and he'd go, *That's a dollar twenty you're throwing away.* And now I do that to my staff.

In the early sixties Julia Child started shopping here. She and my dad just kind of clicked. She loved meat and butchering and she'd go in the cooler and he'd show her this or that piece of meat and she'd say, *Oh, isn't that gorgeous.* She lived right up the street. And then, *boom*, 1967, she was on the cover of *Time* magazine and she mentions Savenor's. And our weekly meat sales went from 5,000 to 15,000 pounds a week.

The people who come in the store are fascinating. I mean we get the president of Harvard, Schlessinger, Erich Segal, Kennedys, Senator Kerry, Robin Cook the author. For the book *Toxin*, I took him out to see what meat processing was. And in his book he thanks me for "overcoming a particular barrier" in his research. I was laughing like a bastard inside. It just goes to show you the sky's the limit.

I'm third generation, so I was supposed to ruin it, right? I almost did lose the business. The place burned down from an electrical fire in March of '92. It's funny because I say I'll never forget that day and every year my wife reminds me that I've forgotten that day. Through great business advice from a family friend, Louis Kane, founder of Au Bon Pain, we moved to Charles Street in Beacon Hill, which is the single wealthiest square mile in Boston. Because of demand, we reopened the store at the original Cambridge location in 2005. We are also the premier meat wholesaler in the Boston area and supply to some of Boston's finest restaurants.

I'm natural at this because it's easy. I have great products to work with and customers who appreciate them. Honestly though I feel like the old-fashioned butcher is a dying breed. You can't just get a pallet of sirloins and say, *Okay, cut these.* That's not a butcher, that's just someone with a knife. Every steak that goes out of here is like a work of art. That's our company's signature. I'm a self-proclaimed master butcher who passes my skills on to my staff. I'm only as good as my staff.

RON SAVENOR

SAVENOR'S MARKET, MA

Ron's resume reads like a Ken doll catalog: race-car driver, gymnast, pro skateboarder, and butcher. He is about as relaxed as a tightrope. But the storyline here is generations of continuity. From Lithuanian immigrants running a franchise grocery store, to the 1960s pomaded sheen of the Julia Child boom, to the "Crazy Ronnie" years of wholesale success and farm-sourced meats, the family has remained happily entrenched in small business ownership.

"IN THE EARLY SIXTIES JULIA CHILD STARTED SHOPPING HERE. SHE AND MY DAD JUST KIND OF CLICKED."

TURKEY MEATLOAF

Turkey meatloaf is healthy, delicious, and above all, comforting, on a chilly winter night. Serve it with potatoes and a salad for a meal that's both healthy and hearty.

1 medium onion, minced
1 stalk celery, minced
1 carrot, minced
1 tablespoon olive oil
1½ pounds ground turkey
½ cup dry bread crumbs

1 large egg
6 tablespoons ketchup, plus ⅓ cup for topping
2 cloves garlic, minced
2 tablespoons club soda
¼ teaspoon salt
¼ teaspoon pepper

Preheat the oven to 350°F. Sauté the onion, celery, and carrot in the olive oil until the onion is translucent. Combine sautéed vegetables with remaining ingredients in a large bowl. Mix well, then shape into a loaf and place on a foil-lined sheet pan, or press the mixture into a 9 by 5 by 3-inch loaf pan or a casserole dish. Spread ketchup over top. Bake for 50 minutes, until thoroughly cooked.

Serves 6

CHICKEN POTPIE

This should be a staple on every family's menu. It's easy and and a great weekend treat for kids.

4 cups unsalted chicken broth
3 chicken breasts, poached and cubed
4 to 5 cups cooked cubed vegetables (any mixture of carrots, leeks, celery,
    mushrooms, pearl onions, zucchini, corn, green peas)
3 tablespoons butter
4 tablespoons flour, plus extra for rolling out dough
1 cup heavy cream
Salt and pepper
9 ounces pastry dough, store-bought or homemade
1 egg

Preheat the oven to 400°F. Boil the chicken broth until it is reduced by half. Set aside. Mix the chicken and cooked vegetables and put in a round baking dish. Melt the butter in a saucepan, add flour, and cook, whisking, over medium-low heat for 2 to 3 minutes. Add broth and heavy cream. Cook, whisking, until thickened, another 3 to 4 minutes. Add salt and pepper, to taste, and pour over the chicken and vegetables.

On a lightly floured surface, roll pastry dough out to fit the shape of your baking dish, adding 1½ inches for an overlap. Whisk the egg and use some of it to brush the outside rim of the baking dish. Lay pastry on top of the dish and crimp the edge, using a fork to give it a decorative look. Brush more egg over crust. Make a few small cuts in crust for steam to escape. Bake for 20 minutes. Reduce heat to 375°F and bake for another 15 to 20 minutes, until golden brown.

Serves 4

TRACY SMACIARZ

HERITAGE MEATS, WA

Heritage Meats is a much-needed plant in a heavily agricultural area of Washington state. The owner, second-generation butcher Tracy, has been introducing the fine-dining world of Seattle to the ranchers of the rest of the state, especially Tracey Baker of Gleason Ranch, his grass-fed co-conspirator. He takes care of the whole process, from a mobile slaughter unit to smoking, stuffing and spicing. Tracy has this twinkle in his eye like he just pulled a fast one. Maybe it's because he knows this business better than any of the chefs and young butchers he meets. Or because he can break down a beef carcass faster than anyone I've seen. Maybe it's because he's so damn tickled that other people think his work is as cool as he does.

Not too shabby, is it? I'm the only certified organic-meat processor in the state. The shop opened in 1977. Dad grew up on a farm, out killing cows. His grandfather had cattle. His father had about 120 head of Hereford, a cow-calf operation. Dad moved away to Pe Ell. So, he went to work at Safeway as a meat cutter and then started his own meat shop, on the side, in a detached two-car garage.

In the late seventies and early eighties, they started taking the meat shops out of all of the grocery stores. As a seven- or eight-year-old, I would help my father take the rail out of the Safeways. And I helped him put the rail in the new shop.

It just started growing and growing and growing. In 1988, he quit Safeway and went full-time in his own shop. I was there the whole time, doing farm slaughter and making sausage. I was the only son. In 1996, his health had gone. I was in Seattle, working for the phone company. I liked it, but I wasn't happy. He couldn't run the business anymore and I came back and took over the shop. Ten years later, I built this facility and moved from state- to USDA-inspection.

About 2000 is when I saw the industry really starting to change. Grocery-store meat cutters were being replaced by centralized meat-processing plants. I also saw the need for local farmers, who I had been working with all my life, to be supported in order to survive. And so, I said, *This is what I need to do, I need to sell locally raised meat.*

There's total transparency in what I do and in what Tracey Baker does. She and I just went to the James Beard Awards in New York. It was pretty exciting, we had an amazing meal with her beef.

When I started talking to chefs: *Well, I have smokehouses, and I have a shop, and I cure meats, and make pepperoni, and I've slaughtered*, they were like, *You've done all of that?* A lot of people just don't speak beef.

"ABOUT 2000 IS WHEN I SAW THE INDUSTRY REALLY STARTING TO CHANGE. GROCERY-STORE MEAT CUTTERS WERE BEING REPLACED BY CENTRALIZED MEAT-PROCESSING PLANTS."

GRILLED NEW YORK STEAK

New York steaks are my favorite to grill. I prefer a steak thick enough to grill without overcooking and yet fast enough to cook so you are not a "grill jockey" for a long period of time. I have served this dish to a former Kansas State meat inspector, who said they were the best steaks he'd ever had and asked me for the recipe. Inspectors usually aren't impressed with much!

2 1-inch-thick grass-fed New York strip steaks *
1 cup balsamic vinegar
½ cup red wine
1 tablespoon sugar
2 teaspoons onion powder
½ stick butter
Freshly ground kosher or sea salt
Freshly ground black pepper
4 ounces blue cheese

Marinate the steaks in a mixture of the vinegar, wine, sugar, and onion powder in the refrigerator for 2 to 4 hours. Place steaks in a baking dish and let them come to room temperature. Melt butter, either in micro-wave or on cool side of grill in a bowl. Butter and generously season one side of steaks with salt and pepper. The butter will add to the flavor of the steaks and help keep them from sticking to the grill.

Prepare a charcoal grill by putting the charcoal on one side of the barbecue. Once the coals have ashed over and are white-hot, place the steaks on hot side of grill first, seasoned side down, for 1 to 2 minutes. Cover the grill (this step gives you those nice grill marks). For checkerboard grill marks, start the steaks crosswise to the grill bars, rotating them 90 degrees, parallel to the bars, halfway through.

Move steaks to cooler side of grill and cook indirectly for 6 to 8 minutes. For grilling beef—or for that matter any meat—low and slow is best, especially for a thicker steak, which will burn on the outside before cooking internally if heat is too high.

Butter and season tops of steaks. Flip over and cook on cool side of grill for another 7 to 10 minutes for medium to medium-rare. Let steaks rest for 3 to 5 minutes, covered with foil to keep warm, on a clean plate. This way, the flavorful juices will stay in the steak and not run all over your plate. Crumble blue cheese over steaks and serve.

Serves 2

* Grass-fed beef from the Pacific Northwest is best, April or May through September or October.

PERSONALITIES OF STEAKS

Nearly any part of an animal can be **CUT** into steaks. These **FIVE** steaks provide a range of **MOODS** and cooking **STYLES** and can be matched to almost any type of **GUEST**.

FILET MIGNON (the Dandy): This cut comes from the tenderloin. The fact that this muscle hardly ever gets used makes it tender but not deeply flavorful. Filet mignon is expensive. This is a show-off dish, requiring precise timing and is most at home when enrobed in a decadent sauce.

PORTERHOUSE to **T-BONE** or **STRIP** (the Dear Friend): The short loin, when cut into steaks, includes the porterhouse and T-bone. Both have a T-shaped bone, with one side having the meat of the top loin and one side the meat of the tenderloin. The porterhouse has a larger section of tenderloin, and when the tenderloin and bone are removed, we are left with strip steaks. The fattiness of these makes them rather forgiving and delicious.

FLANK (the Ill-Advised Lover): The belly of the beast. The abdomen is tough and the  beefiest in flavor. You must either cook this dish very quickly or very slowly if you don't want the texture to turn against you. Generally prepared with peppers, shallots, and other provocations.

RIB EYE (the Cowboy): This cut prefers dry, arid cooking, maybe under a full moon. It doesn't require much beyond salt and pepper; it carries its flavor in its deep rivulets of fat that melt at high heat. You may only desire this intense steak every great once in a while, and that's no more or less than how it should be.

CHUCK EYE STEAK (the Convict): The chuck is the shoulder and it is full of gristle, fat, and bone. The chuck eye is a bit more  tender, so you can grill it instead of braising. An inexpensive cut, but you may have to ask your butcher to separate this part for you because it isn't always sold in the counter separate from the rest of the chuck. Marinate it a good long time and it will be redeemed.

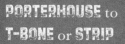

ADAM TIBERIO

DICKSON'S FARMSTAND, NY

Jake Dickson methodically studied the meat business before opening up this Manhattan shop, which sells only from whole carcasses that Jake himself hauls back from an upstate slaughterhouse. And he learned a very important lesson, hand over the butchering to a true butcher, "Even if it's an unfamiliar cut, Adam can make them familiar. They look really good, even though you don't know the names. I think a lesser butcher would make it a bigger challenge."

Adam is all sepia tones, enthrallingly old-fashioned. He is a journeyman butcher. This "have skill and knives, will travel" lifestyle has died out as butchering became a less vaunted and less lucrative path. Yet here he is, like a photo of your grandma—a knockout—on a date with someone who didn't end up being your grandpa.

I was just looking for a job and meat cutting paid well. After supermarkets, I did the slaughterhouse for two years. It was a small USDA plant in New Hampshire, just over the state line. We were producing stuff for everyone in New England—beef, pork, lamb, veal, goat, emu, caribou, moose. It was very difficult work. I wouldn't be where I am right now, if I hadn't gone through that. My mentor there was kind of a meat genius—slaughter, cutting, everything.

Then, I cut my hand with a band saw. We had a workman's comp dispute. They sent me the bill. So I went to a shop in Concord, Massachusetts. That was the first opportunity I had to strike out on my own, develop cuts, set prices. I decided what our cutting standards were, what we would sell. I think there's way too much making it up as you go, especially with younger guys. I pretty much go by the Meat Buyer's Guide.

I was a journeyman for one operation, working store to store to store, maybe five stores in a week. There were thirty stores in the Boston area. I've cut for small supermarkets all the way up to Whole Foods. Most of the meat is pretty much the same. You have to make it look nice and put it in nice packages.

On a busy Saturday, there'll be kids all over the place watching because where I cut the meat is completely open. They get really into it.

"I'VE CUT FOR SMALL SUPERMARKETS ALL THE WAY UP TO WHOLE FOODS. MOST OF THE MEAT IS PRETTY MUCH THE SAME. YOU HAVE TO MAKE IT LOOK NICE AND PUT IT IN NICE PACKAGES."

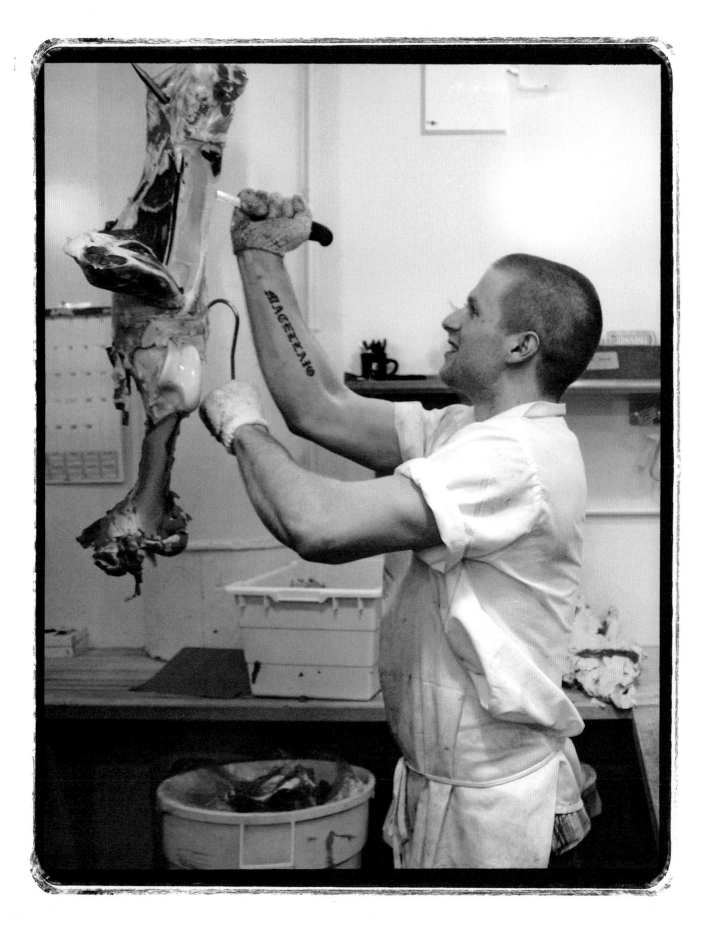

SLOPPY JOE

Guilty pleasure of suburban days of yore no more! There is nothing ironically kitschy about this wholesome, messy plate of homemade love. Remember to stock up on the napkins. This recipe is by our chef, Gabriel Ross.

Chili Paste
1½ teaspoons ground cumin
3 teaspoons ancho chili powder
2 teaspoons chipotle powder
3 teaspoons freshly ground black pepper
1½ teaspoons ground allspice,
3 teaspoons ground coriander
3 teaspoons sweet paprika
1½ teaspoons dried thyme
3 teaspoons mustard powder
6 cloves garlic, peeled and minced
½ cup vegetable oil

2 large onions, minced
2 tablespoons tomato paste
2 (12-ounce) cans crushed tomatoes,
    liquid reserved

5 pounds boneless beef shin
¼ cup vegetable oil
1 to 2 cups meat stock (any good-quality stock
    will do—preferably homemade)
Sugar and salt

To prepare the chili paste, grind and combine spices (cumin, ancho chili, and chipotle powders, black pepper, allspice, paprika, thyme, and mustard powder).

Fry garlic in vegetable oil until it begins to turn golden brown, add onions, and cook until soft. Add ground spice mixture, and cook until fragrant and onions are coated. Add tomato paste. Cook, stirring frequently until mixture begins to dry out.

Add tomato solids and cook until liquid in pan evaporates. Transfer to a container and refrigerate until ready to use. Can be prepared up to one one week in advance.

To prepare the chili, preheat oven to 350°F. Cut meat into 1- to 2-inch chunks. Over medium-high heat, brown meat in a sauté pan with vegetable oil. In a large oven-safe casserole, combine browned meat with liquid from tomatoes, stock, and chili paste. Liquid should cover two-thirds to three-quarters of the meat. Lay a piece of parchment paper on top of meat and cover with lid or foil (this will help retain moisture and prevent the surface from drying out). Turn oven down to 250°F and braise for 6 to 8 hours. (This can also be done in a slow cooker if you prefer.)

To test for doneness, remove one piece of meat and crush it with the back of a spoon. If it shreds effort-lessly, it is done. Strain off cooking liquid into a pot and bring to a gentle simmer, 5 to 10 minutes to reduce slightly. Add sugar and salt to taste.

Transfer meat to a stand mixer with paddle attachment, and mix until the meat is finely shredded—keeping an eye out for bits of tendon and sinew that have not fully broken down during the cooking process. The shredding can also be done by hand with a potato masher or similar utensil.

Combine shredded meat and seasoned liquid. Taste and adjust seasoning. To serve, mix in ketchup or hot sauce of your choice. We love to use a sweet and spicy sauce from Malaysia called Ligham's.

Serves 6

SALT-AND-PEPPER JERKY

A great, easy-to-make basic jerky you can do easily in your oven. You really have no excuse to not have jerky available at all times . . . you will greatly improve relations with your neighbors and visiting dignitaries. This recipe is by our chef, Gabriel Ross.

> 5 pounds beef bottom round (alternative cuts: eye round or lean chuck,
>   such as chuck tender)
> 4 tablespoons kosher salt
> 1½ tablespoons freshly ground black pepper
> 2 tablespoons light brown sugar
> 1 tablespoon whole yellow mustard seeds (optional)

Trim beef of all external fat and gristle. Freeze meat for 15 to 20 minutes for easier slicing. Slice as thinly as possible—no thicker than ¼ inch—across the grain at a 45-degree angle. It is very important to have uniform slices.

Mix all dry ingredients together in a bowl and divide in half. In a glass or ceramic baking dish, put down a layer of meat and sprinkle it with seasoning. Lay a second layer of meat on top and season it, and repeat until you have seasoned all of the meat using half the seasoning mixture. Next, transfer the meat, one layer at a time to the second baking dish, turning over and seasoning the other side. Repeat until both sides of all of the meat slices have been seasoned, and all of the mixture has been used. Cover tightly with plastic wrap and refrigerate for 24 hours

Preheat oven to 150°F. Arrange meat slices in a single layer on wire cooling racks and place in oven for about 8 to 10 hours. Meat is done when it is stiff but not brittle. If the meat is not dry enough, continue drying in oven until desired texture is achieved. Drying times may vary due to moisture and fat content of meat.

If storing, let meat cool before putting into sealed container in refrigerator. The jerky will keep for 1 to 2 months.

Makes approximately 2 pounds jerky

LEFTOVERS

There is something so **UNSATISFYING** about finishing everything. One of the great pleasures of home cooking is wrapping up the **EXTRAS** and making plans for **LUNCH** and **DINNER** the next day. I take the majority of my culinary pride from creating something **DELICIOUS** and surprising from elements skulking around in the fridge and pantry. These dishes are **CLASSIC** leftover catharses to keep in your rotation. Like anything you love, they are flexible, forgiving, and a reflection of yourself just as you are right now.

LE MIROTON

This is a casserole you can make from any type of roast that is at the end of its journey. You can add vegetables that are already cooked and I sometimes grate a hard cheese, like Parmesan, and mix it with the bread crumbs.

2 medium onions, thinly sliced

3½ tablespoons olive oil

1½ tablespoons flour

½ cup red wine

1 tablespoon tomato paste

1 cup beef broth

1 cup beef gravy

2 tablespoons Dijon mustard

12 thin slices leftover roast beef

1 cup bread crumbs

Preheat oven to 400°F. In a skillet, cook onions in 2 tablespoons oil over medium heat, stirring occasionally until golden. Add flour and cook for 2 more minutes, stirring to combine. Stir in wine, tomato paste, broth, and gravy. Simmer the sauce, stirring, for 3 to 5 minutes. Stir in mustard.

Spoon half of the sauce into a baking dish. Place the roast slices on top, overlapping them slightly, so that the bottom of the dish is covered. You can add leftover roasted, mashed, or boiled potatoes, tucking them around the edges of the dish alongside the meat. Spread the remaining sauce over the top. Sprinkle bread crumbs over the top and drizzle with the remaining 1½ tablespoons of olive oil. Bake in the upper third of the oven until just bubbling around the edges, approximately 10 minutes. If crumbs are not golden, put the miroton under the broiler for 1 to 2 minutes.

Serves 4

PYTTI PANNA

A Swedish favorite that will buffer nearly any kind of leftover meat: pork, poultry, or beef; cubed, shredded, or ground. I find that anything described as short-order cookery tends to make everyone feel like they have the night off. Well accompanied by a fried egg, some crusty rye bread, and a salad of bitter greens.

4 tablespoons butter
1½ pounds potatoes, peeled and cubed
1 tablespoons olive oil
2 onions, thinly sliced
2 tablespoons parsley, finely chopped
salt and pepper to taste
¾ to 1 pound leftover meat (bacon, sausage,
   or roast, ground or shredded meat)
pickled beets

In a skillet, heat 1 pat of butter. Add the potatoes and sauté until they are tender and golden. Remove the potatoes and let them rest in a bowl. Melt the rest of the butter in the pan and add the olive oil. Add the onions and sauté until they begin to brown. The lower and longer you cook them, the more flavor you will extract.

Add the onions, parsley, and salt and pepper to the bowl with the potatoes. Fry the meat on high heat until it is warm and gets a bit of delicious crust. Add the potato mixture and combine everything. Serve hot and garnish with pickled beets.

Serves 4

SOUP

I like to play it fast and loose when it comes to soup. I try to keep my stock stocked, and from there I push the boundaries of "throw things into a pot" cooking. In celebration of the eleventh hour, here are the basic guidelines.

Meats all have their natural dancing partners, which are nice to keep in mind before you begin the beguine. Poultry and mushrooms, cream, rice, celery. Beef and tomatoes, potatoes, hefty pastas. Lamb and peas, herbs, substantive grains like barley and oats and rye. Pork and braising greens, cabbage, white beans, hominy.

Sweat onions in butter and sauté hearty raw veggies in the soup pot first. Add leftover meat, shredded or chopped. If the meat is still clinging to a bone and your soup will cook for a bit, leave it. Liquid can be added at this point.

Bones have gelatin and marrow, both of which are dense in flavor, texture, and nutritional value. If you have stock of the same species, this is the moment the stock has been awaiting. You can add water or coconut milk as well.

Next comes any pasta, rice, or beans, added after being cooked al dente in another pot. Finish the soup with salt, pepper, herbs, heat, and a splash of cognac.

GERRIT VAN DEN NOORD
SONOMA DIRECT, CA

Gerrit is the butcher at my meat-processing plant. He had worked for the previous owner and agreed to come on board when we bought the business. I can't imagine a universe where there is a Sonoma Direct without Gerrit. It is fitting that he sits in alphabetical order next to Cole Ward in this book, because I imagine they would make great friends. They are both adventurers and incredibly skilled, in a way that is both macho and humble. Gerrit has a sense of pride in his work that is almost daunting. In his world, butchering means taking care of his meat cutters and taking care of the building, as well as taking care the carcass. His masterful knowledge of meat has made it possible for Sonoma Direct to become a resource for local ranchers who want to sell their meat, teaching them about the cuts and their applications. Plus, he is endlessly full of good stories.

I was an orphan at sixteen and they wanted to put me in a camp. I knew a butcher and his wife and they wanted me to live with them instead. They had two kids of their own, a butcher shop downstairs, and they lived upstairs. They paid me under the table. I always had money then. The lady of the house would come down every night and take whatever was left for dinner. I never had a bad meal. There's no such thing as a bad cut, it's all about how you cook it.

Then I went to school for butchering, two days a week for three years. I joined the service, and when I came back I went into carpentry for a while. When I got back to butchering, I worked for a company from Australia. They bought up cattle from all over Europe and they would call me up and say, *Gerrit, we've got 500 head in Italy or Austria or France, go take care of it.* I did everything. I had thirty-five butchers working for me. That was a lot of fun. We all stayed in a hotel. Paris was a lot of problems because the people there would take a four-hour lunch break and drink wine. When I brought my guys, if they drank wine, they wouldn't come back. A lot of the meat came from France, they raised them so the front was small and the back was really big because that's where the money is.

Then, in Antwerp, we took the meat outside to cut, there were no regulations. Wherever the meat hall was in town, that's where all the bars and the prostitutes were. In the slaughterhouses there was always a bottle of brandy in every corner, they said it was to keep the flies away. People could drink as much as they wanted and no one said anything. Insurance changed all that. Now pople get cut and forget about it.

For several years, I had my own union. We didn't have unions in Europe then. I knew all the butchers from Holland and Belgium, so the big grocery companies would call me when they were short. I would call my people up and send them out. I got bigger and bigger. I got so tired of it because of taxes. I told Jack, my first hire, that he could have the company and I moved to the United States.

I didn't know any of the American names for the cuts, but that was easy to learn. Then I went to Tambolinis, and in three months I was running the place. There were two young kids doing all the ground, making $4 an hour. I gave them both a dollar-an-hour raise and Tambolini got so pissed. He said you run the place, but no raises.

I came to this plant to look for work when Simon Samson owned it. I walked in and couldn't believe it was him. I'd seen Simon around in Holland but I had no idea he had moved here.

My first boss would pick up every little scrap I missed, *It's all pennies and nickels, Gerrit, pennies and nickels.* Of course then, I was making twenty dollars a week. So meat was much more expensive then, relatively. That's how I learned.

HUNGARIAN GOULASH

Contrary to popular belief, true gulyas does not include sour cream or tomato. What it does require, however, is genuine paprika, imported from Hungary. You can find it at specialty food stores, as well as many supermarkets. Some recipes recommend the addition of sauerkraut, which you can add at the very end, if desired. Serve with egg noodles.

2 tablespoons butter
2 large onions, peeled and chopped
2 pounds beef or pork for stew, cut into 1½- to 2-inch cubes
¼ teaspoon caraway seeds
½ teaspoon fresh or dried marjoram leaves
2 cloves garlic, minced
5 tablespoons imported Hungarian paprika
2 cups beef stock
1 cup water
4 large potatoes, peeled and cut into chunks

Melt the butter in a large pot over medium heat. Cook the onions until they are soft and translucent. Add the beef and brown it on all sides.

Add the caraway seeds, marjoram, garlic, and paprika. Cook for a minute or two to soften the garlic and release the flavor of the paprika. Add the stock and water, and cover.

Simmer the beef over very low heat for 2 hours. (Alternatively, use an oven proof casserole and cook the goulash in a 300°F oven.)

Add the potatoes and cook until they are tender, about an hour. Season to taste and serve.

Serves 6

GRANDMA ESTHER'S GREEN CHILI

This recipe is from a dear family friend and I have enjoyed it many, many times along with fresh tortillas made with the rendered pork fat. The fat and cracklings are delightful by-products. The jalapeño amount can be tinkered with to suit your palate for heat.

4 to 5 pounds poblano (pasilla) chiles
2 ounces jalapeño peppers, for heat
Cooking oil
2 to 5 cloves garlic, sliced
4- to 5-pound pork roast (old style, lots of good pork fat)
3 tablespoons flour
Salt

In a 450°F oven, place chiles on a rack and roast until the skins blister. Place the hot chiles in a plastic bag and seal. This will steam the skins off.

Remove skin and stems but not the seeds. Place the chiles in a large bowl and add 8 cups of water. Lightly coat your hands with cooking oil, to avoid burning your skin with the oil from the peppers. Squish chiles and water with your hands to a paste. Add garlic to mixture and set aside chili paste.

Cut all fat from the pork. Dice fat and meat into ¼-inch cubes. Place fat in heavy large pot. To render pork grease, add ¼ cup water and place on low heat, stirring occasionally. Cracklings will sink to the bottom (remove and have as a treat!). The rendered fat can be stored for several months in the fridge.

Place 6 tablespoons of rendered fat in large pot over medium heat. Add cubed pork when hot. Stir pork to coat completely in the fat. Cover pork and continue cooking until the liquid has evaporated. Add flour to make a roux by stirring continually and letting the flour and pork fat combine and darken. Add chili paste to pork and cook just until it boils. Add salt to taste.

Serves 8

COLE WARD
GREEN TOP MARKET, VT

It is physically painful to me to edit out any of my many hours of discussion with Cole. He is a Dickensian hero, all twinkle and humility and somehow deeply entrenched and simultaneously a few inches above the fray. And he plays jazz accordion. Besides his many charms, this man knows the grocery-meat counter, he has been behind one for forty-five years. He doubled the meat sales at Green Top Market in six months. The pride he takes in his work is something that travels with him. Like many butchers of his generation, he gets itchy feet. But he never leaves a store without some of that twinkle permanently embedded. Green Top Market, where he now rules the counter, is attempting to make farm-direct meat a staple. The owner, Joe, knows he's got a good thing in Cole: "When people buy a piece of meat from him, they feel good. They believe in him."

Our parents learned how to cook from their butcher. When you were first married, the butcher would tell you how to make dinner.

In the seventies and eighties, you were on your own in the supermarket. The average supermarket takes a kid off a grocery floor who isn't going to go to college to cut meat. The kid lights up because he's getting nine dollars an hour when he was making seven before. All he's doing is slicing prepackaged meat. When I started, you had to know how to get that piece of meat out of the side of beef or you were lost. We were paid on the scale of electricians and plumbers.

My mother got an apartment over this little mom-and-pop store and she became friends with the owners. I wanted to be a butcher or piano player. I ended up a little bit of both. Notice I have all my fingers. The owner of the store was an old-time butcher and he became my godfather. When I was fourteen, he gave me a job for twenty cents an hour washing meat trays and stuffing sausage. I thought, *Boy, I love this.* The big joke when I started was, we had a

clean-up committee: I was the chairman, the vice president, and the secretary.

When I was sixteen, I was working part-time in a gas station, and one night the meat manager for this IGA store came in. He'd been raccoon hunting and he was drunk and offered me a job as a meat cutter's apprentice. So the next day, I ran home on my lunch hour and changed my clothes, ran across town, and he hired me. It was almost a dollar an hour, and I was making sixty cents an hour at the gas station.

The owner of the store took me under his wing. He made me go to church and I would sit in the back. He'd get me move up closer every week. I was very difficult but he saw potential.

I hadn't learned how to break beef yet and I kept pressing, but he wouldn't let me. So, I got the opportunity to manage a little country store and it was all hanging carcasses. I never saw boxed beef until 1972. When I gave my notice he wasn't upset. He went to his manager and said, *This man's leaving in two weeks. He needs to learn how to break beef, teach him.* I got a crash course.

I discovered that people buy meat with their eyes. We would take lettuce leaves to decorate the meat counter. I didn't know anything about kale back then, I was just a kid.

I went out to California in '77 on a whim with my kid brother. We got there in the wee hours of the morning, sat up drinking, and I finally flopped on a friend's couch. At eight am the phone rang. Some lady said, *Did you apply for a meat cutter's position?* And I'm thinking to myself, *I just got here.* But I said, *Yes, I did.* Apparently, the lady dialed the wrong number.

The man I worked for said, "Forget everything you've learned. I don't want speed. I want quality." I thought he was going to be nasty to work for. I look back and he did me the greatest favor. I used to do all the meat props for CBS Studios, displays for national TV commercials. My customers were Billy Crystal, Glenn Ford, Raymond Burr. We had a fifty-foot retail meat case. I'd be at the store at 4 am and sometimes find myself still there at four the next morning. But I was young.

I've driven back and forth across the country nineteen different times. I've always maintained there were three styles of US cutting: Chicago, California, and Texas. If somebody asks me for a tri-tip, I say, *What part of California are you from?* If somebody wants a full cut of round steak, they're from Texas.

The government has lowered the standards on many of the product terminologies so that corporate America can cash in. People are fooled into thinking they're being healthy when they pick up a package of all-natural chicken. It means nothing. I can taste the difference. The commodity chicken tastes rotten to me now.

You have to be a salesman, but you have to believe in your product too and gain the trust of your customers. I have a lady who follows me from store to store. There will always be a market for quality and good customer service.

"I'VE ALWAYS MAINTAINED THERE WERE THREE STYLES OF U.S. CUTTING: CHICAGO, CALIFORNIA, AND TEXAS. IF SOMEBODY ASKS ME FOR A TRI-TIP, I SAY, WHAT PART OF CALIFORNIA ARE YOU FROM? IF SOMEBODY WANTS A FULL CUT OF ROUND STEAK, THEY'RE FROM TEXAS."

PIG IN A FLANKET

I have been making this for twenty years. Family and friends love it, especially around the holidays. You can try it with sun-dried tomatoes and Parmesan instead of the roasted peppers and cheddar.

1 flank steak, 1½ to 2 pounds
1½ teaspoons Old Quebec style dry seasoning
    (can substitute with any dry seasoning)
1 (8-ounce) bag fresh spinach, washed well

6 thin slices of mild cheddar cheese
4 to 5 roasted red peppers (from a jar)
1 small whole pork tenderloin

Butterfly the flank steak (or ask your butcher to do it). Lay it out flat and trim off ends to make it fairly uniform. Sprinkle with steak seasoning. Place a layer of spinach on top followed by a layer of cheese, followed by another layer of spinach. Place the roasted peppers evenly on top and follow with a final layer of spinach. Lay the pork tenderloin in an overlap on the spinach, with its grain aligned with the flank steak's. With grain running lengthwise, and starting with the pork edge, use both hands to roll up like a jelly roll, as tightly as possible. Tie with cooking string, first in the center, and then on each end. Tie more strings between these strings until you have 1 about every inch. Slice into 2-inch-thick slices (important that each slice has 2 strings). Lay them flat in a pan and bake uncovered in a 350°F oven for 25 to 30 minutes.

Serves 4 to 6

ASPARAGUS-PROSCIUTTO CHICKEN ROULADE

This roulade has been a great hit with our customers for 25 years.

2 whole boneless, skinless chicken breasts
8 slices prosciutto
8 slices (approximately 7 ounces) slicing cheddar

1 bunch asparagus (thin stalks are best)
1 cup thick, Old World–style buttermilk
2 cups unflavored bread crumbs or panko

Cut each breast in half and butterfly each half open, or ask your butcher to do it. For each serving, lay 2 slices of prosciutto side by side, overlapping them by about an inch. Lay 2 slices of cheddar cheese on top of the prosciutto. Cut the tough bases off the asparagus stems and discard. Cut asparagus in half to make 2½- to 3-inch-long pieces. Bundle 4 to 6 pieces of asparagus together and put on the prosciutto and cheddar cheese. Roll it up tightly. Place on top of a butterflied chicken breast half. Fold the chicken over the rolled-up asparagus, cheese, and prosciutto and squeeze together. Repeat for each serving. Put buttermilk and bread crumbs into 2 separate bowls. Dip chicken bundles into buttermilk, being careful to hold them together, and then roll them in bread crumbs and squeeze gently.

Place in a lightly greased baking pan and bake uncovered in a 350°F oven for about 30 minutes.

Serves 4

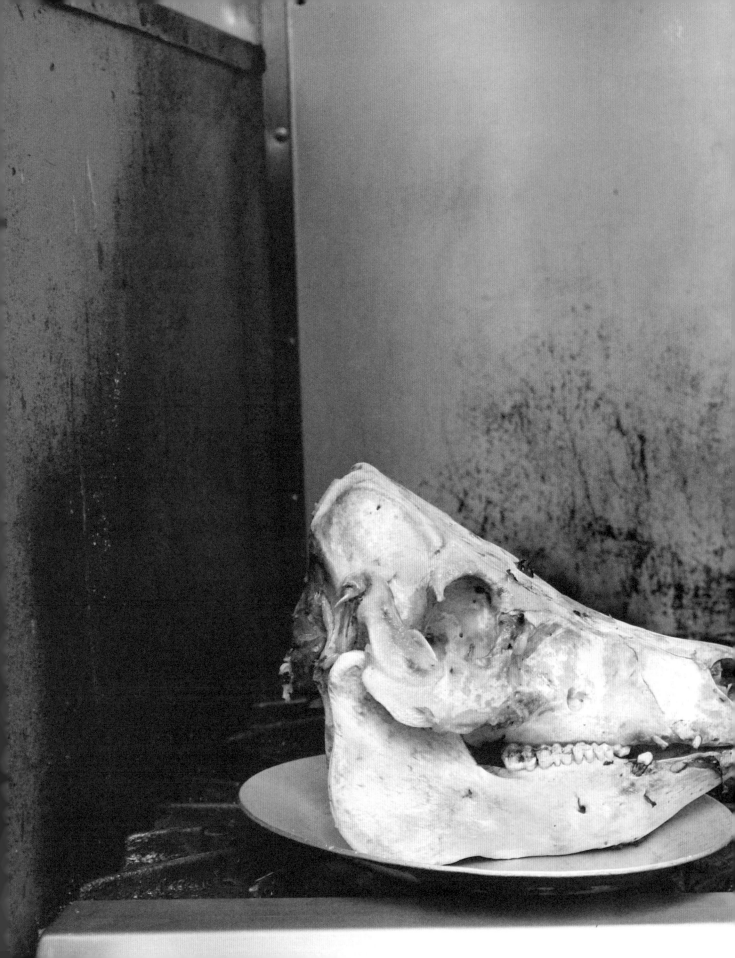

BUTCHER DIRECTORY

Below is a directory of the butchers included in this book, along with websites for some of the local purveyors, producers, and businesses they support:

Josh Applestone
Fleisher's Grass-fed & Organic Meats
307 Wall Street
Kingston, NY 12401
(845) 338-6666
info@fleishers.com; www.fleishers.com

Pete Balistreri
Tender Greens
2400 Historic Decatur Rd Suite 104 P
San Diego, CA 92106
(619) 226-6254
www.tendergreensfood.com

Blue Heron Farm: www.blueheronfarm.com
Crows Pass Farm: www.crowspassfarm.com
Mountain Meadows Farm: www.mountainmeadowfarms.org
Suzie's Farm: www.suziesfarm.com

Dan Barber
Blue Hill at Stone Barns
630 Bedford Road
Pocantico Hills, NY 10591
(914) 366-9606
www.bluehillfarm.com

Anson Mills: www.ansonmills.com
Forest Harvest: www.forestharvest.com
Four Season Farm: www.fourseasonfarm.com
Herondale Farm: www.herondalefarm.com
Jamison Farm: www.jamisonfarm.com
Mas Masumoto: www.masmasumoto.com
Migliorelli Farm: www.migliorelli.com
Norwich Meadow Farms: www.norwichmeadowfarms.com
Polyface, Inc.: www.polyfacefarms.com
Rancho Gordo Beans: www.ranchogordo.com

Jason Barwikowski
Olympic Provisions
107 SE Washington Street
Portland, OR 97214
(503) 954-3663
jason@olympicprovisions.com
www.olympicprovisions.com

Carman Ranch: www.carmanranch.com
Creative Growers: www.creativegrowers.com
Sweet Briar Farms: www.sweet-briar-farms.com
Viridian Farms: www.viridianfarms.com

Jamie Bissonnette
Coppa
253 Shawmut Avenue
Boston, MA 02118
(617) 391-0902
jamie@coppaboston.com
www.coppaboston.com; www.toro-restaurant.com

River Rock Farm: www.riverrockfarm.com
Moon in the Pond: www.mooninthepond.com
Stillman Farm: www.stillmansfarm.com
Round the Bend Farm: www.howonearth.net

Taylor Boetticher
Fatted Calf
644 1st Street
Napa, CA 94559
(707) 256-3684
taylor@fattedcalf.com; www.fattedcalf.com

Cattail Creek: www.cattailcreeklamb.com
Devil's Gulch Ranch: www.devilsgulchranch.com
Full Belly Farm: www.fullbellyfarm.com
Heritage Foods USA: www.heritagefoodsusa.com
Marin Sun Farms: www.marinsunfarms.com
Mariquita: www.mariquita.com
Prather Ranch: www.pratherranch.com
Riverdog Farm: www.riverdogfarm.com
Star Route Farm: www.starroutefarms.com

Scott Boggs
Hudson Ranch
5398 Carneros Highway
Napa, CA 94559
(707) 251-8557; (707) 255-1455
www.hudsonia.com

David Budworth
Marina Meats
2395 Chestnut Street
San Francisco, CA 94123
(415) 673-6700
www.marinameats.com

Atkins Ranch: www.atkinsranch.com
Creekstone: www.creekstonefarms.com
Estancia Beef: www.estanciabeef.com
Superior Beef: www.superiorfarms.com

Scott Buer
Bolzano Artisan Meats
Milwaukee, WI 53212
(414) 426-6380
info@bolzanomeats.com; www.bolzanomeats.com

Christian Caiazzo
Osteria Stellina
11285 Highway 1
Point Reyes Station, CA 94956
(415) 663-9988
www.osteriastellina.com

Barinaga Ranch: www.barinagaranch.com
Lunny Ranch: www.drakesbayfamilyfarms.com
Star Route Farms: www.starroutefarms.com

Tanya Cauthen
Belmont Butchery
15 N. Belmont Street
Richmond, VA 23221
(804) 422-8519
belmontbutchery@gmail.com; www.belmontbutchery.com

Ayrshire Farm: www.ayrshirefarm.com
Buffalo Creek Farm: www.buffalocreekbeef.com
Faith Farms: www.faithfarmfoods.blogspot.com
Gryffon's Aerie: www.gryffonsaerie.com
Skyline Premium Meats: www.skylinepremiummeats.com

Nick Chaset
Bullmoose Hunting Society
1919 19th St NW. Apt 304
Washington, DC 20009
nick@bullmoosehunting.com; www.bullmoosehunting.com

Gabriel Claycamp
The Swinery
3207 California Ave SW
Seattle, WA 98116
www.swinerymeats.com

Thundering Hooves: www.thunderinghooves.net
Wolftown Agricultural Program: www.wolftown.org

Chris Cosentino
Incanto Restaurant and Wine Bar
1550 Church Street
San Francisco, CA 94131
(415) 641-4500
chris@incanto.biz; www.incanto.biz; www.boccalone.com;
www.offalgood.com

Prather Ranch Meat Company: www.prmeatco.com
Range Brothers: www.rangebrothers.com

Mike and Chick Debach
Leona Meat Plant, INC
RD #2 Leona Road
Troy, PA 16947
(800) 416-3968
sales@leonameatplant.com; www.leonameatplant.com

Emile DeFelice
Caw Caw Creek
709 Woodrow Street #220
Columbia, SC 29205
(803) 917-0794
happyhams@cawcawcreek.com; www.cawcawcreek.com

FIG: www.eatatfig.com
Rosewood Market and Deli: www.rosewoodmarket.com
Terra: www.terrasc.com

Mark M. DeNittis
Il Mondo Vecchio Salumi
1174 South Cherokee Street
Denver, CO 80223
(303) 744-MEAT (6328)
www.mondovecchio.net

Canyon Ranch: www.canyonranch.com
Colorado's Best Beef Company: www.naturalbeef.com
Jumpin' Good Goat Dairy: www.jumpingoodgoats.com
Wine Experience Café & Wine Cellar:
    www.wineexperiencecafe.com

Andrew Dorsey
Marlow & Daughters
Brooklyn, NY 11211-6030
(718) 388-5700
www.marlowanddaughters.com

Vinny Dotolo and Jon Shook
Animal
435 N Fairfax Avenue
Los Angeles, CA 90048
(323) 782-9225
info@animalrestaurant.com; www.animalrestaurant.com

Niman Ranch: www.nimanranch.com

Ben Dyer
Laurelhurst Market
3155 East Burnside Street
Portland, OR 97214
(503) 206-3099
ben@laurelhurstmarket.com; www.laurelhurstmarket.com

Cattail Creek Lamb: www.cattailcreeklamb.com
Groundwork Organics: www.groundworkorganics.com
Sauvie Island Organics: www.sauvieislandorganics.com
Viridian Farms: www.viridianfarms.com

Christopher Eley
Goose the Market
2503 North Delaware Street
Indianapolis, IN 46205
(317) 924-4944
chris@goosethemarket.com; www.goosethemarket.com

Apple Family Farm: www.applefamilyfarm.com
Big City Farms Indianapolis: www.bigcityfarmsindy.com
Cook's Bison Ranch: www.cooksbisonranch.com
Fischer Farms: www.fischer-farms.com
Good Life Farms: www.goodlifefarms.com
Gunthorp Farms: www.gunthorpfarms.com
Heritage Farms: www.heritagefarms.com
Schacht Farm: www.schachtfleecefarm.com
Strauss Feeds: www.straussfeeds.com
Traders Point Creamery: www.traderspointcreamery.com
The Swiss Connection: www.swissconnectioncheese.com
Viking Lamb: www.vikinglamb.com

Nick Fantasma
Mario Fantasma, Teresa Fantasma, Louis Fantasma
Paradise Locker Meats
405 W. Birch Street
Trimble, MO 64492
(816) 370-6328
nick@paradisemeats.com; www.paradisemeats.com

Arrowhead Specialty Meats: www.gamemeat.com
Heritage Foods USA: www.heritagefoodsusa.com
MO Assoc. of Meat Processors: www.missourimeatprocessors.com
The Steak Knife Restaurant: www.thesteakknifestaurant.com

Brad Farmerie
PUBLIC
210 Elizabeth Street
New York, NY 10012
(212) 343-7011
info@public-nyc.com; www.public-nyc.com;
www.doublecrown-nyc.com

Ryan Farr
4505 Meats
I Ferry Plaza
San Francisco, CA 94111
meats@4505meats.com; www.4505meats.com

Ingel-Haven Ranch: www.magrudergrassfed.com

Nathan Foot
Northern Spy Food Co.
511 East 12th Street
New York, NY 10009
(212) 228-5100
nathan.foot@gmail.com; www.northernspyfoodco.com
Fleisher's Grass-fed & Organic Meats: www.fleishers.com

Robert Grant
The Butcher Shop
552 Tremont Street
Boston, MA 02118
(617) 423-4800
rgrant@thebutchershopboston.com
www.thebutchershopboston.com

Allandale Farm: www.allandalefarm.com
Carlisle Farmstead Cheese: www.carlislefarmsteadcheese.com
Cato Corner Farm: www.catocornerfarm.com
Cellars at Jasper Hill: www.cellarsatjasperhill.com
Consider Bardwell Farm: www.considerbardwellfarm.com
PT Farm: www.newenglandmeat.com
Siena Farms: www.sienafarms.com
Twig Farm: www.twigfarm.com
Verrill Farm: www.verrillfarm.com

Jesse Griffiths
Dai Due Supper Club and Butcher Shop
(512) 524-0688
www.daidueaustin.net

Alexander Family Farm:
    www.alexanderfarmdoc.wordpress.com
Bastrop Cattle Company: bastropcattlecompany.com
Broken Arrow Ranch: www.brokenarrowranch.com
Countryside Farms: www.countryside-farms.com
Home Sweet Farm: www.homesweetfarm.com
Richardson Farms: www.richardsonfarms.com
Thunder Heart Bison: www.thunderheartbison.com

Tia Harrison
Avedano's
235 Cortland Avenue
San Francisco, CA 94110-5556
(415) 285-6328
www.avedanos.com

Bellwether Farms: www.bellwethercheese.com
Golden Gate Meats: www.goldengatemeatcompany.com
Magruder Ranch: www.magrudergrassfed.com
Royal Hawaiian Seafood: www.royalhawaiianseafood.com
Sonoma Direct: www.sonomadirect.com
Soul Food Farm: www.soulfoodfarm.com

Chris Hughes
Broken Arrow Ranch
3296 Junction Highway
Ingram, TX 78025
(800) 962-4263
chris@brokenarrowranch.com; www.brokenarrowranch.com

Rob Levitt
Mado Restaurant
1647 North Milwaukee Avenue
Chicago, IL 60647
(773) 342-2340
madorestaurant@att.net; www.madorestaurantchicago.com

Nichols Farm: www.nicholsfarm.com
Seedling Fruit: www.seedlingfruit.com
Slagel Family Farm: www.slagelfamilyfarm.com
The Stewards of the Land: www.thestweardsoftheland.com

Scott Leysath
The Sporting Chef
106 Catlin Court
Folsom CA 95630
(916) 351-1079
sportingchef@comcast.net; www.huntfishcook.com

Donald Link
Cochon Butcher
930 Tchoupitoulas
New Orleans, LA 70130
(504) 588-PORK
info@linkrestaurantgroup.com; www.cochonbutcher.com

Ryals Dairy: www.rockingrboers.com

Mike Lorentz
Lorentz Meats
705 Cannon Industrial Blvd
Cannon Falls, MN 55009
(507) 263-3618
mlorentz@lorentzmeats.com; www.lorentzmeats.com

Cedar Summit Farm: www.cedarsummit.com
Grass Run Farm: www.grassrunfarm.com
High Plains Bison: www.highplainsbison.com
Organic Prairie: www.organicprairie.com
Thousand Hills Cattle Co.: www.thousandhillscattleco.com
Verity Meats: www.verityfarms.com

Morgan Maki
Bi-Rite Market
3639 18th Street
San Francisco, CA 94110-1531
(415) 241-9760
info@biritemarket.com; www.biritemarket.com

Becker Lane Organic Farm: www.beckerlaneorganic.com
Niman Ranch: www.nimanranch.com
Jim Reichardt: www.libertyducks.com

Marsha McBride
Café Rouge
1782 Fourth Street
Berkeley, CA 94710
(510) 525-1440
marshamcbride@sbcglobal.net; www.caferouge.net

Tom Mylan
The Meat Hook
100 Frost Street
Brooklyn, NY 11211
(718) 349-5032
Tom@the-meathook.com; www.the-meathook.com

Kinderhook Farm: www.kinderhookfarm.com

Scott Pampuch
Corner Table Restaurant
4257 Nicollet Avenue
Minneapolis, MN 55409-2014
(612) 823-0011
www.cornertablerestaurant.com

Castle Rock Creamery: www.castlerockfarms.net
Green Pastures Creamery: www.greenpasturesdairy.com

Mike Phillips
Craftsman Restaurant
4300 East Lake Street
Minneapolis, MN 55404
(612) 232-3793
mikeyp42@gmail.com; www.craftsmanrestaurant.com

Hidden Stream Farm: www.hiddenstreamfarm.com
Fischer Family Farms Pork: www.fischerfamilyfarmspork.com
Star Thrower Farm: www.starthrowerfarm.com
Venison Steaks: www.venisonsteaks.com

Berlin Reed
The Ethical Butcher
1902 NW 24th Avenue
Portland, OR 97210
(347) 409-2504
theethicalbutcher@gmail.com; www.theethicalbutcher.com

Boondockers Farm: boondockersnaturals.com
Deck Family Farm: www.deckfamilyfarm.com
Dolce Farm and Orchards: www.dolcefarm.com
Heritage Farms Northwest: www.heritagefarmsnw.com

Jim Reichardt
Sonoma Country Poultry–Liberty Ducks
P.O. Box 140
Penngrove, CA 94951
(707) 480-0379
scpducks@aol.com; www.libertyducks.com

Ari Rosen
Scopa
109A Plaza Street
Healdsburg, CA 95448
(707) 433-5282
ari@scopahealdsburg.com; www.scopahealdsburg.com

Joel Salatin
Polyface Farm
115 Pure Meadows Lane
Swoope, VA 24479
(540) 885-3590
www.polyfacefarms.com

Olivia Sargeant
Farm 255
255 W. Washington Street
Athens, GA 30601
(706) 549-4660
farm255.com; farmburger.net

Backyard Harvest: www.backyardharvest.org
Crystal Organics: www.crystalorganicfarm.wordpress.com
Full Moon Farms: www.fullmooncoop.org
Love is Love Farm: www.loveislovefarm.com
Moore Family Farms: www.moorefarmsandfriends.com
Red Mule Grits: www.redmulegrits.com

Riverview Farms: www.grassfedcow.com
Sequatchie Cove: www.sequatchiecove.com
Sparkman's Dairy: www.sparkmancreamvalley.com
White Oak Pastures: www.whiteoakpastures.com

Ron Savenor
Savenor's Market
90 Kirkland Street
Cambridge, MA 02138
(617) 576-0214
customerservice@savenorsmarket.com
www.savenorsmarket.com

Boyden Farm: www.boydenfarm.com
US Wellness Grassland Beef: www.grasslandbeef.com

Tracy Smaciarz
Heritage Meats
18241 Pendleton Street SW
Rochester, WA 98579
(360) 273-2202
tsmaciarz@comcast.net; www.heritagemeatswa.com

The Gleason Ranch: www.thegleasonranch.com
Puget Sound Meat Producers Cooperative: www.psmpc.com

Adam Tiberio
Dickson's Farmstand
75 Ninth Avenue
New York, NY 10011
(212) 242-2630
adamunderscoretiberio@hotmail.com
www.dicksonsfarmstand.com

Herondale Farm: www.herondalefarm.com
The Pig Place: www.thepigplace.homestead.com
Stony Brook Farm: www.stonybrookfarm.wordpress.com
Stuart Family Farm: www.stuartfamilyfarm.com
Wrighteous Organics: www.dicksonsfarmstand.com

Gerrit Van Den Noord
Sonoma Direct
PO Box 5223
Santa Rosa, CA 95402
(707) 795-1283
www.sonomadirect.com

Devil's Gulch Ranch: www.devilsgulchranch.com
Gleason Ranch: www.gleasonranch.com
Salmon Creek Ranch: www.salmoncreekranch.

Cole Ward
Green Top Market
639 Morristown Corners Road
Morrisville, VT 05661
(802) 881-1468
info@greentopmarket.com; www.greentopmarket.com

SOURCES AND RESOURCES

Organizations:

American Grassfed Association
www.americangrassfed.org; (877) 774-7277
An organization promoting, supporting, and certifying
grass-fed producers and products.

Eat Well Guide
www.eatwellguide.com
An indispensable guide to local, sustainable, and organic
food.

Local Harvest
www.localharvest.org; (831) 515-5602
The best search engine for farmers' markets, family
farms, and other sources of locally grown food in your
area.

Eat Wild
www.eatwild.com; (866) 453-8489
Lists of farms that sell grass-fed products by state
including beef, lamb, goats, bison, poultry, pork, and
dairy.

Slow Food USA
www.slowfoodusa.org; (718) 260-8000
Carlo Petrini's vision for the future of food production and
consumption has inspired followers the world over. Slow
Food USA is the ultimate resource for learning about the
movement in the United States.

California Certified Organic Farmers
www.ccof.org; (831) 423-2263
A leading and full service trade association and organic
certifier since 1973, and a trusted source for organic
education and political advocacy. It provides resources
about organic farming, certification and even a state by
state list of farmers' markets

The Robyn Van En Center of Wilson College
717-264-4141, ext. 3352
www.csacenter.org
Robyn Van En introduced the idea of the CSA in 1985.
RVEC national holds a CSA database that includes over
1400 farms from all over the country.¬

Retail:

American Grass Fed Beef
www.americangrassfedbeef.com; (866) 225-5002
Virtual aisle upon virtual aisle of quality, certified, grass-
fed beef.

American Prairie Partners
www.americanprairiepartners.com; (507) 283-4915
Open tallgrass prairie grass-fed Longhorn beef. No
hormones, antibiotics, or hot feeding.

Hearst Ranch
www.hearstranch.com; (866) 547-2624
Central California coast, humane-certified, grass-fed beef,
beef jerky, lamb, and Heritage Berkshire pork.

Niman Ranch
www.nimanranch.com
Humanely raised, beef, pork, lamb, and poultry, as well as
unusual cuts free of hormones and antibiotics.

Blackwing Quality Meats
www.blackwing.com; (847) 838-4888
Antibiotic- and hormone-free, organic meats and jerky;
unusual options such as free range buffalo, ostrich,
pheasant, Muscovy duck and Berkshire pork.

D'Artagnan
www.dartagnan.com; (800) 327-8246
Gourmet and organic meat, organic poultry, pâté, truffles
and more.

Thousand Hills Cattle Company
www.thousandhillscattleco.com; (507) 263-4001
100% grass-fed beef grown on family farms in the
Midwest, raised using humane, sustainable farming
practices.

Salumi Artisan Cured Meats
www.salumicuredmeats.com
An artisan factory equipped to produce high-quality,
gourmet, cured meats and other traditional Italian foods,
including guanciale and pancetta.

Black Pig Meat Co.
www.blackpigmeatco.com; (707) 523-4814
Bacon with a celebrity and chef following; made from
Pure Country Pork, the first sustainable hog operation in
the U.S.

La Quercia
www.laquercia.us; (515) 981-1625
Artisan salumi made from traditional dry curing. Strict
focus on humane, organic animal production.

The Sausage Maker:
www.sausagemaker.com; (888) 490-8525
The source for all of your curing and casing needs,
including pink salt.

Colonel Bill Newsom's Aged Kentucky Country Ham
www.newsomscountryham.com; (270) 365-2482
All things pork, including aged Kentucky Country Ham,
gourmet prosciutto, and sausages. Almost 100 years of
experience and international acclaim.

Edwards of Surrey, Virginia
www.edwardsvaham.com; (888) 320-0902
A website for specialty foods, food service, and grocery
professionals. Wholesale producers of genuine Virginia
Country Hams, premium hickory-smoked bacon, and
sausage for over 80 years.

INDEX

TABLE OF SUGGESTED COOKING TEMPERATURES

Cut of meat	Inner doneness	Inner temperature of food		
Beef	Medium Rare	145°F	or	63°C
	Medium	160°F	or	71°C
	Well Done	170°F	or	77°C
Pork	Medium	160°F	or	71°C
	Well Done	170°F	or	77°C
Ham	Fully Cooked	140°F	or	64°C
Lamb	Medium Rare	150°F	or	66°C
	Medium	160°F	or	71°C
Turkey	Breast	170°F	or	77°C
	Dark Meat	180°F	or	82°C
	Whole (bone in)	180°–185°F	or	82°–85°C
Chicken	Whole pieces (bone in)	180°F	or	82°C
	Boneless	165°F	or	74°C
Duckling		180°–185°F	or	82°–85°C

NOTE: Cooking continues after removal, so you may want to remove the meat a little early.

MY THANKS TO

My parents, Ritz and Margo, who have been even greater examples in adversity than in success and who have proven that grace and generosity are matters of spirit and not of circumstance. And for feeding me so well, all these years.

Douglas Gayeton. Thought I might just take this whole page to say "Thank you, Douglas" in 140 point type but then I couldn't say how much *Slow: Life in a Tuscan Town* has inspired me and how this book would not be here without your transcendental meddling.

Laura Howard-Gayeton, you always know just what should be done. I have so often relied upon that.

The people of Welcome Books are practically co-authors in their commitment and passion for this book and I am certain that this is a rare and beautiful experience in author-publisher relations. Thank you to Lena Tabori, Gavin O'Connor, Kristen Sasamoto, David Spencer Seconi, Emily Green, and Taylor Sperry. And to Clark Wakabayashi, whose design makes me very proud of this book. Thank you, Clark, for creating a space with dignity and beauty, a space fit for the country's best butchers.

Thank you to every butcher in this book, you have been lessons and inspirations for me. Especially to those of you who shared your couches, your dinner tables, your Sunday afternoons.

Sarah Domke, my Secret Eating Society co-founder and my favorite collaborator and farmer, always nurturing the fertile ground.

Dario Cecchini, for being a saint of butchery, one I have prayed to often for special dispensation.

Andrew Zimmern for your thoughtful words and adventurous spirit.

My friends at Slow Food Russian River, who gave food a beautiful context and with whom I have shared countless lovely evenings of ideas, project-planning, and great meals. And all my Slow Food compatriots, outside the Russian River: Anya Fernald, Sarah Weiner, Gibson Thomas, Alli Ghiorse, so many others.

The employees of Sonoma Direct, who are dedicated and loyal and have kept us in business.

Deni Guggiana, for keeping the SS Sonoma Direct righted.

All the ranches that work with Sonoma Direct to create a local food system: Gleason Ranch, Devil's Gulch, Open Space Meats, Tara Firma Farms, Son-Rise Ranch, Rossotti Ranch, Magruder Ranch, Salmon Creek, and others.

Carrie, Liselle, Sadie, and Bruce Springsteen, for keeping me company through 11,000 miles of freeway and back roads.

The recipe testers, who defied the limitations of butcher shops, New York-sized kitchens and culinary aversions to make sure every recipe in this book is spectacular, including Jeff Bobula and Paula Shatkin.

Patrick Logsdon of Red Bat Photography, for the lessons.

To friends who housed, fed and distracted me during my travels, namely The Vetsches, Tamar Adler, The Cardenas, The Christensens.

Esther Newman for some of my most cherished food awakenings, like sitting at the kitchen table with homemade tortillas and chicharrones, or realizing that Molly & Polly were hamburger.

Christian Caiazzo for hatching the book title.

Edible Communications, HARO, Slow Food chapters, Postcard Communications for suggestions and support all over the country.

And from a cavern deep, deep in the low country of my heart, thanks to Katrina Fried and Alice Wong, my editors, who have mentored, cajoled, incited, and nurtured this book out me with tremendous diligence, talent and vision.

—M.G.

CAUTION

The following recipes involve curing meats over a long period of time and/or the use of curing salts, and require special precautions: Bacon (page 233), Bresaola (page 143), Butcher's Cobb Salad (page 23), Corned Veal Tongue (page 55), Hot Dogs (page 142), Little Smokies (page 125), My Boudin (page 184), Rustic Ham (page 216), Salami (page 144). Please see page 144 regarding safety issues in dry curing. Curing salts are dangerous if ingested accidentally, so use exactly as stated in the recipes and keep them out of the reach of children.

Published in 2010 by Welcome Books®
An imprint of Welcome Enterprises, Inc.
6 West 18th Street, New York, NY, 10011
(212) 989-3200; fax (212) 989-3205
www.welcomebooks.com

Publisher: Lena Tabori
Associate Publisher: Katrina Fried
Project Director: Alice Wong
Project Assistants: Gavin O'Connor, Kristen Sasamoto,
    Taylor Sperry, Staci Spritzer, Emily Green, and
    David Spencer Seconi
Recipe Testers: Jeff Bobula, Paula Shatkin, Lenore Dolin,
    and Nicki Kalish
Copyeditor: Ellen Leach
Illustrations on pages 180–181 and 261 by Zach Hewitt
Illustrations on page 46–47, 116–117, 226–227, and
    endpapers by Cary Bernstein Architects
Recipes on pages 155 and 156 are from *Stir: Mixing It Up
    in the Italian Tradition* by Barbara Lynch, Published by
    Houghton Mifflin, 2009.

Designed by H. Clark Wakabayashi

ISBN 978-1-59962-088-6

Library of Congress Cataloging-in-Publication Data

Guggiana, Marissa.
  Primal cuts : cooking with America's best butchers / by
Marissa Guggiana.
      p. cm.
  ISBN 978-1-59962-088-6 (hardcover)
  1. Cookery (Meat) I. Title.
  TX749.G965 2010
  641.6'6--dc22

                    2010016654

First Edition
10 9 8 7 6 5 4 3 2 1
Printed in China

For further information about this book
please visit online:
www.welcomebooks.com/primalcuts

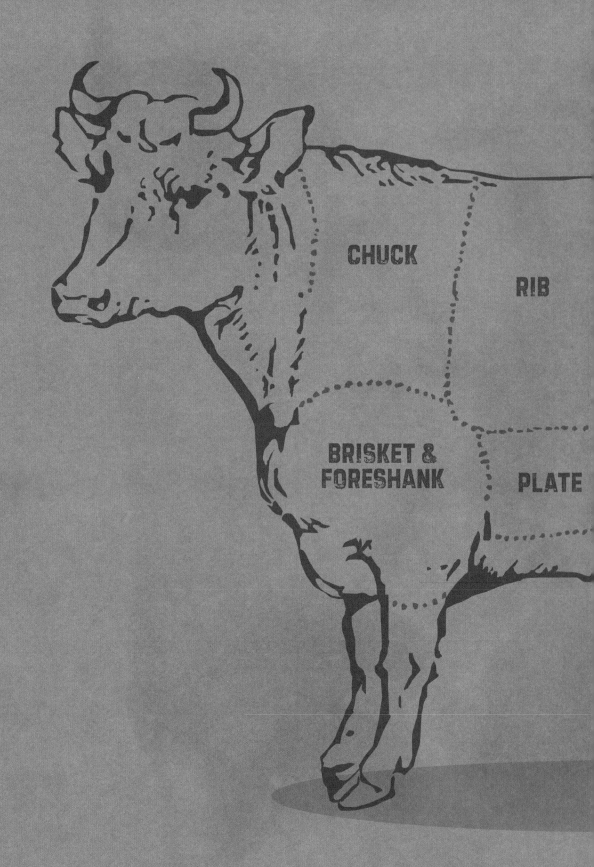